Resistance in the Era of Nationalisms

US–CHINA RELATIONS IN THE AGE OF GLOBALIZATION

This series publishes the best, cutting-edge work tackling the opportunities and dilemmas of relations between the United States and China in the age of globalization. Books published in the series encompass both historical studies and contemporary analyses, and include both single-authored monographs and edited collections. Our books are comparative, offering in-depth communication-based analyses of how United States and Chinese officials, scholars, artists, and activists configure each other, portray the relations between the two nations, and depict their shared and competing interests. They are interdisciplinary, featuring scholarship that works in and across communication studies, rhetoric, literary criticism, film studies, cultural studies, international studies, and more. And they are international, situating their analyses at the crossroads of international communication and the nuances, complications, and opportunities of globalization as it has unfolded since World War II.

Resistance in the Era of Nationalisms

Performing Identities in Taiwan and Hong Kong

Edited by Hsin-I Cheng and Hsin-i Sydney Yueh

MICHIGAN STATE UNIVERSITY PRESS | *East Lansing*

Michigan State University Press
East Lansing, Michigan 48823-5245

Library of Congress Cataloging-in-Publication Data is available
ISBN 978-1-61186-456-4 (Paper)
ISBN 978-1-60917-730-0 (PDF)
ISBN 978-1-62896-493-6 (Kindle)

Cover design by Erin Kirk
Cover photo: Demonstration by Taiwan's Legislative Yuan in supportive of Hong Kong.
Photographed by Ke Chin-Yuan on June, 16, 2019.

Visit Michigan State University Press at *www.msupress.org*

ON THE INTERSECTION OF EDGE BALL AND COURTESY: NOTES ON SCHOLARSHIP IN THE AGE OF GLOBALIZATION

Like America or France or Brazil, China is a nation-state riven with fault-lines along region and race, ethnicity and education, linguistics and libido, gender and more general divisions. Media in the United States tend to portray Chinese society as monolithic—billions of citizens censored into silence, its activists and dissidents fearful of retribution. The "reeducation" camps in Xinjiang, the "black prisons" that dot the landscape, and the Great Firewall prove this belief partially true. At the same time, there are more dissidents on the Chinese web than there are living Americans, and rallies, marches, strikes, and protests unfold in China each week. The nation is seething with action, much of it politically radical. What makes this political action so complicated and so difficult to comprehend is that no one knows how the state will respond on any given day. In his magnificent Age of Ambition, Evan Osnos notes that "Divining how far any individual [can] go in Chinese creative life [is] akin to carving a line in the sand at low tide in the dark." His tide metaphor is telling, for throughout Chinese history waves of what Deng Xiaoping called "opening and reform" have given way to repression, which can then swing back to what Chairman Mao once called "letting a hundred flowers bloom"—China thus offers a perpetually changing landscape, in which nothing is certain. For this reason, our Chinese colleagues and collaborators are taking great risks by participating in this book series. Authors in the "west" fear their books and articles will fail to find an audience; authors in China live in fear of a midnight knock at the door.

This series therefore strives to practice what Qingwen Dong calls "edge ball": Getting as close as possible to the boundary of what is sayable without crossing the line into being offensive. The image is borrowed from table tennis and depicts a shot that barely touches the line before ricocheting off the table; it counts as a point and is within the rules, yet the trajectory of the ball makes it almost impossible to hit a return shot. In the realm of scholarship and politics, playing "edge ball" means speaking truth to power while not provoking arrest—this is a murky game full of gray zones, allusions, puns, and sly references. What this means for our series is clear: Our authors do not censor themselves, but they do speak respectfully and cordially, showcasing research-based perspectives from their standpoints and their worldviews, thereby putting multiple vantage points into conversation. As our authors practice "edge ball," we hope our readers will savor these books with a similar sense of sophisticated and international generosity.

—Stephen J. Hartnett

We dedicate this book to the people in Taiwan, Hong Kong, and all those around the world who continue to fight for self-determination. May these voices be heard and recognized with peace and respect.

Contents

Introduction

In the past decade, the world has heard the resisting voices of dissidents across Asia. In 2014, Taiwanese youth-led activists ignited the Sunflower Movement by occupying Taiwan's Legislative Yuan to protest the ruling party's unilateral passage of a comprehensive economic agreement with the Beijing government.[1] Months later, across the Taiwan Strait, Hongkongers occupied the city demanding "true universal suffrage" and the resignation of Leung Chun-Ying, the pro-Beijing chief executive.[2] In that same year, anti-government protests were held in Thailand, where demonstrators marched against government corruption.[3] Since then, we continue to witness mass protests in nations such as Indonesia, Malaysia, India, and Myanmar, to name a few.

Although some authoritarian governments reacted with brutality against these demonstrators, especially during the COVID-19 pandemic,[4] these dissents have not been muzzled. Many of the protesters exploited digital media and expressed support for one another across geographic boundaries. One example was the "Milk Tea Alliance," which started in April 2020, when young Thai netizens fought against cyberattacks against two Thai celebrities who expressed support for Taiwan and Hong Kong's independence.[5] After these celebrities received backlash from the

People's Republic of China (PRC) and nationalistic Chinese internet trolls, young Thai activists engaged in a "Twitter" war with the Chinese government and its nationalistic netizens over the "One-China" principle as a way to demonstrate their solidarity with Taiwanese and Hongkongers against the authoritarian Beijing government.

Scholarship on resistance has shifted from large-scale revolutions, such as the peasant and subaltern opposition during the 1960s, and the anti-war protests of the 1970s, to the localized resistance of the 1990s.[6] The support by "#Milk Tea Alliance" for Hong Kong and Taiwan illustrates the fluidity and agility of resisting forms against oppressive governments in Asia. Indeed, this endorsement offers a glimpse of the dynamism in one of the most volatile geostrategic regions, in which Taiwan, Hong Kong, China, and the United States are major actors.

This collection engages in a "culture-centered" approach to study cases of *glocalized resistance* as a communicative process. Specifically, we focus on how people in Taiwan and Hong Kong, two postcolonial, cosmopolitan societies, strive for autonomy over their democratic ways of life. Although each has its unique historical and contemporary realities, residents in both places face the same obstacle: the PRC is either blocking their path to freedom (in Hong Kong), or threatening their democratic way of life (in Taiwan). The essays in this volume examine how Taiwanese and Hongkongers express their desire to achieve self-rule, practice democracy, fully embody local identities, and become global citizens despite the tumultuous relationship between China and the United States threatening to overwhelm them. Occupying a critical stance on the margins, the local perspectives and international relations of Hong Kong and Taiwan challenge a China-centric narrative and those solely focused on the U.S.–Sino power struggle. By shifting the focus onto the actions Taiwanese and Hongkongers are taking to intervene in China's aggressive campaigns and policies to rein in the will of the people, we bring much-needed scholarly attention to these marginalized societies. In focusing on the "geocultural identity-in-the-making"[7] of the Taiwanese and Hong Kong people, these chapters offer valuable insight into societies under imminent threat by aggressive neighbors.

Nationalisms in a Fragmented World

More than half-a-century after WWII, one of the most unimaginable atrocities took place in Europe. On February 24, 2022, Ukrainians were forced, once again, to counter Russian aggression. However, unlike the response to Russia's illegal annexation of Crimea in 2014, the global community recognized the threats posed by Putin's aggressive nationalism.[8] Today, the world is witnessing the pervasive fermentation of nationalistic enthusiasm in the form of expansion (e.g., China, Russia) and secession for self-rule (e.g., Catalonia, Hong Kong, South Sudan, Tibet). It is certainly risky to paint a broad stroke across groups with vastly different histories, cultures, memories, and geopolitical positions based on the binary of "unifiers" versus "separatists." Lumping diverse population's desires for self-determination under the label of secession erases unique pasts and present experiences conditioned by local, regional, and global events. These movements respond to a rapidly growing sense of deep longing, complicated by history, transnational influences, and regional circumstances, for freedom and autonomy. For example, Hong Kong and South Sudan, although both former British colonies, have different aspirations and demands for the government to provide an adequate quality of life. As in any society, Hongkongers and Sudanese continue to struggle over a desire for autonomy due to heterogeneous and competing interests, many of which are the result of the British colonial government's manipulation of local ethnic or religious identity to divide and rule.[9] Nevertheless, critical masses demand their freedom.

At the same time, Ukraine, Taiwan, and Kosovo face immense obstacles to be recognized as global or regional members due to the aggressive interference of their nationalistic neighbors like China and Russia.[10] Even after Russian shelling on the Ukrainian people, homes, schools, and hospitals, it remains impossible for Ukraine to be part of the North Atlantic-Treaty Organization (NATO).[11] These external pressures inevitably conjure collective emotions to form a stronger union unencumbered by foreign impositions—a will for independence seen particularly after World War II. In various parts of Asia, the Middle East, Africa, and Europe, we now see a quest for self-rule continue to rise from the margins in nation-making efforts. Currently, Ukrainians represent the most unfortunate but formidable example of such brave struggles. Meanwhile, race- and ethnicity-based nationalism have become mainstreamed in powerful nations such as China, Russia, and the United States.[12] Complicated historical and geostrategic relationships result in various expressions of nationalism. For example, Taiwanese student activist Chen Wen-ting distinguishes "good" nationalism—aiming for self-rule—from "bad" nationalism, which is exploitative in nature.[13] Similarly, Taiwanese political scientist Wu Rwei-ren separates the aggressive form of nationalism practiced by powerful nations such as China from the self-protective kind developed in less robust nations such as Ukraine and Taiwan.[14]

Because national consciousness is a collective imagination catalyzed by a strong sense of identification, it is imperative that we examine the triggers for—and means to—sustain these strong affects. For example, communication scholars have observed that the current Chinese nationalism, also known as "cyber nationalism" or "fandom nationalism," is performed by "informed nationalists,"[15] many of whom are young people who voluntarily attack any entity that criticizes China.[16] While these nationalistic actions could be regarded as a response to China's humiliating past as Western imperialism's prey,[17] the current rise of nationalism is also about individually rationalized public performance through what Yang calls "cultural skills."[18] Indeed, China is not the only nation in which the internet is a prominent space for nationalistic expression. Since the 2000s, the internet, with its easy anonymity, has become a breeding ground for alt-right white nationalism in the United States.[19] Fortified by powerful politicians and traditional media, this cyber culture of exclusionary and violent nationalism takes place in off-line public spaces.[20] However, China and the United States are dramatically different nations. In the United States, the growth of chauvinistic nationalism has met with significant public dissent, while in China such attitudes are "a top-down and bottom-up phenomenon."[21]

Taiwan and Hong Kong are two current examples of Wu's nationalism of less powerful countries with fresh memories of colonial pasts. Heavily affected by China's aggressive nationalism, Hong Kong and Taiwan face challenges on multiple fronts as described in the phrase 內憂外患 (*nei you wai huan*, internal and external troubles). Absent a central governing authority as in previous decades of U.S.-led dominance after the Cold War,[22] many Taiwanese and Hongkongers who live under the threat of the Beijing government have been speaking out; yet their hopes to chart their future continue to be impacted, perhaps impaired even, by more powerful global actors such as China and the United States.

Historical Contexts of Hong Kong and Taiwan as Former Colonies

Both Hong Kong and Taiwan are multicultural postcolonial Sinophone societies. Toward the end of the nineteenth century, in the eyes of the Qing Empire, which ruled these two places, Hong Kong and Taiwan were insignificant and expendable for the sake of preserving the declining empire. Thus, Hong Kong was ceded to the British Empire after the Qing lost the Opium War in 1842. Taiwan was ceded to the Japanese Empire after the first Sino-Japanese War in 1895. The separation from the Qing's rule made Hong Kong and Taiwan develop their own local cultures, even as they were enveloped in the early networks of colonialism in Asia.[23]

The Qing Empire collapsed in 1911, and the two world wars exploded respectively from 1914 to 1918 and 1937 to 1945. Immediately after WWII, the Chinese Civil War broke out on the Chinese mainland, until the Chinese Communist Party (CCP) won and established the PRC in 1949.[24] Chiang Kai-shek, leader of the defeated Republic of China (ROC), brought his nationalist Kuomintang (KMT) military troops and followers to Taiwan, as Japan had handed the colony over to the ROC government in 1945. Under Chiang's rule, Taiwan returned to the Sinophone cultural circle, although it stood with the United States as an anti-communist ally during the Cold War.[25] In contrast, Hong Kong was still under British rule until the United Kingdom and the PRC signed the Sino-British Joint Declaration in 1984, determining the time of the handover of Hong Kong to the PRC as 1997.[26]

During the British colonial era, Hongkongers developed a distinctive identity that combined Chinese traditions and Western customs.[27] The colonial government helped create a local Chinese business elite that valued the rule of law, impartial civil service, and a liberal and democratic political climate.[28] Under the circumstances, there was no clear local Hong Kong identity that grew beyond their Chinese identity. As Kai Khiun Liew argues, the deep-seated cultural uncertainties for Hong Kong's future in the 1980s did not result from the perceived loss of a local Hong Kong identity, but rather, from worries about Beijing's interference in people's democratic and cosmopolitan culture; that is, they feared how encroaching CCP domination over their city would enforce changes in their lifestyle.[29]

By the time of the 1997 handover, many Hongkongers rushed to emigrate to Canada and other countries. Although the Sino-British Joint Declaration stated that "one country, two systems" would be the main constitutional architecture of Hong Kong for fifty years, those who worried about potential changes chose to leave. Those who stayed might have had a more optimistic view and more confidence about adjusting to their dual cultural identities. For example, Anthony Fung maintains that people started to face the reality of adopting a new dual Hong Kong–China identity, an identity aligned and hybridized between local and national identity.[30]

However, after a decade, the PRC gradually increased its control over Hong Kong's freedom of speech and political participation, which set limits to growing a national identity with China. Hongkongers' nostalgia for the British colonial past is a genuine way to fight the PRC's neocolonialism.[31] Their localist thinking also expresses a strong feeling about their cultural difference from mainland China.[32] For example, Article 23 in Hong Kong's Basic Law requires Hong Kong to make rules for its national security. In 2003, Hong Kong lawmaker Regina Ip proposed the National Security Bill, claiming it would fulfill such a requirement. Enactment of this bill triggered massive protests toward this "provision that outlaws treason, sedition, secession, and subversion" in Hong Kong.[33] Many Hongkongers were concerned that their freedoms would be severely compromised in the name of "national security." The 2015 Hong Kong movie *Ten Years* captures the crisis, despair, and anxiety provoked by the apparatus of Chinese authoritarianism in Hong Kong.[34] The PRC banned the movie from even being mentioned on the mainland. However, the dystopian Hong Kong prophesied in *Ten Years* seemed to come true—we witnessed the broken promise of the Joint Declaration from the Beijing authorities, and increasingly desperate—sometimes violent—protests from citizens in Hong Kong.

After the 2014 Umbrella Movement, recognition of an independent Hong Kong identity escalated. In 2019, another wave of local consciousness led to critical local activism against "Sinocentric nationalism."[35] In the wake of these protests, the Beijing Central Government imposed a Hong Kong National Security Law (NSL) in 2020 to evoke the 2003 Article 23 attempt. Amnesty International warned against this Chinese-forced NSL for its vagueness, expansiveness, and potential human rights violations. In fact, the law has since been used to suppress free expression in Hong Kong.[36] After a series of intimidations and arrests of pro-democracy lawmakers, pro-Beijing "patriots" won the 2021 December election in a landslide, with only a 30 percent turnout—half of the turnout in 2016.[37] Without any political opposition in the legislature, former chief executive Carrie Lam swiftly announced that Hong Kong would create a national security law to achieve the goal of Article 23 of the Basic Law, dismissive of the fact that the majority of Hongkongers showed strong opposition to such a law in 2003.[38]

Unlike Hong Kong, Taiwan has never been ruled by the PRC regime established in 1949. While the term "postcolonial Hong Kong" refers to the status of Hong Kong as part of the PRC territory after 1997, "postcolonial Taiwan" has different connotations. In Leo T. S. Ching's analysis, Taiwan is part of postwar postcolonial East Asia, along with the PRC and South Korea, in need of dealing with the sentiment toward Japanese colonization.[39] Therefore, the era of postcolonial Taiwan began after Japan's war defeat in 1945.

After the KMT government took over Taiwan in 1945, tension, distrust, and favoritism of mainland officials/soldiers over local Taiwanese resulted in various conflicts. A major demonstration on February 28, 1947, turned into uncontainable turmoil, followed by the KMT's severe military crackdown in which tens of thousands of people were killed and arrested. The 228 Incident signaled the beginning of the "white terror" era of the 1950s, the ruthless authoritarian rule of the KMT to squash political dissent and exercise ideological control.[40] Although the KMT government deliberately deconstructed Japanese colonial monuments and buildings to impose a China-centric historiography, traces of the Japanese past have been revisited in the 1990s.[41] This was owing to the process of Taiwanization that started as early as the 1970s and 1980s—concurrent with the period of Taiwan's ascendancy to its economic miracle.[42]

As Lee Teng-hui ascended to the presidency in 1988, Taiwan moved toward a democracy. According to Bruce Jacobs, with democratization, Taiwan began a process of decolonization and Taiwanization that emphasized "identification with Taiwan, consciousness of Taiwan, and even a Taiwan nationalism." In terms of cultural and historical perspectives, the process led the Taiwanese to reconstruct a Taiwan-centered historiography, revisit the colonial legacies of the past four hundred years, and reevaluate the roles of Chinese, Japanese, Manchu, Spanish, Dutch, and various Indigenous groups in shaping Taiwanese culture.[43] This Taiwanese identity reached a new peak with the PRC's heightened pressure against Taiwan. Under these conditions, the contributors to this volume view recent resistance in Hong Kong and Taiwan, two highly sophisticated capitalistic and postcolonial societies, against rising Chinese nationalism and imperialistic expansion as continuous efforts for self-determination.

Taiwan and Hong Kong under the U.S.-China Interactions

Since President Richard M. Nixon's historic visit to the PRC in 1972, which reopened U.S.–China relations, the two nations have more or less sought means of compromise. That all changed with the arrival of Donald Trump, who, from as early as the campaign season of 2016, launched repeated attacks on China. Since then, the PRC and the United States have engaged in an overt power struggle as the world's two most powerful nations. Armed with the spirit of "Make America Great Again," Trump waged a war of American white nationalism to compete with Chinese leader Xi Jinping's goal of creating a "Chinese Dream" and restoring China's national and international greatness through the massive international initiative known as "One Belt One Road."[44]

Not to be overlooked in this struggle are its impacts on the postcolonial societies of Taiwan and Hong Kong, particularly under China's "One-China" principle. While each society has responded to and been impacted by the disputes between the United States and China in different ways, what they share is the perception that any attempt to create a distance from the aims and governance of the PRC is interpreted as an effort by the United States to "split" the unity of the "Chinese" motherland. Hence, a tweet sent in support of Hong Kong by an NBA basketball manager in 2019 was framed by the PRC as an affront to the feelings of the Chinese nation.[45] Viewed through this lens, an act or message, no matter how small, has the potential to fuel feelings of distrust between these competing nations. Under Xi Jinping's leadership, the PRC government has practiced so-called wolf-warrior diplomacy. After the outbreak of COVID-19, the PRC government became more belligerent and defensive in efforts to evade international criticism. The latest example of wolf-warrior diplomacy is the use of the U.S.-based social media platform, Twitter, where more than 170 Chinese diplomats "bicker with Western powers, promote conspiracies about the coronavirus, and troll Americans on issues of race."[46]

On February 10, 2021, U.S. president Joseph Biden had his first phone call with Xi Jinping. During their conversation, Biden raised concerns over the crackdown in Hong Kong, human rights abuses in Xinjiang, and Taiwan's security under China's increasing activities in the region. These issues were communicated with very different weight to citizens in these two nations. The *New York Times* specifically identified and featured these issues at the beginning of the article, while the *Chinese Central Television* mentioned them vaguely in one sentence toward the end of its report.[47] Since this phone conversation, China continued tightening its grip over Hong Kong's democratic system,[48] arresting many pro-democracy figures such as Jimmy Lai, winner of the 2021 Gwen Ifill Press Freedom Award and owner of Hong Kong's *Apple Daily*. Lai's popular newspaper was forced to close in June 2021 for being critical of the Chinese government's oppressive actions.[49] China's erosion of Hong Kong's democracy became more comprehensive by raiding, intimidating, and indicting pro-democracy news practitioners,[50] arresting activists in the name of national security, and removing the "Pillar of Shame" statue—the monument to those massacred in Tiananmen Square—from the public eye.[51] Across the strait, Beijing's overt pressure on Taiwan has also increased in asserting its "one country, two system" doctrine. On June 15, 2021, China sent twenty-eight military planes—an unprecedented number—into Taiwan's airspace after the Taiwanese government began publicizing these aggressive activities in 2020.[52] Despite these threatening acts, people in Taiwan and Hong Kong continue to express their resistance against pressure from China while managing their delicate relationships to Western nations. Nevertheless, the most threatening aspect of the dilemmas facing Hong Kong and Taiwan all flow from the CCP's "One-China" principle.

Hong Kong and Taiwan in the "One Country, Two Systems" Framework

The idea of "one country, two systems" originated in the 1960s when Mao Zedong asserted that Taiwan would be "returned to the motherland."[53] Such a view reflected Mao's continuous frustration with the "U.S. and allied activities aimed at creating 'two Chinas'" after seeing the U.S. government's actions supporting Taiwan's defense against the Chinese Communist threat.[54] This belief was cemented when Deng Xiaoping created the "one country, two systems" principle in the early 1980s to stress the existence of only 'One China.'[55] The United States initially accepted Deng's position of "One China"; however, its ambiguous meaning continues to evolve (See Cheng in this volume for more information about United State's One-China policy).

Currently, Hong Kong subscribes to the One-China principle, not without contestation however.[56] As Daniel Garrett shows in *Counter-Hegemonic Resistance in Hong Kong*, Hongkongers embody a long tradition of protests against injustice in the city and the world. As "a city of protests," Hong Kong endured subjugation under British colonialization and later Chinese neocolonialism through mainlandization.[57] Sonny Lo, a political scientist, describes mainlandization as a process of convergence with the PRC through political and economic policies. In Hong Kong, this process was accelerated under Chief Executive Tung Chee-hua after the 1997 handover, in which China's (one country) interests prevailed over those of Hong Kong (two systems). The result is Hong Kong's dependency on China, further facilitated by local pro-Beijing elites to diminish support for democracy in Hong Kong. As Lo writes, if "patron-client politics" is a characteristic in Hong Kong under the British rule, mainlandization in Hong Kong is a "recolonization . . . where the political loyalists of Beijing have been awarded with influential positions throughout the policy-making institutions."[58] In the sociocultural realm, patriotic curriculum such as "mother-tongue language" education was launched after the retrocession in the hopes of converging the Chinese and Hongkongers' identities.

Against the backdrop of mainlandization is the well-and-alive culture and lifestyle of demonstrations and protests, which were a "cultural object and symbol" of Hong Kong under the "one country, two systems" framework.[59] This "way of life" was not aggressively repressed until 2014, when Hongkongers protested against Beijing's increasing involvement in Hong Kong's selection process of its chief executive position. Since March 2019, a series of demonstrations have condemned the extradition law, which would allow Beijing to further infringe upon Hong Kong's autonomy.[60] In their contributions to this collection, both Andrew Gilmore and Micky Lee showcase Hongkongers' strategies to counter Beijing's efforts to impede their way of life.

Due to the PRC's early adoption of a soft style of mainlandization through economic integration and Chinese pop cultural influence, Hong Kong had arguably already become "another PRC colony," as of 2008.[61] The decade from 1997 to 2007 saw a slight decrease in how people in Hong Kong self-identify, which dropped from 44 percent to 37 percent, compared to the Chinese identity, which rose from 24 percent to 27 percent.[62] However, the oppressive policies the CCP used to "mainlandize" Hong Kong since 2018 has backfired, as locals identifying with Hong Kong have risen dramatically. According to the 2021 Hong Kong public opinion survey, the percentages of respondents identified as "Hongkonger + Hongkonger in China" in 2007, 2018, and 2021 were 54.9 percent, 66.8 percent, and 70 percent, respectively. The numbers for those identified as "Chinese + Chinese in Hong Kong" decreased from 43.2 percent in 2007, to 32 percent in 2018, and to 28.4 percent in 2021. Further, 23.5 percent of the respondents used Hongkongers as an identifier in 2007, which rose to 38.6 percent in 2021.[63] The message is clear: the harder the CCP pushes to control Hong Kong, the more Hongkongers reject that pressure.

In Xi Jinping's 2019 speech marking the twentieth anniversary of the return of Macau to the Chinese Communist Party's rule, he indirectly spoke to Hongkongers and warned that "external forces," including the United States, have been instigating the unrest in Hong Kong.[64] The Beijing-backed chief executive, Carrie Lam, echoed this sentiment about resisting Western influences. Ming Xie and Chin-Chung Chao's chapter in this volume reveals that Hong Kong's mainstream media highlighted Lam's defiant statements, hence defending her from criticism from the Western media. This trope of "external meddling" is important to our study, as it shows how the CCP tends to blame local political unrest on outside forces. This tactic means that activists in Hong Kong and Taiwan are often labeled "splittists," "Western stooges," or "spies," designations that enable the CCP to displace political turmoil from local causes onto the alleged subterfuge of foreign powers.

In the PRC's selling of the mainlandizing policies of "one country, two systems" and its vision of the "Great China" to people in Hong Kong, Taiwan remains resistant to becoming another Hong Kong–like Special Administrative Region (SAR) under PRC's rule. Taiwan has played an integral role in China's ambition for "Chinese unification" ever since Mao's China in the 1960s. After the KMT retreated to Taiwan, the United States signed the Mutual Defense Treaty (MDT) to protect U.S. interests in the region.[65] In 1979, the U.S. Congress passed the Taiwan Relations Act (TRA) to sustain U.S. strategic interests and maintain its "One China" policy, which stresses a mutual and peaceful resolution between both sites of the Taiwan Strait without U.S. intervention.[66] Taiwan's current president, Tsai Ing-wen, refuted the nebulous understanding of "One China" in the 1992 consensus, an alleged agreement between the KMT party and the PRC through works by nonofficial representatives. In 2019, Xi equated the alleged "1992 Consensus" with its "one country, two systems" principle.[67] This move drew significant negative reaction from Taiwan toward this framework.[68]

While Taiwan and Hong Kong, each with its unique challenges, are fighting against Beijing's self-imposing "one country, two systems" principle, conflicts between China and the United States have become much more public. Yu Bin states that the U.S. government's increasing criticism of China's "misbehavior" on trade started in early 2005.[69] As mentioned, U.S.-China relations further intensified under the Trump administration. Starting in mid-2018, the United States placed heavier tariffs on China's imports. In return, China placed retaliatory tariffs on U.S. imports. In May 2019, the United States banned Huawei Technologies, the Chinese telecommunications giant from buying from and selling to U.S. companies. No substantial progress was made between China and the United States until October 2020. Around the same time, U.S. secretary of the state Mike Pompeo issued a warning in a press briefing about the "continued erosion of the 'One Country, Two Systems'" framework.[70] From 2019 to 2020, U.S. Congress showed support for both Hongkongers and Taiwanese through a series of legislations.[71] U.S. support for Taiwan has increased China's frustration.[72] While COVID-19 spread across the globe, China and America blamed each other for the virus, and President Trump further pressured China to assume responsibility for the pandemic.[73] The Biden administration continues to pursue potential connections between the virus and the CCP.[74] As two of the most nationalistic countries,[75] these two powerful nations are unlikely to subdue their tumultuous relationship in the near future. This trajectory further complicates how people in Taiwan and Hong Kong, who developed localized and flexible resistant strategies, express their desire to seek self-rule, practice democracy, fully embody local identities, and become global citizens.

Resistance as Hybridizing Communicative Processes

According to the PBS News Hour program, by the end of 2019 "there have been protests in Spain, Sudan, Russia, Egypt, Uganda, Indonesia, Ukraine, Peru, Hong Kong, Zimbabwe, Colombia, France, Turkey, Venezuela, The Netherlands, Ethiopia, Brazil, Malawi, and Algeria."[76] Globally, many youth-led movements ushered the unjust plight of those suffering under oppressive regimes and capitalism to the forefront. Communication as a field has collectively examined resistance against powerful establishments as researchers explicate strategies that express opposition through utilizing public spaces, both physical and online,[77] rhetorical mediations,[78] and everyday participations.[79]

Much of this visibility is credited to (uneven) communication infrastructures and technologies, which facilitate information dissemination and event organizing.[80] Online and off-line "insurgent spaces" are created, appropriated, and reproduced by urban- and city-dwellers.[81] Social media platforms are major vehicles for disseminating (mis)information within and across these spaces. Consequently, the marginalized resorted to new media to express their plight. For example, during the 2010 Jasmin Revolution and 2014 Hong Kong Umbrella movement, the whole world saw activists appear in the streets to demand justice and reform. At the same time, authoritative regimes targeted digital media to surveil, control, and regulate free speech as a final resort to maintain power.[82] Leaders such as Xi in China, Putin in Russia, Modi in India, Duterte in the Philippines, and—to a certain extent—Trump in the United States, have either shut down the internet, censored information flow, spread false information, and/or hijacked conversations on social media sites.[83] All have done so in the name of (misguided) nationalism and (the pretense of) national security to control defiant voices from its own society and abroad. Whether digital organizing has sustained structural impacts is debatable.[84] Nevertheless, access to and ownership of these cyber spaces remain contentious and significant spheres in fighting over who controls what narratives to communicate to the masses within and beyond national borders. One aim of the resisting efforts is to ensure that truthful accounts are available and amplified. Using Taiwan—one of the most targeted nations for misinformation—as an example, Chiaoning Su and Wei-Ping Li's chapter highlights challenges and strategies to sustain the culture of openness and democracy by nullifying false information circulated on the internet.

Digital space is a significant political terrain in which resistive communication occurs. At the same time, Marwan Kraidy reminds us that "the human body is the indispensable political medium" through which dissent has been embodied and made visible. According to Kraidy, protesting bodies perform "a posture of active resistance" when they "self-immolated, posed naked, sprayed graffiti, enacted street theater, confronted police and regime goons, and occupied urban squares and boulevards." Animated as such, bodies articulate the complex innerworkings of power structures that online texts, such as viral memes, inside jokes, historical and local references, express. In these performances, what Kraidy calls "corporeal docility"[85] is broken to reflect a smorgasbord of dissent presented on social media, and to poignantly present what people are willing to put their bodies on the line for.[86] Human bodies along with "digital artifacts" communicate resistance in the form of "icon, meme, and metaphor."[87] *Resistance in the Era of Nationalisms* includes cases in Hong Kong and Taiwan in which social media and human bodies serve to express defiance. With the aid of social media, we witness these localized concerns connect to regional and global geopolitical terrain. Wen Liu's chapter explores the subversive power held within these mundane cyber spaces, arguing that, through visceral connections, ironic memes have the potential to mend hardened positions. Some scholar advocate examining resistance as a continuum, a communicative process that has cumulative effects.[88] We take the view of examining "glocalized resistance"—strategies infused with local practices and globalized logics—as active processes in constant dynamic interaction with local culture and transnational ideas.

Why Focus on Resistance in Asia?

In the early 2000s, the Malaysian prime minister Mahathir Mohamad mentioned his "Look East Policy"—both a critique of formal colonial practices and a showcase for successful Asian experiences, such as those in Japan. He asserted that "Asia lies not in a distinctive and clear set of values but rather in practices that can be rationalized as resistance and defined against a West."[89] This policy has drawn much attention in a region that suffered from rampant imperialism. The shared experiences of colonialism sowed the seeds for Asian nations such as China to seek power within themselves to counter presumed foreign foes. In the name of resisting Western influence, China's growing nationalistic zeal has turned into imperialistic aggression.

Armed with the economic success that propelled China's "peaceful rising" since the late 1970s, today's CCP employs its "sharp power" to coerce potential allies and isolate enemies. However, there remains scarce research on China's active engagement and impacts on neighboring democratic development and practices, and to a larger extent, global society.[90] In *The Struggle for Democracy in Mainland China, Taiwan, and Hong Kong*, Andreas Fulda details how, for example, China's United Front Work developed concerted efforts to coopt and coerce peoples in China, Taiwan, and Hong Kong.[91] Fulda's work is significant in that it closely examines how the Chinese central government utilizes communication technologies to effectively control its targeted populations. Rather than treating Taiwan and Hong Kong as passive "peripheries" of the PRC, essays in this book shift the focus onto actions Taiwanese and Hongkongers have taken to intervene in China's aggressive campaigns and policies to reign in the people's will in these two societies. This movement to emphasize the resistive communication in Taiwan and Hong Kong, two imperative geostrategic actors in the region and global stage, calls upon scholarly efforts to attend to these marginalized societies. Scholarship on experiences in Taiwan and Hong Kong is particularly urgent due to the potential military conflict between China and the United States if China and Taiwan engage in a direct confrontation.[92] Analyses on how Taiwanese and Hongkongers engage in the strained relations with the Beijing government—and people in mainland China, to a certain degree—afford critical insights into resistance movements in this volatile part of the Indo-Pacific—a region that the United States "has, is and always will be part of," as U.S. secretary of state Antony Blinken stated.[93]

Sociologist Alaine Touraine insists that researchers study tension in order to seek possibilities for progress. In so doing, political forces will no longer be dissociated from economic forces. Consequently, subjects are viewed as actors whose efforts to construct themselves are worthy of attention—as opposed to regarding them as passive products subordinated to "a logic of order."[94] Actions that subjects perform in movements, whatever the scale may be, offer a lens through which to scrutinize sociocultural and politico-economic landscapes, both locally and globally. Focusing on resistance in Asia, this collection examines these resistive acts as the "aporetic space of representation," spaces that become sites for tackling "empirical and analytical subalternity." Tariq Jazeel and Stephen Legg invoke Gayatri Chakravorty Spivak's description of subalternity as "a position without identity . . . an absence of a possibility of the abstract structures of the state."[95] Although most Taiwanese and Hongkongers have opportunities to travel, receive an education, and exercise political decisions, collectively they lack direct access to global governance as independent agents. Homi Bhabha calls these spaces of a "thirdness," in which "speaking subjects" make histories as subaltern agents and produce *their own* "life-story" amid contradictions or fragmentations. In this volume, we document these marginalized experiences and resistant strategies to speak up by tracing the "recrudescence of subaltern agency."[96]

Hongkongers and Taiwanese often express their subversion of Chinese state violence and domination through (dis)identification. These populations wield political, economic, and ideological consciousness anchored in self-knowing as speaking subjects negating the PRC. Iam-Chong Ip's chapter in this volume delineates such ideological struggles over consciousness in Hong Kong. Indeed, without expanding "personal reflections" to "a general and operative national-popular consciousness," revolutionary changes cannot take hold.[97] Hsin-i Sydney Yueh's chapter on the vernacular discourses of an online community demonstrates influences over the everyday identity negotiation of Taiwanese identity through negating Chinese identity. The incremental and collective consciousness of a people as subjects of their own destiny propels macro-level changes free from external social, cultural, economic, and political interference.

Both Taiwan and Hong Kong resemble Spivak's analytical concept of the subaltern,[98] caught in being "spoken over," translated, and reinterpreted repeatedly by multiple power holders, such as China and the United States. Taiwanese and Hongkongers, although each a heterogenous group, struggle to self-represent. Only through continuous fights for more influence are resistive voices from these two places increasingly being heard. That the PRC's aggressive behavior toward Hongkongers and Taiwanese is regularly reported in the U.S. mainstream media attests to this new beginning. Taiwan and Hong Kong are examples of incorporating the figurative lens of subalternity, creatively using their extremely restrictive autonomy to seek recognition and sustained freedom. For example, Taiwanese president Tsai Ing-wen's rhetoric expresses postcolonial resistance with hybridized cultural influences and Taiwan-centered epistemology, as Hsin-I Cheng argues in her chapter.

The PRC's dominance via its global financial and technological power has been described as both neocolonial and neoimperialist.[99] Since the 1980s, China, through its Sinonization process such as the Belt and Road Initiative (BRI), has increased its economic, cultural, political, technological, and military influences over its neighboring societies and beyond.[100] China's expansions are symbiotic—not absent of contractions, however, with Western neoliberalism.[101] During the economic reform era, China worked closely with Western neoliberal institutions to speed up its integration into the global economy, while simultaneously breaking the free-market-driven rules set by these Western nations.[102] Early in this process, Hong Kong, a cosmopolitan city, became China's connection to international capital (also see Ip's chapter in the volume). The transition toward "state neoliberalism" simultaneously generated an "ideological vacuum" for rising nationalism.[103] China's economic power constitutes its aggressive nationalistic zeal. In this volume, Micky Lee illustrates how Hong Kong protesters utilized their familiarity with global capitalism and local culture to voice their struggle for democracy. At the same time, she contends that market-based resistance strategies, which have roots in neoliberal practices, cannot address Hongkongers' plight.

After opening its market in the 1980s, China transformed into an embodiment of exploitative "state neoliberalism," in which the CCP designated where resources were devoted and who benefited from state subsidies both inside and outside China.[104] Under Xi Jinping's "New China," neoimperialistic edifices were further fortified;[105] for example, China's foreign-aid policy aimed at developing nations so that it could gain accesses to energy and raw materials. China's foreign aid increased nearly five times—from $7.6 billion per year during the 2000s to $38 billion annually in the 2010s. China instigated the New Development Bank (NDB) and the Asian Infrastructure Investment Bank (AIIB), both with neoimperialistic characteristics comparable to those of the World Bank (WB) and International Monetary Fund (IMF).[106] And, just a few decades ago, the Tricontinental Conference in Havana forged African–Asian–Latin American solidarity and internationalized revolutionary efforts against imperialism. At that historical meeting, the Chinese delegates claimed that the capitalistic United States was an imperialistic power, and pushed for Afro-Asian solidarity to protect resources in countries of "the South."[107] No longer the China at the time of the Solidarity, Xi's New China has fully embraced an ethos of exploitative capitalism and imperialistic policies of "development" to advance the PRC's national interests and global ambitions.

As mentioned, Xi's China employs oppressive practices through carrots, like monetary assistance. For those who defy its authoritarian demands, China uses its economic and military supremacy to deliver the sticks, punishing policies that dovetail with Chinese jingoism. Stephen J. Hartnett asserts that the CCP's core rhetoric, "traumatized nationalism," has guided its leaders to establish a nationalist myth by promoting patriotism and wiping out national humiliations of the past. Since the 2006 policy to create a "socialist countryside [and] a harmonious society,"[108] the newly emerged capitalist middle class has been absorbed into China's economic elites, supportive of the CCP and less resistant to Xi's authoritarian leadership.[109] Today, the Beijing government orchestrates military and civilian citizens to serve as its cyber warriors (網軍*wang-jun*) who wage "hybrid warfare" with an unprecedented amount of misinformation on controversial issues, such as same-sex marriage, to polarize Taiwan.[110] Furthermore, in China and overseas, masses of "young, Communist-red Chinese nationalists," known as "little pinks," use "the internet as a patriotic battlefield to fight those who [they deem are disparaging] China."[111] These cyber soldiers are armed with the ethno-nationalistic zeal to issue attacks that advance China's expansive interests.

Meanwhile, the Beijing government rhetorically positions itself as a victim of the "West," led by the United States, in its managing of "internal affairs." For example, the Beijing government has labeled its dissidents in Hong Kong and Xinjiang as "terrorists," a smokescreen meant to divert from the fact that these locations play a key role in China's continuous development of authoritarian capitalism.[112] Facing China's expansion, the Taiwanese and Hongkongers remain vigilant, with "the power of the multitude."[113] As groups under existential threat, they exercise such power to generate resistance against an increasingly shrinking space for autonomy, voices, and agency for self-narration.[114] People in these two societies forge strategies with abundant local support and growing international attention with the hope of rendering their situations visible. At this historical juncture, charged with the tensions between the United States and China competing for global market and leadership, each society navigates ways to counter the current "postcolonial colonialism" and neoimperialistic efforts from China.[115]

Mohan Dutta explicates marginalization as a communicative process through which groups are perpetually constructed as outsiders afforded "limited opportunities for participation in discursive spaces" by legitimizing global structures such as media conglomerates, the United Nations, and the World Health Organization.[116]

They experience symbolic and material forms of marginalization—both are interconnected to perpetuate exclusions of the "Other." For example, during the COVID-19 pandemic, Taiwan initially could not secure vaccines for its people due to China's interference in Taiwan's purchasing attempts.[117] Finally, during an outbreak in Taiwan, Japan and the United States donated vaccines in June 2021. Such humanitarian actions drew strong objections from Beijing, which put more pressure on those who assisted Taiwan.[118] The Taiwanese government has since become more public about China's active ostracism of the Taiwanese people. As Dutta asserts, the cycle of symbolic and material marginalization must be disrupted in the "transformative politics of resistance."[119] To this end, it is imperative that diverse peoples actively participate in public affairs that impact their lives. Being pushed to the margins, people in Hong Kong and Taiwan have organized ingenious ways to formulate their identity and articulate their stories to shift the tides of oppression. The chapters in this book illustrate venues and forms of these resisting performances and practices, born out of localized experiences and shaped by regional and global geopolitics.

Organization of the Book

Resistance in the Era of Nationalisms engages in a "culture-centered" approach to study cases of glocalized resistance as a communicative process. Each essay focuses on the voices and agency of the marginalized to further their self-representation for their needs. The strategies discussed in this book range from macro- and meso- to micro-level.[120] Collectively, the chapters shed light on the "coagulating"[121] effects that individual and communal resistance strategically speaks against, and with, growing nationalism in China, Taiwan, and Hong Kong amid rising challenges toward America's global leadership since the Cold War. Each location allows for unique storytelling through "things" such as public spaces, and performing resistances through their "bodies"[122] and digital discourses.

People in both Taiwan and Hong Kong are strategizing ways to expand their autonomy within the undercurrent of tumultuous U.S.-China relations. This book has two parts. The first section discusses the experiences of Taiwan, a postcolonial nation that continues to experience marginalization in global society due to the Chinese-imposed and the U.S.-acknowledged "One-China" framework. The second part includes experiences in Hong Kong as an advanced capitalistic society under China's "one country, two systems" policy. Authors examine Hongkongers' grassroots activism as performances that communicate their unique experiences in this historical moment in which post-colonialism intersects with the influences of mainlandization.

The U.S. influence in Taiwan and Hong Kong is a constant factor in their struggle to relate to China. Cheng argues that Taiwan's first woman president, Tsai Ing-wen, from a marronage standpoint, engages in the "transformative rhetoric of realness" to resist China's aggressions toward Taiwan. Affirmations from the United States and other global powers become sources of the reality of Taiwan's existence. In the process, Tsai articulates an inclusive form of nationalism rooted in Taiwan's cultural diversity and collective memories. Across the Taiwan Strait, Hong Kong also had a woman leader for the first time. Chao and Xie examine media coverage of the leadership of Hong Kong's former chief executive Carrie Lam, and find that it was reported in a polarized fashion due to her alignment with the central government in Beijing and her defiant stand against U.S. and UK policies. These oppositional portrayals are symptoms of the identity struggles in Hong Kong vis-à-vis Chinese nationalism.

The struggle for autonomy and self-identification also occurs in online spaces. The chapters by Yueh and Ip show how social media allows for imagination and future-crafting through linguistic creativity. Ip argues that the term *laam caau* or *lanchao* (攬炒, mutual destruction), which was widely shared on social media, conjures actions on the ground and paints a vivid picture for Hong Kong's future. Focusing on what he calls "compressed temporal experience" that *laam caau* creates, Ip articulates the massive agency generated through the idea of mutual destruction in Hong Kong's current struggle. In her chapter, Yueh demonstrates how Taiwanese netizens use the term *hari* (哈日, Japan-worshipping) to negotiate the meanings of Taiwanese and to express their resistance to China. Through informal debates and confrontations, netizens "collaborate" to perform their national identity. Both chapters affirm Abbott's claim that social media has a democratizing impact,[123] and illustrate how online spaces afford accumulative power to those with access, to challenge, expand, or complicate the meaning of collective consciousness.

Social media has the unique ability to elicit immediate emotions. Grounding her chapter in the skepticism toward U.S.-centered "decryptive" epistemology, Liu advocates for a "weak theory" that "is descriptive" for openness and curiosity. She argues that humorous memes render reparative potential through palpable affects. Using the COVID-19 pandemic as an example, she analyzes how memes were effectively used in Taiwan to fend off the perils of misinformation in cyber space. The online world has the power to provoke quick impressions and tenacious reactions for exploitation, particularly of the vulnerable. Taiwan is one of the most targeted countries for misinformation from China. Because of its vulnerability to China's information war, Su and Li provide a critical assessment of three fact-checking platforms in Taiwan. Although fact-checking became prevalent in the United States, their chapter advances the urgent need to understand non-Western resisting tactics against a pressing crisis of knowledge and misinformation being (re)produced on social media. Both chapters introduce timely topics at the height of U.S.-China competition over (mis)information.

Online spaces cannot act alone, however; nor can they be viewed as a de facto arena for countering pressure from authoritative regimes.[124] They are part of transformative changes made through public participation. Demonstrations on the streets remain popular strategies for people to voice their opinions. Gilmore anchors his chapter in the rhetorical power Hong Kong activists performed by utilizing public transportation during the 2014 Umbrella Revolution and 2019 Hard Hat Revolution. Through Paul Ricœur's lens of historicity, Gilmore's analysis shows distinctly different visions of Hong Kong's past, present, and future in the ways that protesters have engaged with public transportation. Lee highlights the miscalculation of China's democratization ensuing from its globalized economy. The global and local dynamic is messy and interactive, particularly in postcolonial Hong Kong. Lee argues that a "glocal consumer identity" embodied by Hong Kong's protesters to resist the Extradition Bill falls short in challenging a global surge of racist and xenophobic nativism. These two chapters point to the ongoing development of Hongkongers' opposition to Beijing's expansion of power while negotiating the shifting terrain of global (re)arrangement. This book ends with an interview with Taiwan's digital minister, Audrey Tang. In our interview, Tang shared their experiences as a mega-community organizer who firmly believes in and practices "radical transparency" as a way to deepen public communication and participation in Taiwan—the only thriving democracy in the Han-dominated societies. Minister Tang articulated their belief in democracy as a technology of resistance.

Resistance in the Era of Nationalisms documents localized resistive communication in two postcolonial societies, each impacted by China's superpower in different ways. At the same time, both sites continue to develop localized identities in response to the reenergized race/ethnicity-based masculine nationalisms in the United States and China. Each chapter elucidates contemporary struggles for self-expression in one of the most dynamic regions in the world. The authors tackle the variegated impacts of China's dominance with careful attention to the complex historical and political trajectories in Hong Kong and Taiwan, and their relations to the West. Collectively, this book offers analyses of resistance from what Michael Hardt and Antonio Negri refer to as an "intersectional multitudes" perspective.[125] These accounts show that resistance to authoritarian regimes, under the monstrous neoliberalist ethos of China, is messy, cumulative, and full of contradiction. However, these efforts are also imperative to forging a path for the people to reach what Achille Mbembe's calls "the universal right to breathe."[126] This book aims to start the conversation about resistance to the expansion of imperialistic nationalism through military, monetary, bio-technology, and cultural dominance by focusing on China, Taiwan, Hong Kong, and the United States.

NOTES

1. James X. Morris, "A Visual Dialogue of the 2014 Sunflower Movement, 5 Years Later," *The Diplomat*, April 26, 2019.
2. Jonathan Kaiman, "Hong Kong's Umbrella Revolution—the Guardian Briefing," *Guardian*, September 30, 2014.
3. "Thailand Protests: Anti-Government March in Bangkok," *BBC News*, March 29, 2014.
4. Nithin Coca, "What's Next for Asia's Social Movements?," *The Nation*, May 13, 2020.
5. Nicola Smith, "#MilkTeaAlliance: New Asian Youth Movement Battles Chinese Trolls," *The Telegraph*, May 3, 2020.
6. Lila Abu-Lughod, "The Romance of Resistance: Tracing Transformations of Power through Bedouin Women," *American Ethnologist* 17, no. 1 (1990): 41–55.
7. We are grateful to the anonymous reviewer for this term.
8. Steven Pifer, "Crimea: Six Years after Illegal Annexation," *Brookings*, March17, 2020.
9. Kim Searcy, "Sudan in Crisis," *Origins: Current Events in Historical Perspective*, Ohio State University, https://origins.osu.edu/article/sudan-darfur-al-bashir-colonial-protest; Ming K. Chan, "The Legacy of the British Administration of Hong Kong: A View from Hong Kong," *The China Quarterly* 151 (1997): 567–582.
10. Both nations practice ethnonationalism, which is antagonistic toward ethnic minorities, while deploying armed forces into neighboring territories. For more on nationalism in Russia, see Pål Kolstø, "Introduction: Russian Nationalism Is Back—but Precisely What Does That Mean?," in *The New Russian Nationalism: Imperialism, Ethnicity and Authoritarianism 2000–2015*, edited by Pål Kolstø and Helge Blakkisrud, 1–17 (Edinburgh: Edinburgh University Press, 2016).

11. "Ukraine Conflict: What is NATO and How Has It Responded to Russia's Invasion?," *BBC News*, May 3, 2022.
12. Heather Woods and Leslie Hahner, *Make America Meme Again: The Rhetoric of the Alt-Right* (New York: Peter Lang, 2019).
13. Leo T. S. Ching, "Anti-Japan: The Politics of Sentiment in Postcolonial East Asia" (Durham: Duke University Press, 2019).
14. Rwei-ren Wu, *Prometheus Unbound: When Formosa Reclaims the World* (Taipei: Acropolis, 2016).
15. Guobin Yang, "Performing Cyber-Nationalism in Twenty-First-Century China," in *From Cyber-Nationalism to Fandom Nationalism*, edited by Hailong Liu, 1–12 (New York: Routledge, 2018).
16. Rongbin Han, "Defending the Authoritarian Regime Online: China's 'Voluntary Fifty-Cent Army,'" *The China Quarterly*224 (2015): 1006–1025.
17. Hongmei Li, "Understanding Chinese Nationalism: A Historical Perspective," in *From Cyber-Nationalism to Fandom Nationalism: The Case of Diba Expedition*, edited by Hailong Liu, 11–31 (New York: Routledge, 2019).
18. Yang, "Performing Cyber-Nationalism," 6.
19. Woods and Hahner, *Make America Meme Again.*
20. Barton Gellman, "Trump's Next Coup Has Already Begun: January 6 Was Practice," *The Atlantic*, December 6, 2021.
21. Jo Kim, "The Chinese People Step Up to Enforce China's Nationalist Propaganda," *The Diplomat*, May 5, 2020. Also see Peter Gries, Derek Steiger, and Tao Wang, "Social Media, Nationalist Protests, and China's Japan Policy: The Diaoyu Islands Controversy, 2012–13," in *The Internet, Social Media, and a Changing China*, edited by Jacques deLisle, Avery Goldstein and Guobin Yang, 161–179 (Philadelphia: University of Pennsylvania Press, 2016).
22. Yasemin Nuhoğlu Soysal, *Transnational Trajectories in East Asia* (New York: Routledge, 2015).
23. Fang-Long Shih and Carol Jones, "Introduction to Taiwan and Hong Kong in Comparative Perspective: Centres-Peripheries, Colonialism, and the Politics of Representation," *Taiwan in Comparative Perspective* 5 (2014): 1–20.
24. Odd Ame Westad, *Decisive Encounters: The Chinese Civil War, 1946–1950* (Stanford: Stanford University Press, 2003), 7.
25. Warren Tozer, "Taiwan's 'Cultural Renaissance': A Preliminary View," *The China Quarterly* 43 (1970): 81–99.
26. Ming K. Chan, "Hong Kong: Colonial Legacy, Transformation, and Challenge," *The Annals*

of the American Academy of Political and Social Science 547, no. 1 (1996): 11–23.

27. Siumi Maria Tam, "Eating Metropolitaneity: Hong Kong Identity in Yumcha," *The Australian Journal of Anthropology* 8, no. 1 (1997): 291.
28. John M. Carroll, *Edge of Empires: Chinese Elites and British Colonials in Hong Kong* (Cambridge, MA: Harvard University Press, 2005).
29. Kai Khiun Liew, "Intersecting Anglicization and Sinicization," *Cultural Studies* 26, no. 5 (2012): 778–779.
30. Anthony Fung, "Postcolonial Hong Kong Identity: Hybridizing the Local and the National," *Social Identities* 10, no. 3 (2004): 399.
31. Wing Man Liza Kam, "Colonial Nostalgia? Demolition of Colonial Space and Its Aftermaths in Hong Kong," in *Exploring Nostalgia: Sad, Bad, Mad and Sweet*, edited by Anita Dremel and Daniel Juckes (Oxford: Inter-Disciplinary Press, 2016), 57.
32. Wing-sang Law, "Decolonization Deferred: Hong Kong Identity in Historical Perspective," in *Citizenship, Identity and Social Movements in the New Hong Kong*, edited by Wai-man Lam and Luke Cooper (London: Routledge, 2018), 13.
33. Sonny Lo, "The Mainlandization and Recolonization of Hong Kong," in *The Hong Kong Special Administrative Region in Its First Decade*, edited by Joseph Cheng (Hong Kong: University of Hong Kong Press, 2007), 181.
34. Satish Kolluri and Joseph Tse-hei Lee, "Representing Crisis and Crisis of Representation: Screening Postcolonial Hong Kong in *Ten Years* (2015)," *Cine-East: Journal of East Asian Cinemas* 1 (2018): 41.
35. Law, "Decolonization Deferred," 26–27.
36. "Hong Kong's National Security Law: 10 Things You Need to Know," *Amnesty International*, July 17, 2020, https://www.amnesty.org/en/latest/news/2020/07/hong-kong-national-security-law-10-things-you-need-to-know/.
37. Mee Kam Ng, "Hong Kong," *Disp* 46, no. 180 (2010): 6–15.
38. "Hong Kong to Draw Up Own 'National Security' Law," *Al Jazeera*, January 12, 2022.
39. Ching, *Anti-Japan*, 15.
40. Ibid., 94.
41. Yoshihisa Amae, "Pro-colonial or Postcolonial? Appropriation of Japanese Colonial Heritage in Present-day Taiwan," *Journal of Current Chinese Affairs* 1 (2011): 24.
42. Yoshihisa Amae and Jens Damm, "Whither Taiwanization? State, Society and Cultural Production in the New Era," *Journal of Current Chinese Affairs* 40, no. 1 (201): 6; Stephen J. Hartnett, Patrick Shaou-Whea Dodge, and Lisa B. Keränen, "Postcolonial Remembering in Taiwan: 228 and Transitional Justice as 'The End of Fear,'" *Journal of International and Intercultural Communication* 13, no. 3 (2020): 238–256.

43. Bruce Jacobs, "Wither Taiwanization? The Colonization, Democratization and Taiwanization of Taiwan," *Japanese Journal of Political Science* 14, no. 4 (2013): 575, 576.
44. OBOR is composed of two routes, the land-based "Silk Road Economic Belt," which connects the countries in Central Asia, West Asia, the Middle East, and Europe, and the oceangoing "Maritime Silk Road," which links the countries in Southeast Asia, Oceania, and North Africa. See Chris Buckley and Keith Bradsher. "Xi Jinping's Marathon Speech: Five Takeaways," *New York Times*, October 18, 2017.
45. "Daryl Morey Backtracks after Hong Kong Tweet Causes Chinese Backlash," *BBC News*, October 7, 2019.
46. Jessica Brandt and Bret Schafer, "How China's 'Wolf Warrior' Diplomats Use and Abuse Twitter," *Tech Stream*, October 28, 2020.
47. Michael Crowley, "Biden Raises Concerns with China's Xi in First Call Since Election," New York Times, February 10, 2021; "习近平同美国总统拜登通电话" (Xi Jinping and U.S. president Biden hold phone call), Chinese Central Television, February, 11, 2021.
48. Keith Bradsher and Chris Buckley, "How Chinese Plans to Control Hong Kong's Elections and Elevate 'Patriots,'" *New York Times*, March 11, 2021.
49. The Editorial Board, "Honoring Jimmy Lai: In Hong Kong, a Valiant Attempt to Keep Publishing the Truth," *Wall Street Journal*, June 21, 2021.
50. "Another Hong Kong News Site Shuts as Pro-Beijing Lawmakers Sworn In," NPR, January 3, 2022.
51. "Pillar of Shame: Hong Kong's Tiananmen Square Statue Removed," *BBC News*, December 23, 2021; Kang-chung Ng and Clifford Lo, "Hong Kong Activist Arrested again for Allegedly Violating Bail Terms," *South China Morning Post*, January 12, 2022.
52. John Ruwitch, "China Sends a Record 28 Military Planes into Airspace Controlled by Taiwan," NPR, June 15, 2021.
53. Ministry of Foreign Affairs of the People's Republic of China, "A Policy of 'One Country, Two Systems' on Taiwan," https://www.fmprc.gov.cn/mfa_eng/ziliao_665539/3602_665543/3604_665547/t18027.shtml.
54. Yafeng Xia and Zhi Liang, "China's Diplomacy toward the United States in the Twentieth Century: A Survey of the Literature," *Diplomatic History* 41 (2017): 241–264.
55. Derek Grossman, "One Country, Two Systems, Lots of Problems: Beijing's Soft Sell to Taiwan and Hong Kong Is Falling Apart," *Foreign Policy*, June 21, 2019.
56. Derek Grossman, "Where Does China's 'One Country, Two Systems' Stand in 2020?," *The Diplomat*, February 13, 2020.
57. Daniel Garrett, *Counter-Hegemonic Resistance in China's Hong Kong: Visualizing Protest in the City* (New York City: Springer, 2015), 2, 11.

58. Lo, "The Mainlandization of Hong Kong," 55.
59. Ibid., 10.
60. James Pomfret, "EU Lodges Formal Diplomatic Note Against Contentious Hong Kong Extradition Bill," *Reuters*, May 24, 2019.
61. Lo, "The Mainlandization of Hong Kong," 71.
62. Ibid., 63–65.
63. Hong Kong Public Opinion Research Institute, "Categorical Ethnic Identity 8/1997–12/2021," https://www.pori.hk/pop-poll/ethnic-identity-en/q001.html?lang=en.
64. "Reading Between the Lines on Macao," *Taipei Times*, December 26, 2019.
65. Ibid.
66. Bonnie Glaser and Michael Green. "What Is the U.S. 'One China' Policy, and Why Does It Matter?," *Center for Strategic & International Studies*, January 13, 2017, https://www.csis.org/analysis/what-us-one-china-policy-and-why-does-it-matter.
67. See Grossman, "Where Does China's."
68. Gary Sands, "Is This the End of the '1992 Consensus'? Tsai Ing-wen Is Promoting Her Alternative 'Taiwan consensus,' but the KMT Remains Committed to the 1992 Consensus," *The Diplomat*, January 11, 2019.
69. Yu Bin, "China's Harmonious World: Beyond Cultural Interpretations," *Journal of Chinese Political Science* 13 (2008): 119–141.
70. Morgan Ortagus, *Department Press Briefing*, Department of State, June 20, 2019, https://www.state.gov/briefings/department-press-briefing-june-10-2019/#post-82620-HONGKONGCHINA.
71. For example, the *New York Times* reported that, in November 2019, President Trump signed the Hong Kong Human Rights and Democracy Act, a bipartisan bill, which would compel the United States to force sanctions on officials and negatively affect trade conditions between the United States. and Hong Kong. See Emily Cochrane, Wong Edward, and Bradsher Keith, "Trump Signs Hong Kong Democracy Legislation, Angering China," *New York Times*, November 27, 2019. In May 2019, the U.S. House of Representatives passed the "Taiwan Assurance Act of 2019" and supported "regular sales and defense articles" to Taiwan and its participation in international organizations. See Bureau of Political-Military Affairs, "U.S. Arms Sales and Defense Trade," U.S. Department of State, January 20, 2021, https://www.state.gov/u-s-arms-sales-and-defense-trade/. In March 2020, during the COVID-19 pandemic, President Trump signed the "Taiwan Allies International Protection and Enhancement Initiative (TAIPEI) Act" into law to enhance bi-lateral relationships with Taiwan. See Stanley Kao, "From Taiwan Relations Act to TAIPEI Act: A Robust Global Partnership Amid Crisis," *The Hill*, April 15, 2020.

72. Graham Allison, "China vs. America: Managing the Next Clash of Civilizations," *Foreign Affairs* (September/October 2017): 80–89; Yu Bin and Young Deng, "Hegemon on the Offensive: Chinese Perspectives on U.S. Global Strategy," *Political Science Quarterly* 116 (2001): 343–365.
73. Ian Bremmer, "China and America's Blame Game Over COVID-19 Hurts Everyone," *TIME*, March 26, 2020; "'Come Clean': US Presses China on Coronavirus After Lab Reports," *Al Jazeera*, April 16, 2020.
74. "Statement by President Joe Biden on the Investigation into the Origins of COVID-19," *The White House*, May 26, 2021, https://www.whitehouse.gov/briefing-room/statements-releases/2021/05/26/statement-by-president-joe-biden-on-the-investigation-into-the-origins-of-covid-19/.
75. Jiayu Wang, "Representing Chinese Nationalism/Patriotism through President Xi Jingping's 'Chinese Dream' Discourse," *Journal of Language & Politics* 16 (2017): 830–848.
76. PBS News Hour, "Why Protest Flourished Across the Globe in 2019," *KQED*, December 25, 2019.
77. For examples of physical and online spaces, see Amy Koerber, "Postmodernism, Resistance, and Cyberspace: Making Rhetorical Spaces for Feminist Mothers on the Web," *Women's Studies in Communication* 24 (2001): 219–243; Anna Feigenbaum, "Resistance Matters: Tents, Tear Gas and the 'Other Media' of Occupy." *Communication & Critical/Cultural Studies* 11 (2014): 15–24; Anastasia Denisova "Democracy, Protest and Public Sphere in Russia After the 2011–2012 Anti-Government Protests: Digital Media at Stake," *Media, Culture & Society* 39, no. 7 (2017): 39; Jessica Lu and Catherine Steele, "'Joy Is Resistance': Cross-Platform Resistance and (Re)invention of Black Oral Culture Online," *Information, Communication & Society* 22 (2019): 823–837; Robert Asen, "Neoliberalism, the Public Sphere, and A Public Good," *Quarterly Journal of Speech* 103 (2017): 329–349; Sarah Sharma, "Because the Night Belongs to Lovers: Occupying the Time of Precarity," *Communication & Critical/Cultural Studies* 11 (2014): 5–14; and Zhiming Cheng, "The Changing Pattern of State Workers' Labour Resistance in Shaanxi Province, China," *Communication, Politics & Culture* 45 (2012): 197–216.
78. For examples of rhetorical mediation, see Anju Chaudhary and William Starosta, "Gandhi's Salt March: A Case Study of Satyagraha with Rhetorical Implications," *Journal of World Communication* 21 (1992): 1–12; Murray Edelman, "The Language of Participation and the Language of Resistance," *Human Communication Research* 3 (1997): 159–170; Jason Black, "Remembrances of Removal: Native Resistance to Allotment and the Unmasking of Paternal Benevolence," *Southern Communication Journal* 72 (2007): 185–203; and Eli Mangold and Charles Coehring, "The Visual Rhetoric of the Aerial View:

From Surveillance to Resistance," *Quarterly Journal of Speech* 105 (2009): 25–41.

79. For examples of everyday participation, see Isaac West, "Performing Resistance in/from the Kitchen: The Practice of Maternal Pacifist Politics and La WISP's Cookbooks," *Women's Studies in Communication* 30 (2007): 358–383; and Jennifer Lena, "Voyeurism and Resistance in Rap Music Videos," *Communication & Critical/Cultural Studies* 5 (2008): 264–279.
80. Jason Abbott, "Democracy@internet.org Revisited: Analysing the Socio-Political Impact of the Internet and New Social Media in East Asia," *Third World Quarterly* 33, no. 2, (2012): 333–357.
81. Rita Padawangi, Peter Marolt, and Mike Douglass, "Introduction to the Special Issue: Insurgencies, Social Media and the Public City in Asia," *International Development Planning Review* 36, no. 1 (2014): 3–14; Mohan J. Dutta, *Voices of Resistance* (West Lafayette, IN: Purdue University Press, 2012), 325.
82. Padawangi, Marolt, and Douglass, "Introduction to the Special Issue," 3–14; Lily Kuo, "China's Great Firewall Descends on Hong Kong Internet Users," *Guardian*, July 8, 2020; Paul Mozur and Aaron Krolik, "Hong Kong Website Doxxing Police Gets Blocked, Raising Censorship Fears," *New York Times*, January 9, 2021.
83. Mozur and Krolik, "Hong Kong Website Doxxing Police"; Kuo, "China's Great Firewall"; Mujib Mashal, Schmall Emily, and Goldman Russell, "Why Are Farmers Protesting in India?," *New York Times*, January 27, 2021; Miles Parks, "Trump Is No Longer Tweeting, but Online Disinformation Isn't Going Away," NPR, March 5, 2021; Lauren Etter, "Rodrigo Duterte Turned Facebook into a Weapon, with a Little Help from Facebook," *Bloomberg*, December 7, 2017.
84. W. Lance Bennett, Alexandra Segerberg, and Curd B. Knuepfer, "The Democratic Interface: Technology, Political Organization, and Diverging Patterns of Electoral Representation," *Information Communication & Society* 21 (2018): 1655–1680.
85. Ibid. Marwan M. Kraidy, "The Body as Medium in the Digital Age: Challenges and Opportunities," *Communication and Critical-Cultural Studies* 10 (2013): 285–290, 288.
86. We have seen such actions not only in places like Hong Kong but also in the United States, including the Capitol insurgency in the United States on January 6, 2021.
87. Kraidy, "The Body as Medium," 289.
88. Michael Hanchard, *Party/Politics: Horizons in Black Political Thought* (New York: Oxford University Press, 2006); Neil Roberts, *Freedom as Marronage* (Chicago: University of Chicago Press, 2015); Dutta, *Voices of Resistance*.
89. David Leheny, "From Resistance to Attractiveness: The Politics of Values and Regionalism in East Asia," in *Transnational Trajectories in East Asia: Nation, Citizenship, and Region*,

edited by Yasemin Soysal, 62–80 (London: Routledge, 2015)., 75.

90. David Leheny, "From Resistance to Attractiveness: The Politics of Values and Regionalism in East Asia," in *Transnational Trajectories in East Asia: Nation, Citizenship, and Region*, edited by Yasemin Soysal, 62–80 (London: Routledge, 2015).
91. Andrea Fulda, *The Struggle for Democracy in Mainland China, Taiwan and Hong Kong Sharp Power and Its Discontents* (London: Routledge, 2019).
92. Kenneth Lieberthal, "Preventing a War Over Taiwan," *Foreign Affairs* 84, no. 2 (2005): 53.
93. Antony Blinken, "A Free and Open Indo-Pacific," U.S. Department of State, December 14, 2021, https://www.state.gov/a-free-and-open-indo-pacific/.
94. Alain Touraine, "Beyond Social Movements?," *Theory, Culture & Society* 9 (1992): 125–145; Alain Touraine, "The Voice and the Eye: On the Relationship between Actors and Analysts," *Political Psychology* 2, no. 1 (1980): 3–14.
95. Tariq Jazeel and Stephen Legg eds., *Subaltern Geographies* (Athens: University of Georgia Press, 2019), 13, 40.
96. Homi Bhabha, *Our Neighbours, Ourselves: Contemporary Reflections on Survival* (New York: De Gruyter, 2011), 21.
97. Ibid., 113.
98. Gayatri Chakravorty Spivak, "Scattered Speculations on the Subaltern and the Popular," *Postcolonial Studies* 8, no. 4 (2005): 475–486.
99. Tukumbi Lumumba-Kasongo, "China-Africa Relations: A Neo-imperialism or a Neo-colonialism? A Reflection," *African and Asian Studies* 10 (2010): 236–266.
100. Mya Maung describes Sinonization as a process through which China gains free access to another country by providing financial and technological support for "economic development." Such a process inevitably has an impact on the socioeconomic and cultural spheres of the local environment. See Mya Maung, "On the Road to Mandalay: A Case Study of the Sinonization of Upper Burma," *Asian Survey* 34 (1994): 447–459. China's "One Belt One Road" initiatives have been viewed as a way to gain access and control of countries that receive its financial and technological support. See Kate Mayberry, "China Signals Belt and Road Shift with Malaysia Rail Project," *Al Jazeera*, April 15, 2019, https://www.aljazeera.com/news/2019/04/china-signals-belt-road-shift-malaysia-rail-project-190415072550955.html; Roger Louis and Robinson Ronald, "The Imperialism of Decolonization," *The Journal of Imperial and Commonwealth History* 22, no. 3 (1994): 462–511.
101. Isabella Weber, "Origins of China's Contested Relation with Neoliberalism: Economics, the World Bank, and Milton Friedman at the Dawn of Reform," *Global Perspectives* 1, no. 1 (2020); Li Zhang and Aihwa Ong, *Privatizing China :Socialism from Afar* (Ithaca: Cornell

University Press, 2008).

102. Weber, "Origins of China's Contested Relation with Neoliberalism."
103. Weber, "Origins of China's Contested Relation with Neoliberalism," 178–179.
104. Alivn Y. So and Yin-wah Chu, "The Transition from Neoliberalism to State Neoliberalism in China at the Turn of the Twenty-First Century," in *Developmental Politics in Transition the Neoliberal Era and Beyond*, edited by Chang Kyung-Sup, Ben Fine, and Linda Weiss, 166–187 (London: Palgrave, 2012).
105. Adrian Hadland, "If the Hat Fits: Revisiting Chinese 'Neo-Imperialism' in Africa from a Comparative Historical Perspective," *Asian Politics & Policy* 4, no. 4 (2012): 467–485.
106. Minxin Pei, "A Play for Global Leadership," *Journal of Democracy* 29, no. 2 (2018), 37–51.
107. Karrim Essack, "Report from Havana: Hsinhua Correspondent, 1979," *Peking Review Economic and Political Weekly* (1979): 1647–1648.
108. Alivn Y. So and Yin-wah Chu, "The Transition from Neoliberalism to State Neoliberalism in China at the Turn of the Twenty-First Century," in *Developmental Politics in Transition the Neoliberal Era and Beyond*, edited by Chang Kyung-Sup, Fine Ben, and Weiss Linda (London: Palgrave, 2012), 177.
109. Fulda, *Struggle for Democracy*; Hsiao Hsin-Huang Michael, ed., *Chinese Middle Classes: Taiwan, Hong Kong, Macao and China* (New York: Routledge, 2014).
110. Puma Shen, "中國認知領域作戰模型初探: 以 2020 臺灣選舉為例," Tssci 22, no. 1 (2021).
111. Li Yuan, "China Students Trapped Abroad by the Coronavirus Are Criticized at Home," *New York Times*, June 24, 2020.
112. Christopher P. Cunningham, "Counterterrorism in Xinjiang: The ETIM, China, and the Uyghurs," *International Journal on World Peace* 29, no. 3 (2012): 7.
113. Michael Hardt and Antonio Negri, *Multitude: War and Democracy in the Age of Empire* (Durham: Duke University Press, 2005), 336.
114. Mohan Dutta, *Voices of Resistance: Communication and Social Change* (West Lafayette, IN: Purdue University Press, 2012).
115. Stephen J. Hartnett, Lisa B. Keränen, and Donovan Conley, eds., *Imagining China: Rhetorics of Nationalism in an Age of Globalization* (East Lansing: Michigan State University Press, 2017); Hadland, "If the Hat Fits."
116. Dutta, *Voices of Resistance*, 20.
117. In February 2021, it was reported that Taiwan's deal with Germany's BioNTch was put on hold due to potential pressure from China. See Ben Blanchard, "Taiwan Says BioNTech Vaccine Deal on Hold, Cites Potential Chinese Pressure," *Reuters*, February 16, 2021, https://www.reuters.com/business/healthcare-pharmaceuticals/

taiwan-says-biontech-vaccine-deal-hold-cites-potential-chinese-pressure-2021-02-17/.

118. Helen Davidson, "How Taiwan's Struggle for Covid Vaccines Is Inflaming Tensions with China," *Guardian*, June 14, 2021. See Nick Aspinwall, "Taiwan Confronts COVID-19 Outbreak, Accuses China of Blocking Vaccines," *The Diplomat*, May 29, 2021.
119. Dutta, *Voices of Resistance*, 7.
120. Shiv Ganesh, Heather Zoller, and George Cheney, "Transforming Resistance, Broadening Our Boundaries: Critical Organizational Communication Meets Globalization from Below," *Communication Monographs* 72 (2005): 169–191.
121. Michael Hanchard, *Party/Politics: Horizons in Black Political Thought* (New York: Oxford University Press, 2006).
122. Bonnie Honig, *Public Things: Democracy in Disrepair* (New York: Fordham University Press, 2017). Kraidy, "The Body as Medium," 285–290.
123. Abbott, "Democracy@internet.org Revisited."
124. Ibid., 351–352.
125. Michael Hardt and Antonio Negri, "Empire, Twenty Years On," *New Left Review* 120 (2019): 67–92.
126. Achille Mbembe and Carolyn Shread, "The Universal Right to Breathe," *Critical Inquiry* 47, no. S2 (2021): S58–S62, doi:10.1086/711437.

PART 1

Resistance in Taiwan

Existence as Resistance

President Tsai Ing-wen's Transformative Rhetoric of Marronage

Hsin-I Cheng

During her reelection campaign in 2019, Taiwanese president Tsai Ing-wen was asked if she supported Taiwan's independence, to which she replied: "If Taiwan is not a country, what is it then?"[1] She followed up with an explanation that Taiwan's government takes care of its own people with its own foreign diplomacy and democratic institutions, and therefore is indeed a nation. Her answer depicted Taiwan's unique situation as a well-functioning and independent political entity that is nonetheless not recognized by most nations in the world. In *Invisible Countries*, Joshua Keating describes eight requirements that constitute a nation; these "bylaws" are supported by the United Nations (UN).[2] One of these rules is that the territory be recognized by the international community. But because the People's Republic of China (PRC), a permanent member of the UN with security council veto power, denies Taiwan's status as a nation independent of China, all but fifteen countries in the world fail to accept Taiwan's nationhood.

While Taiwan is not under the PRC's rule, its autonomy has been severely compromised by Beijing's persistent claim over the island nation, despite the will of the majority in Taiwan, where more than 60 percent of the population self-identifies as Taiwanese instead of Chinese.[3] Interestingly, this identity is closely related to how positively China and the United States are viewed. In Pew's 2019 survey, 68 percent of Taiwanese held a favorable view of the United States compared to 35 percent, who viewed China in a positive light. Moreover, 75 percent of those who identified as Taiwanese-only viewed the United States more favorably than China.[4] When the sovereignty of a people on shared land is threatened by an outside influence, such as that of the Taiwanese by the Chinese government, their lived experiences resemble those under an imperialistic colonial power. As the polling data shared above confirms, accounts of their inability to chart their own destiny propel Taiwanese people to resist their most pressing threat—China.

Such resistance became particularly pronounced during the late 2010s, when relations between the United States and China rapidly deteriorated. From the U.S.–China trade war in 2018 to the fight for accountability in the COVID-19 pandemic in 2020, the struggle for global dominance between the Trump administration and Xi's government was evident.[5] This fierce competition has only escalated in China's interactions with the Biden administration. Considering these geopolitical relations, this chapter argues that President Tsai's articulation of Taiwan's existence as an undeniable fact is a model of resistance to China's threatened encroachments. Scant research has focused on resistance in regions where non-Western powers, such as China, are the perpetrators. Through what I call the "transformative rhetoric of realness,"[6] Taiwan's first female leader connects its people's fate to those who struggle for dignity and self-determination in other societies, such as Hong Kong. This rhetoric accrues transformative power due to its ability to evoke the inner faith and capabilities within audiences. Through directly describing and inviting listeners to accept the reality of Taiwan's existence as an independent nation, President Tsai's rhetoric strives to create an empowering narrative rooted in inclusion and listening, not exclusion and threatening.

This chapter first describes Taiwan's historical engagement with the PRC's "One-China" principle, which continues to underwrite China's threats to Taiwan's sovereignty. It then discusses concepts of marronage and piracy, situating analyses of President Tsai's speeches within Taiwan's long history as a marginal entity on the fringes of empires. Finally, the chapter illustrates how President Tsai's speeches sketch out a Taiwan-style nationalism that is inclusive, flexible, indigenous, and resilient. Through concurrently articulating the two levels of realness in Taiwan—the challenging political reality it faces and its indisputable existence as an island nation—President Tsai's rhetoric transforms Taiwan from an "issue" or a "question" into a given reality, a noncontroversial, independent entity.[7]

China's Claim over Taiwan under "One-China"

On January 2, 2019, at "the 40th Anniversary of the Message to Compatriots in Taiwan," Chinese President Xi Jinping expressed China's determination to continue its "peaceful reunification and one country, two systems."[8] He asserted that peoples on both sides of the Taiwan Straits are Chinese, "a *fact* that can never be altered by any force or anyone" (emphasis added). Given that less than 3 percent of Taiwanese self-identify as Chinese,[9] Xi's claim of the "fact" raises concerns in Taiwan for the credibility of his other assertions. For example, on the one hand, his speech promised that Taiwan's "[democratic] social system and its way of life will be fully respected." On the other hand, Xi threatened that if the principle of Taiwan belonging to China is challenged, "cross-Straits relations will become strained and volatile, and the interests of our compatriots in Taiwan will be harmed." The statements, in the end, are contradictory, indicating how the Beijing government does not respect Taiwan's right to choose what its relationship to the PRC should be. From this perspective, Xi's rhetoric is little more than a road map to renewed Chinese imperialism.

Furthermore, since 2018, Taiwanese, along with the global community, witnessed how the Chinese central government has encroached upon Hongkongers' freedoms of expression. In his speech, Xi stated that "the affairs of us Chinese must be decided by ourselves. The Taiwan question is an internal affair that involves China's core interests and the Chinese people's national sentiments, and no external interference in this issue will be tolerated." His proclamation alluded to the perceived collective wound caused when parts of China were occupied by foreign powers during the mid-nineteenth and early twentieth centuries. This historical memory was wedded to the present rising Chinese nationalism in Xi's closing remarks that "the new era is one . . . [with] a promising future for the rejuvenation of the Chinese nation." His message was by far the most forceful declaration of China's uncompromising stand toward Taiwan's desire for unhindered self-determination. Indeed, Xi's words, "we cannot choose our history," signaled China's inflexibility when it comes to the choices of Taiwanese people to not be included in Xi's "our history."

Xi's remark came just two days after U.S. president Donald Trump signed into law the Asian Reinsurance Initiative Act of 2018, which advises the United States to support Taiwan through regular arms sales and visits from high-level U.S. officials.[10] In addition to ballooning its defense budget by more than $100 billion (compared to that under the Obama administration), the Trump administration sought creative measures to influence the United States's highly ambiguous "One-China" policy.[11]

To the U.S. administration, the "One-China" policy generally includes "the three U.S.-PRC communiqués of 1972, 1978, and 1982; implementation of the Taiwan Relations Act enacted in April 1979 and six assurances."[12] The 1972 Shanghai Communiqué stated that "the United States acknowledges that all Chinese on either side of Taiwan Strait maintain there is but one China and that Taiwan is a part of China. The United States does not challenge that position."[13] Yes this statement must be interpreted within the context of the whole document,[14] and the last part of the statement has been dropped in later U.S.-PRC communiques. Further, in 2000, President Clinton stressed that any resolutions to the cross-Strait relations must include "the assent of the people of Taiwan." The Obama administration enacted an even more flexible interpretation of the "One-China" policy. In 2011, his administration allowed Taiwanese to hold the annual reception to celebrate their National Day at the former Republic of China's (ROC) ambassador's residency before the United States ended its official relations with the ROC in 1979.[15] Clearly, the "One-China" policy of the United States is not the same as Beijing's "One-China" principle, which excludes Taiwan's voice.

Several days after Xi's 2019 address, President Tsai appealed to the international community with the following statement: "It is impossible for me or, in my view, any responsible politician in Taiwan to accept President Xi Jinping's recent remarks without betraying the trust and the will of the people of Taiwan." President Tsai further challenged the possibility of working with the Beijing government, explaining that "there's no need to talk about the 1992 consensus anymore, because this term has already been defined by Beijing [unilaterally] as 'one country, two systems.'"[16] President Tsai's response to Xi's messages revealed a defiant stance, derived from the will of the majority of Taiwanese who reject Beijing's goal of claiming Taiwan.[17] Her words also echoed the United States's clear position that any proposed "unification" is only valid if it reflects the assent of the Taiwanese people.[18]

People in Taiwan had long since begun developing a clear consciousness of be(com)ing Taiwanese, even during Japanese colonization. After decades of struggle against the one-party authoritarian government ruled by the Kuomintang (KMT), the Democratic Progressive Party (DPP) formation of a localized democracy and identity intensified after Lee Teng-hui won Taiwan's first free election for president in 1996. The DPP eventually won its first presidential election in 2000. Since then, the Taiwan consciousness championed by the DPP, as an alternative to the Sinocentric ideology represented by the KMT, continues to grow in Taiwan.[19] With Beijing's mounting aggression in the region and its grip on power in Hong Kong, Taiwanese people have become increasingly vigilant about the PRC's ambitions.[20] One example is the 2014 student-led Sunflower Movement, instigated by the lack of due process by the ruling KMT's rushing through passage of the Cross-Strait Service Trade Agreement (CSSTA).

The CSSTA agreement is a part of a larger Economic Cooperation Framework Agreement (ECFA) meant to further economic integration across the Taiwan Strait. The Sunflower Movement activists protested that these agreements would allow China's penetration of Taiwan's media industry and erode its people's freedom of expression.[21] The rising concerns over Taiwan's sovereignty ushered in the DPP's second presidential election win, by President Tsai, in 2016. Across the Taiwan Strait, the Chinese Communist Party (CCP) became perturbed by President Tsai's popularity. Stephen Hartnett offered analyses on the 2016 "internet war" waged by Chinese nationalistic netizens trolling President Tsai and her supporters through misogynist and dehumanizing messages.[22] The irony of these attacks is that these soldier-like "little pinks" had to use illegal mechanisms such as VPNs to bypass China's Great Firewall to perform their jingoistic assails against President Tsai on Facebook, which is banned in China.[23] The island nation continued to resist the PRC's dominating coercive measures to marginalize Taiwan, which have further ramped up since Taiwan's 2016 election and deteriorating U.S.-China relations.[24]

Marronage, Piracy, and Transformational Rhetoric in Taiwan

In *The Art of Not Being Governed*, James Scott describes marginalized communities in Southeast Asia as "a zone of refuge . . . of relative equality and physical mobility . . . and an ecocultural identity that was nearly a mirror image of lowland identities."[25] On the one hand, these marginalized spaces represent an imperative trading partner with their adjacent major powers, while on the other hand, they are under constant threat of being incorporated by these influential neighbors. Consequently, they engage in what Neil Roberts describes as marronage,[26] seeking to be free from and independent of the authority that attempts to claim their land and ways of life. China has long viewed Taiwan as a renegade state. Although not directly ruled by the Beijing government, Taiwanese people continue to be subject to covert and overt intimidation from the PRC regime. Taiwan's precarious condition casts it as a maroon society—a zone of refuge hovering on the fringes of power, a liminal space threatened by others yet struggling for independence. As a maroon society, Taiwanese citizens persist in a long-lasting space of flight, resisting formidable pressure from China.

Roberts writes that "marronage defies inertia," and identifies four types of marronage: petit, grand, sovereign, and sociogenic, to explain the micro and macro actions taken by slaves to seek freedom from "the zone of nonbeing." Sovereign marronage is initiated by political leaders to address structural oppressions experienced by the colonized, while sociogenic marronage includes acts that denote "a revolutionary process of naming and attaining individual and collective agency, non-sovereignty, liberation . . . and the cultivation of a community that aligns civil society with political society." These strategies not only declare the sovereignty of a people but also further solidify the legitimacy of the colonized to represent the land in which they reside.[27] Through self-proclamation, connections through indigenous symbols, and reimagining societal structures anchored in the desires of local populations, marronage propels the processes of freedom-seeking. It would be a far stretch to equate Taiwanese with slaves from Africa, and I do not wish to make such a claim. Rather, the conditions that force the colonized to seek survival in interstitial spaces, where support was sought and rendered in secret, resonate with Taiwanese people's lived experiences under Beijing's growing suppression and rising chauvinistic nationalism. People in Taiwan have engaged in the "perpetual flight from [being subjugated, searching for] an economy of survival" under China's threats. As Roberts writes, "freedom is not a place; it is a state of being."[28] Thus, despite Beijing's eminent military, economic, and diplomat forces aiming to suffocate Taiwan's independence, the Taiwanese people and our leaders, inheriting experiences from previous generations, have demonstrated ingenuity in learning to thrive in an interstitial space of possibility and resilience.

This marronage identity is rooted in history. The island of Formosa, Taiwan, has been a jewel for outsiders such as the Western imperial powers and Chinese courts. Due to its strategic location, the island embodies the spirits of those who cleverly found means to survive. In *Forbidden Nation*, Jonathan Manthorpe documents the formidable pirate Li Tan, a multilingual cosmopolitan trader who was active in the region of Taiwan, Japan, Southeast Asia, and China during the early 1600s.[29] On the one hand, Li acted as a go-between for the Dutch and English East India Company in their desires to penetrate Japanese and Chinese markets. On the other hand, Li established a pirate kingdom in Taiwan that lasted nearly forty years. He passed down his legacy to Cheng Chih-lung and consequently to Chih-lung's son, Cheng Chen-gong (the pirate chieftain known as Koxinga, who is celebrated throughout the region). Both Chih-lung and Chen-gong were multilingual and multicultural individuals who built a well-trained navy and controlled trading activities across today's Indonesia, the Philippines, Macau, southeast Chinese provinces, and Kyushu in Japan. From the outset, this independent island offered refuge to those outside of the establishment to *be* through astute negotiations with multiple powerful stakeholders vying for their own self-interests. We continue to witness this pirate-like spirit and multiculturalism in Taiwanese's emerging subjectivity as a collective people seeking "a [free] state of being." In this sense, President Tsai's rhetoric of marronage is a clear descendant of Koxinga's nation-building piracy.

Esther Fitzpatrick and Kelly Freebody assert that piracy can be seen as "a cultural phenomenon that occurs in response to systems that control and limit the potential of certain populations."[30] As an island with a deep connection to piracy in seeking ways to keep freedoms of belief, cultures, and languages, Taiwanese leaders and peoples have devised various strategies for resisting China's threats.[31] Not unlike pirates who exist in the liminal spaces deprived of legitimacy in the global community, Taiwanese society, through President Tsai's leadership, engages in marronage to guard its freedoms. Inheriting a pirate-like spirit seeking "grand marronage,"[32] President Tsai has continuously sought to convey Taiwan's reality against China's imperialistic threats.

Cultural sociologist Bob Kurik states that "resistance as an experience produces effects, which may transform, reconfirm, or even strengthen the existing identities of subjects." Because revolutions within the self are imperative for any lasting resistance,[33] how to conjure such effects remains challenging for any leader. Meryl Brodsky DeLaure used African American human rights activist Ella Baker's speeches as an exemplar for revolutionary rhetoric. According to DeLaure, such rhetoric reaches its transformative power in its ability to evoke the inner faith and capabilities within audiences.[34] Transformational rhetoric invites listeners to the conversation. Speaking as feminists who work to move the world toward a more equitable place for the marginalized, many rhetors, including President Tsai, took on the roles of not only persuaders but also deep listeners. As Baker and Tsai demonstrate, inspirational transformation is accomplished through deep engagement with interlocutors. Through such rhetoric, resisting subjects are (re) constituted. Resistance is (re)invented within a particular locale to assert, not always in opposition, but always for the freedom from oppression and exploitation.[35] A leader's transformational rhetoric engenders possibilities for structural change that enables the development of emotional/bodily poetic acts and rational/technological calculations for change. Working from the standpoint of marronage, combined with Taiwan's history, and imbued with a pirate-like spirit, this chapter examines President Tsai's significant speeches to illustrate how she performs resistance.

President Tsai's Speeches

Taiwanese elected Tsai Ing-wen in 2016 as the Republic of China's fourteenth-term president and reelected her in 2020.[36] Researchers have examined the impacts of President Tsai's presidency on the cross-Strait relations mostly from a political perspective.[37] Such research agendas primarily focus on Beijing's reactions to President Tsai's positions and policies over Taiwan's independence. This chapter examines the rhetorical strategies of Taiwan's first woman president. With an emphasis on Taiwan, this analysis provides insight into what President Tsai communicated to Taiwanese people in times of heightened U.S.-China relations. Since assuming the presidency, President Tsai has delivered annual speeches on important days such as National Day, Lunar New Year's Eve, New Year's Day, and of course, at the inaugurations. These speeches offer opportunities to communicate to people, on the island and abroad, about her vision and accomplishments for Taiwan. At the time of this essay, ten such speeches are published on the Office of the President website, two of which are inauguration speeches and four are speeches on National Day. Starting in 2018, President Tsai also delivered addresses on the Lunar New Year and the New Year. The length of these speeches ranged from ten to forty minutes, and

TABLE 1. President Tsai's Speeches to Taiwanese People

YEAR	OCCASION	TITLE
2016	Inaugural Address	Our Gratitude and Responsibilities
2016	National Day Address	Forging Ahead: Achieving Reforms to Make the Country Great
2017	National Day Address	Better Taiwan
2018	Lunar New Year Address	N/A
2018	National Day Address	Democratic Taiwan Lights Up the World
2019	Lunar New Year Remarks	N/A
2019	National Day Address	Nation of Resilience, Forward into the World
2020	Inaugural Address	A Taiwanese Community
2020	National Day Address	2020 Proud of Taiwan
2020	New Year's Address	N/A

Source: Office of the President Republic of China (Taiwan) Website, https://english.president.gov.tw/Page/35.

are transcribed in both Mandarin and English. Table 1 provides basic information on the speeches analyzed in this chapter.

Combining the concepts of sovereign and sociogenic marronage, as well as transformational rhetoric as the analytical prism, I will show that these speeches articulate a resistance rhetoric of freedom for Taiwanese people based on their lived reality. President Tsai's speeches engender a sense of radical empowerment, self-determination, and imagination to coexist with the PRC in the world.

Transformational Rhetoric of Realness as Resistance

President Tsai's speeches communicated an ontological (i.e., lived experiences) and epistemological (i.e., known idea) reality of Taiwan's existence. Sekimoto Sachi claims that an identity "*becomes* real" not only by discursive repetitions but also by "one's subjective experience of such ideologies as experientially and ontologically real." In this sense, one's knowledge is both "perceptual and embodied."[38] Indeed, A-Chin Hsiau argues that the early Taiwanese social movements derived from "a realistic recognition" of the fact that the ROC only controlled Taiwan, not China.[39] Such a recognition was inseparable from the social, cultural, political, and historical experiences of Taiwanese. This *realness* is not static; rather, it continues to evolve according to dynamic global geopolitical relations, particularly those between the United States and China. The following analyses highlight President Tsai's rhetorical transformation of these realities for Taiwanese people and beyond.

Rhetoric of Flexible Endurance

President Tsai's speeches instilled a sense of burgeoning national pride for the Taiwanese. This consciousness is a historical product of this land since it first experienced foreign powers.[40] Her rhetoric solidifies the existence of Taiwan, a political entity different from China, as an undisputable fact. On National Day in 2016, President Tsai stated, "the reality that the Republic of China exists," and then repeatedly stressed its "continued existence" during her next National Day speech in 2017. In her second inauguration speech, she declared that "the Republic of China can be united. Taiwan can be safe. Being Taiwanese can be an honor that makes you hold your head high." The ways in which President Tsai continued to fluidly interweave "ROC" and "Taiwan" signals her acknowledgment of the presence of the Republic of China in Taiwan, thereby recognizing the reality that although more than 60 percent of people identified as Taiwanese, 30.1 percent of those identified as both Taiwanese and ROC Chinese.[41] At the same time, she underscores *be(com)ing Taiwanese* as a source of pride. By naming Taiwan(ese) and evoking its people's shared desire for strong national esteem and international recognition, she employs the techniques of sociogenic marronage to create a sense of safety and freedom, both known and embodied, for the island's people.

President Tsai's words elevated the spirit of Taiwanese people and delineated the differences between Taiwan and China. On February 3, 2019, President Tsai delivered a Lunar New Year address. In her remarks, she noted that the Taiwanese will "maintain our cultural tradition, while also enjoying freedom and democracy." Distinguishing Taiwan's cultural and political identity has been a clear point in her presidency since 2016. Taiwan, as a polity of "united democracy, efficient democracy, and pragmatic democracy," where "courage, dignity, unity, confidence, justice" are valued, has clearly demarcated itself from the Beijing Chinese government. Her rhetoric adopted the "both . . . and" strategy for Taiwan to radically exist outside the binary on the question of "whether Taiwan is Chinese."[42] By maintaining cultural traditions while furthering freedom, democracy, and transitional justice on the island, President Tsai on National Day vowed to deepen reforms so that "20 years from now, when Taiwanese look back on 2020, they will remember this as the year . . . to overcome challenges and throw off their shackles, giving them a chance to determine their own future."[43] Once again, through "non-fleeting acts,"[44] her rhetoric depicted an image of a free people who are able to self-determine their preferred way of life. She practiced sociogenic marronage to highlight the importance of holding onto locally cherished values such as observing the Lunar New Year. Her rhetoric offers space for Taiwanese to transcend the confined definitions of being Taiwanese from external political entities while changing Taiwan into an even more democratic polity.

Although these speeches engendered a radical imagination for the listeners of a free, self-determining, and expansive future rooted in local histories, they also expressed the need for structural reforms to adeptly respond to volatile global and regional geopolitics. In her 2018 National Day address, President Tsai explained that Taiwan is "naturally subject to tremendous pressure" for being "on the frontline of the Western Pacific," especially under "the U.S. and China trade dispute . . . [and complex relations] in the Indo-Pacific region." In this uncertain historical moment, her rhetoric provided stability, hope, and courage to find Taiwan's "survival niche" based on its "distinctive resilience." That resilience is how Taiwan "will maintain strategic flexibility to be responsive to changes." She reminded listeners that "as a president, protect[ing] sovereignty is not a provocation [but] a responsibility."[45]

Stating that because of its strategic location, Taiwan is "naturally" under pressure during this particularly tumultuous time, the rhetoric of realness is combined with a sense of making the resistant process count. She alluded to resolving into Taiwan's past experiences, similar to its early pirate settlers, in nimbly finding resources to survive and to stand firmly amid challenges from outside the island. There exists the reality that Taiwanese people have a sovereign nation, and they are charged with finding ways to counter the dynamic international arena when the PRC puts a crushing amount of pressure on Taiwan and its few international allies.

President Tsai's rhetoric depicted a people with a collective past, present, and future. Her reference to "throw(ing) off shackles" figures an enchained Taiwanese people and casts the CCP as fettering the Taiwanese people and impeding their survival. She further called upon the Taiwanese people to utilize the "distinctive resilience" accumulated throughout their history to find their "survival niche." A history of battling various subjugations well prepared them for the current challenges. Their experience in finding means to survive has equipped Taiwan to defend its deeply held democratic values and cultivate flexible steadiness. Through phrases like "steadiness," "throw off shackles," and "survival niche," President Tsai rhetorically drew connections between the past and present to imagine a future for Taiwanese people based on a real understanding of their challenging political position and their ability to face down any obstacles.

Rhetoric of Reserved Invitation

While President Tsai enacted the rhetoric of realness to differentiate Taiwan from China, she also engaged in what I term the "rhetoric of reserved invitation." Sonja Foss and Cindy Griffin have written that invitational rhetoric aims for more than mere persuasion but is a conversation through an active listening process. Rooted in the feminist tradition of "equality, immanent value, and self-determination," President Tsai's speeches are examples of the rhetorical form of "offering," in that the rhetor creates an environment for different perspectives to be expressed in a safe, ethical, and free environment.[46] Moreover, her rhetoric embraces reservations and "interdiscursivity,"[47] in which different voices are amalgamated. The goal is to persuade and invite for a *mutually* respectful conversation.

One of the ways political leaders convey agendas is through linguistic coupling and repetition.[48] In President Tsai's remarks, Taiwan is frequently connected to the word "peace." For example, her 2017 National Day address on "Better Taiwan" described Taiwanese as a "peace-loving people who can make more meaningful contributions to the international community." Taiwanese were said to play an "irreplaceable role in the peace, stability, and prosperity of the Asia-Pacific region . . . with like-minded countries."[49] Her speeches pronounce a rhetorical construct of "good Taiwan" versus "bad China," Manichean framing that narrows the potential for mutual listening and understanding.[50] However, a shift in such framing seems to have occurred after 2017.

As mentioned earlier, in January 2019, cross-Strait relations further deteriorated after President Xi issued a resolute address about his "One-China" stance. In October, President Tsai stated that the chaotic condition in Hong Kong was the result of a failing "one country, two system" policy. A year later, she enacted the tactic of "re-sourcement,"[51] which presented a new source to reframe Beijing's authority as a potential actor of peace-seeking in the region, and extended an invitation for further engagement between Taiwanese and Chinese governments. On National Day 2020, President Tsai noted that

> I am also aware that the leader across the Strait has publicly stated in a video message to the United Nations General Assembly that China will never seek hegemony, expansion, or a sphere of influence. As countries in the region and around the world are now concerned about China's expanding hegemony, we hope this is the beginning of genuine change.

Although not a completely reconciliatory statement, President Tsai highlighted President Xi's message of restraint rather than aggression. At the same time, President Tsai held a firm position and called for an open ear by stating that "if Beijing can heed Taiwan's voice, change the way it handles cross-strait relations, and jointly facilitate cross-strait reconciliation and peaceful dialogue, I believe that regional tension can surely be resolved."[52] During her second inaugural address, in 2020, she reached out once again by calling for a conversation based on the principles of "peace, parity, democracy, and dialogue." While expressing a willingness for engagement, she firmly rejected Beijing's unilateral interpretation of "one country, two systems" over Taiwan's freedom to choose its relations with the PRC. Once again, she demonstrated reservations while being encouraging in her statements.

As Taiwan's leader, President Tsai engaged in both axes of "horizontal interdiscursivity" and "vertical interdiscursivity." Horizontal intertextuality involves a subject–addressee relationship in which the remarks of another speaker are invoked. The vertical axis refers to the text–context relationship in which spoken or written words are situated within a broader context. President Tsai's invitations with reservations are to be analyzed in this essay along with the overt conflicts and intensified democratic struggles between the United States and China in Hong Kong since 2018. By invoking President Xi's previous statement at a different occasion about China's role in the rapidly changing world, she showed herself to be listening closely to Xi's words. At the same time, she situated her remarks within China's confrontational interactions with the Trump administration and protesters in Hong Kong. President Tsai's words are the "'results from a complex of relationships linking' current with past (or future) discourse."[53] Her invitation for a dialogue with the PRC is reticent, which signaled her concerns over China's actions toward those it deemed as interfering in its interests as well as her resolve for Taiwan to be treated judicially when interacting with the Beijing government.

Although President Tsai underscored ways that Taiwan and China are distinctly different societies, she acknowledged that many Taiwanese citizens—like all ethnic Chinese peoples—share cultural traditions as many PRC citizens. On 2018 Lunar New Year's Eve, she explained that "the Lunar New Year is the most important holiday of the year on both sides of the Taiwan Strait. We have very similar traditional customs that run from New Year's Eve and New Year's Day through the Lantern Festival." President Tsai closed her remarks by wishing "our friends in the mainland China and ethnic Chinese around the world a happy Lunar New Year." This speech struck a more intimate note, as Lunar New Year's Eve is a time for family to gather in order to *chu jiu bu xin* (除舊佈新; rid of the old to welcome the new) and *shou sui* (守歲; stay up late until the arrival of the first day of the new year as a way to further lives of the elderly family members). This occasion allowed President Tsai to blur the private-public rhetorical boundaries. The Lunar New Year holiday became an opportunity to bridge the political gap between people on both sides of the Taiwan Strait. President Tsai reminded her audiences of the political reality faced by both nation-states when she declared that "I will not be provoked into confrontation or conflicts that endanger cross-strait relations, nor will I deviate from the will of the people, and sacrifice Taiwan's sovereignty." Her words reflected the real desire of the majority evident in a 2016 poll, which showed that almost 75 percent of Taiwanese preferred immediate independence if no military threats from the PRC were present.[54] Once again, President Tsai emphasized the existence of Taiwan based on her regard for its people's wishes while simultaneously signaling good will to meaningful engagement for peace. In practicing reserved invitational rhetoric, Taiwan and China are positioned in a dialectical relation delicately balanced with an unwavering stance supported by her people's will and an openness based on genuine respect.

Rhetoric of Sustainable Survivability through Diverse Relationality

President Tsai's remarks illustrated a way to counter what Stephen Hartnett calls "rhetoric of marginal significance,"[55] used by the United States to purposely make its commitment to Taiwan ambiguous. Instead, President Tsai adopted a rhetorical strategy of significance that amplified Taiwan's role on the global stage. At the same time, her rhetoric communicated the deeply rooted cultural sense of intimacy mitigated through "relationality."[56] These two concepts inform one another to articulate a sense of resistance expressed from a space of *outsideness*, inhabited by pirate-like personae non gratae. This island of significance offers its people opportunities and resources to authentically be(come) Taiwanese, further nurturing relationships within and beyond its geographic bounds.

Roberts engages in Édouard Glissant's concept of "*pays* (land, country)" to explain resistance. *Pays* refers to "the intersections of country, nation, state, and soil with the landscapes of a people."[57] In this sense, the liberation of becoming one's own people on their soil is the essence of resistance. In President Tsai's first inauguration speech in 2016, she referred to Taiwan as an agent who "faces" challenges and "shoulders" the burdens to guard democracy with the world. In her words, Taiwan was understood as both the land and the people "to carry the future of this country." In her many addresses, she called Taiwan a "home" that people come to and that "belongs to the 23 million people." Further, President Tsai articulated her policies to address unique needs for different Taiwanese populations. For example, on the 2019 National Day, she spoke of how the broadband infrastructure is rolled out in "tribal homelands and remote areas" to "narrow the urban-rural gap" in Taiwan. The temporal homebuilding project is part of the transitional justice work of facing and correcting mistakes from previous administrations that harmed the marginalized groups. The sustainable housing program aims to ensure that those who have historically been disadvantaged could benefit from Taiwan's transitioning into a more just and equitable society.[58] The ongoing transitional justice effort in Taiwan is juxtaposed with labelling Taiwan as "a beacon" for "our friends who are pursuing democracy in Hong Kong, in mainland China, and around the world." These examples expressed a desire to build Taiwan as *pays* in which the less powerful could be cared for. Such a desire is rooted in its people's understanding of oppression. This embodied knowledge furthers the significant role that Taiwan holds in the Indo-Pacific region, where democracy and human dignity undergo much contestation.[59]

In President Tsai's transformative rhetoric, Taiwan becomes a "zone of refuge" or a "shattered zone,"[60] seeking survival with localized knowledge and lived experiences at the edge of the Chinese expansion. This search involves work to progress to the ideal of justice, both on the island and of it. *Be(com)ing Taiwanese* means to resist all colonial and imperial arrogance. It also means confronting the legacy of exploitation and oppression performed by the KMT government after the Asian-Pacific war, and by Beijing's ever-stronger coercive power over Taiwan since Xi's reign. Acts in the realm of democratic policy reforms, as well as in President Tsai's words of solidarity directly spoken to "our friends . . . in Hong Kong," revealed the covert and nonconfrontational resistance to the PRC's authoritarian governance.[61] Five years after Taiwan's 2014 Sunflower Movement, people in Hong Kong organized unprecedentedly large protests out of deep concern over the extradition bill in Hong Kong. President Tsai in her 2019 National Day address explicitly connected efforts for justice and democracy witnessed both in Taiwan and Hong Kong, where people continue to struggle to free themselves from the CCP-imposed "One-China" principle.

President Tsai, in her 2020 National Day's speech, included the COVID-19 pandemic as another of China's threat to Taiwan. Due to China's objection, Taiwan remains excluded from major global organizations including the World Health Organization. Even during the global pandemic, Taiwan was not welcomed to the seventy-third meeting of the World Health Assembly (WHA), an exclusion that "neglects the health and human rights of Taiwan's 23.5 million people."[62] In her speech, President Tsai thanked everyone on the island for having "helped make Taiwan a happy, safe, and prosperous place" in the middle of a global pandemic. President Tsai further stressed that "Every single person in Taiwan is a hero," including all members in Taiwan's movement for freedom. Inclusivity remains key to sustaining Taiwan's resistance to the PRC's singular effort to isolate its people.

In addition to articulating ways of be(com)ing Taiwanese in the past, present, and into the future, President Tsai's rhetoric calls for every Taiwanese to take up the responsibility to live out its most powerful resource: *qing* (情; connective feelings).[63] In her 2018 Lunar New Year's Eve remarks, President Tsai expressed her appreciation toward "friends from the international community" who provided assistance after Taiwan experienced a devastating earthquake of a 6.4 magnitude in early February.[64] She reminded Taiwanese to never forget the support they had received. President Tsai vouched that the Taiwanese would reciprocate if there were ever an opportunity to demonstrate "the authentic spirit of friendship; the *qing* of Taiwanese (*tai wan ren de jen qing* 台灣人的真情)." On National Day 2018, President Tsai stated that "The US Congress recently passed many Taiwan-friendly legislative bills. . . . Japan . . . has also spoken up for Taiwan in international gatherings. . . . [T]he European Parliament passed a resolution to recognize Taiwan's democratic development." These activities were viewed as more than gestures of support but, indeed, of efforts to forge close relationships. Highlighting the cultural salience of *qing*, President Tsai reminded Taiwanese that key global powers recognize Taiwan's significance to the world and have advocated for their cause. Her rhetoric continuously underscores a sense of friendship based on *qing*, a concept recognizable to all Taiwanese, between Taiwan and those President Tsai referred to as "forces of good."[65]

In President Tsai's speeches, all agents envision liberation by developing a sense of accountability to continuously build relationships within and outside the island nation. Speaking of people at the political margins, her rhetoric reflects "the act of marronage as a continual process of becoming." Such freedom can only be accomplished through a "rhizome-like" process whereby connections are ceaselessly established in multiple spheres of human activity.[66] These activities inspire Taiwanese to keep cultivating relationships so that they continue to be(come) members of the landscape of *patrie* (nation), *état* (region), and *le monde* (the world).[67]

Transformative Rhetoric of Realness

President Tsai's rhetoric of realness presents radical permission to imagine and be(come) free Taiwanese. Her rhetoric is transformative in remaining aware of China's substantial threat while articulating Taiwan's geocultural identity as rooted in the experience of enduring multiple forms of occupation. Rather than the jingoistic fever heightened by China's leader, President Tsai's nationalistic rhetoric seeks self-determination for a people under a long-period of subjugation. Her form of inclusive and justice-based nationalism radically differs from the CCP's Han-Chinese ethnic nationalism, which the world witnessed in Tibet with the Buddhist Tibetans throughout the 1950s–1970s.[68] More recently, this aggressive nationalism was enacted against the Uighur and other Turkic Muslims in Xinjiang.[69]

A-Chin Hsiau describes Taiwan as a "latecomer to the nationalist club."[70] Although the idea of building a Taiwanese nation is not new,[71] President Tsai is the first incumbent leader to publicly call Taiwan what it is, and to depict how be(com) ing a Taiwanese could feel. By rhetorically conjuring a radically imagined future free from intimidation, President Tsai repeatedly invited all oppressed to maroon together on the journey for dignity and liberation. Her speeches reflect, connect, and contest various voices derived from Taiwanese people's real life. These "*huo sheng sheng* (活生生的)" and lived experiences, including surviving earthquakes, global pandemics, CCP military threats, and Taiwanese flags being erased from regional and world events, forge strong bonds among Taiwanese.[72] President Tsai underscored the pirate-like resilient survival skills Taiwan embodied even before the Dutch arrived on the island. She asked the Taiwanese and the world to recognize this *realness* of

Taiwan's past, current, and future existence, and to resist the "One-China" narrative repeatedly ascribed to Taiwanese by those who have not lived Taiwan's reality. Her rhetoric of flexible endurance evinces how Taiwanese have fashioned their fate in times of change and stability. This flexibility and persistence, according to President Tsai, offers a realness to Taiwan's effort to hold onto traditions to deepen its democracy. While Taiwan and China each has its own distinctive principles, President Tsai engaged in reserved rhetoric to invite the Beijing government to listen to the wishes of Taiwanese people. In her speech, the reality of Taiwan's existence is articulated through events such as protests in Hong Kong and struggles between the United States and China. President Tsai's goal is not only to persuade but also to invite those with willing ears to hear Taiwan's reality. Part of Taiwan's reality is the need to fight for its survival under Beijing's all-encompassing pressures. The rhetoric of sustainable survivability encourages its people to utilize Taiwan's deeply held value—*qing*—to establish more relationships so that the road to freedom can be constructed in solidarity. These rhetorical strategies highlight that Taiwan's very existence resists the PRC's "one country" claim.

Although President Tsai's rhetoric of realness propels a vision of be(com)ing Taiwanese as a form of challenging Beijing's oppression, her rhetoric also addresses the growing ethno-nationalism facilitated by rising political populism.[73] Against the simplified, bifurcating either/or identification of Taiwanese or Chinese, President Tsai's epistemological stance of marronage included and attended to roughly 30 percent of the population, albeit a minority, that self-identifies as both. As a leader, her speeches did not encourage hatred toward people on the mainland—even though Beijing used its "divide-and-conquer economic policy" to successfully create deep fissures in age, class, and ethnicity groups in Taiwanese's national identification during the 1996 election. For example, those who self-identified as Taiwanese might not support Taiwan's independence, fearful for its various military or economic ramifications from China.[74] Without completely subtracting Taiwan from the ROC, her rhetoric recognized the nuanced distinctions within the "pro-unification" and 'pro-independence" camps in cross-Strait relations. Indeed, an approximately equal percentage of the population in Taiwan would like to "maintain the status quo [of Taiwan and] decide at later date" (28.8 percent), to "maintain the status quo, move toward independence" (25.8 percent), or to "maintain the status quo indefinitely" (25.5 percent).[75] Without overtly calling for Taiwan's independence, but rather articulating its existence as a political entity independent of other nations, President Tsai artfully avoided excluding any of these stances. Her rhetoric demonstrates the complicated and competing forces at play in any resistance,[76] providing a radical imagination based on Taiwan's reality shared—and lived—by all.

Conclusion

During President Tsai's reelection campaign, a key component was the theme song by Fire Extinguisher (*miehuoqi*). Fire Extinguisher is a band whose tune "Island Sunrise" stirred many Taiwanese souls and became a driving force in the Sunflower Movement's success in 2014.[77] "Island Sunrise" conjured a consciousness, particularly in young Taiwanese, to no longer be fearful of China's intimidation and to "become brave" in asserting their power to chart their own fate. In 2019, Sam Yang, the band's vocalist, wrote "Confident and Brave: Our Name" for President Tsai's 2020 campaign. The song asks people to put faith in President Tsai's steady leadership to guide her people along "the bumpy road of the island's fate." It challenges people to "stand up" so that their family can "live a simple and peaceful life." The song proclaims that "resolve is [our] name, we are proud children of Taiwan" who are be(com)ing "confident and brave, free and unfettered." This song is the epitome of President Tsai's rhetoric, which offers a clear vision of Taiwanese people's hope to live freely by courageously staying true to their collective reality.

Benedict Anderson centers communication in nationalistic imagination.[78] This chapter moves beyond the power of this collective imagination and focuses on the materiality—or, what Hsiau calls the "social effects"—of these imaginations.[79] All of President Tsai's significant speeches clearly depict and demand a "free and unfettered" Taiwan. No longer satisfied with living under Beijing's constant threat, her "transformative rhetoric of realness" demonstrates a deep desire for Taiwan, as a people in marronage, to be emancipated from China's neoimperialistic power.[80] With deep attachments to its surrounding oceans, the Taiwanese people have inherited a tradition of a pirate-like mentality, adept in survival. Living on an island situated at the intersection of various civilizations, Taiwanese have demonstrated the ability to be "multi-tongued" global citizens embracing diverse views, and practicing vigilance against threats.[81] President Tsai's remarks articulated a clear reality of who the Taiwanese are based on their values, shared history, what they can accomplish, and how they are impeded from pursuing their goals. She enacted marronage resistance against structural oppression that hinders Taiwan's free will. Simultaneously, through "non-fleeting acts" of naming, invoking local values, and establishing policies to reform uneven societal structures, President Tsai practiced resistance based on the unfortunate situation and limited resources afforded to Taiwan. Her rhetorical devices of flexible endurance, reserved invitation, and sustainable survivability through diverse relationality, drew energy from the increasingly mature Taiwanese nationalism while simultaneously fueling its further growth. By speaking explicitly to the unique existence of Taiwanese people, her rhetoric of realness invites Taiwanese to reimagine their future, at the same time, signaling unwillingness to be treated as any country's subject against its people's will.

Stemming from the knowledge and embodiment of marronage and pirate-like survival instincts, these rhetorical strategies are reinvented with an intensified uncertainty between the Beijing government and the United States, and to a larger extent, the European Union.[82] Those who live on the margins—such as pirates—constantly evaluate their strategies for building alliances for self-protection. With Taiwan's isolated position in the interconnected global society, President Tsai articulated existing and potential future resources for the island nation to cultivate as a means of subverting China's global economic and political clout. Instead of focusing on Taiwan's lack of freedom to partake in the global community, her rhetoric and policies underscore the importance of fostering authentic regional and global relations while holding firmly to building a democratic society at home with renewed relationships through transitional justice. These enduring actions are imperative to Taiwan's freedom. She rhetorically frames relationships different from those of patronage; they are friendships based on mutual respect.

Certainly, the emphasis on Taiwan's need for support from influential countries such as the United States could be construed as operating as a "tool" in the doctrine of utilitarianism in international affairs.[83] At the same time, however, this emphasis depicts the reality of Taiwan and anchors its current existence as the basis for its continuing resistance. President Tsai tapped into shared interdiscursive social knowledge about events that have impacted and occurred in Taiwan (e.g., Beijing's intimidation, the youth's desire for an autonomous Taiwan free from outside threats), as well as global activities (e.g., protests in Hong Kong, advocacy for the Uighur people, the COVID-19 pandemic) to animate multiple strains of national consciousness. The outcome is an effervescent nationalism rooted in lived experiences as a response to China's interference in Taiwan's free will.

Roberts asserts that "the act of marronage [is] a continual process of becoming [because] freedom [is] a relational concept."[84] Although the conditions of Taiwanese people cannot be compared to those endured by people of African descent, the concept of marronage, derived from slavery experiences, is a useful heuristic for unpacking the rhetorical strategies of Taiwan's president Tsai Ing-wen. For those at the margins of the global structure—those with limited resources and legitimacy, President Tsai's rhetoric bridges Taiwan's need for both the negative freedom of non-interference and the positive freedom of self-empowered autonomy. Integrating marronage strategies drawn from Taiwan's national consciousness, President Tsai narrates Taiwan's existence as a reality. She further frames such existence as the only way to resist the ever-increasing pressure from the PRC government in its stance toward the fate of Taiwanese people. The road of continuously and collectively be(com)ing Taiwanese is part of the process to freedom.

NOTES

1. Li-lan Chou, "Taiwan bo shi guo jia shi she me?" [What is Taiwan if not a country?] *China Times*, April 5, 2019, https://www.chinatimes.com/realtimenews/20190405002261-260407?chdtv.
2. These rules include "(1) A country is territory defined by borders mutually agreed upon by all countries; (2) A country must have a state that controls (or at least seeks to control) the legitimate use of force within its territory, and a population of citizens; (3) Every spot on the earth's landmass must be occupied by a country; (4) Every person on the planet must be a citizen of at least one country; (5) On paper, all countries have the same legal standing–Tuvalu has just as much right to its nationhood as China, Somalia just as much as Switzerland–even if they are politically and economically highly unequal; (6) Consent of the people with each country is preferred, but not required. Tyranny or de facto anarchy within a country is not grounds for loss of club membership; (7) Under some circumstances, one or more countries may invade or occupy another country, but not eliminate its nationhood or redraw its borders; and (8) The currently existing set of countries and the borders between them should be left in place whenever possible–that is, the club prefers not to admit new members." Joshua Keating. *Invisible Countries: Journeys to the Edge of Nationhood* (New Haven: Yale University Press, 2018), 8–9.
3. According to the most recent survey, 64 percent of Taiwanese self-identify as a Taiwanese rather than Chinese. It is important however to note the nuances in the survey, which extends beyond only "Chinese (Blue) vs. Taiwanese (Green)" identities. Within the so-called Blue vs. Green camps are nuanced identifications such as "deep blue/green"

and "light blue/green." Such phenomena resonate with Trinh's words "All categories leak." See Election Study Center, National Chengchi University, "Taiwanese/Chinese Identity (1992/06~2020/12)," https://esc.nccu.edu.tw/PageDoc/Detail?fid=7800&id=6961. Minh-ha Trinh, *Women, Native Other: Writing Postcoloniality and Feminism* (Bloomington: Indiana University Press, 1989).

4. Devlin Kat and Huang Christine, "In Taiwan, Views of Mainland China Mostly Negative," Pew Research Center's Global Attitudes Project, (2020), https://www.pewresearch.org/global/2020/05/12/in-taiwan-views-of-mainland-china-mostly-negative/.
5. Louisa Ha and Lars Willnat (eds.), *The U.S.–China Trade War: Global News Framing and Public Opinion in the Digital Age* (East Lansing: Michigan State University Press, 2022).
6. Here, the term "realness" resembles Laura Pérez's argument about the "realness" in Chicana/os' collective imagination, Aztlán, and their effort to make such an image visible. Pérez explains that the dominant group's control of the military, political, economic, and social resources is never comprehensive enough to eradicate the cultural significance represented in arts and shared in the imagination of the oppressed. This "realness" is present in the articulations of Taiwan's national imagination and its people's lived experiences. See Laura Pérez, "*El Desorden*, Nationalism, and Chicana/o Aesthetics," in *Between Women and Nation: Nationalisms, Transnational Feminisms, and the State*, edited by Caren Kapaln, Norma Alarcón, and Minoo Mallem, 19–46 (Durham: Duke University Press, 1999).
7. In the past, the need for Taiwanese to self-rule has often been framed as a problem. For example, see the interview "Why the Taiwan Issue Is So Dangerous?," *Frontline*, 2001, https://www.pbs.org/wgbh/pages/frontline/shows/china/experts/taiwan.html. See the next paragraph for President Xi's framing of Taiwan in his speech.
8. Jinping Xi, "Working Together to Realize Rejuvenation of the Chinese Nation and Advance China's Peaceful Reunification," Taiwan Work Office of the CPC Central Committee: Taiwan Affairs Office of the State Council PRC, January 2, 2019, http://www.gwytb.gov.cn/wyly/201904/t20190412_12155687.htm.
9. Election Study Center, National Chengchi University, "Taiwanese/Chinese Identity"; Elizabeth Larus, "Xi Jinping's Message to Compatriots in Taiwan Signals Change in Taiwan Policy," *Taiwan Insight*, January 24, 2019.
10. De Morais, Isabela Nogueira, Ben Lian Deng, and Caroline Rocha Travassos Colbert, "One China Policy: Origins and Implications for the Current US Taiwan Policy," *Mural Internacional* 9, no. 1 (2018): 8–20.
11. This ambiguity has allowed the United States to pursue its interests with China while offering support to Taiwanese people's safety and their democratic government. Dean

P. Chen, "The Trump Administration's One-China Policy: Tilting Toward Taiwan in an Era of U.S.-PRC Rivalry?," *Asian Politics & Policy* 11, no. 2 (Apr, 2019): 250–278, https://onlinelibrary.wiley.com/doi/abs/10.1111/aspp.12455; Isabela Nogueira De Morais, Ben Lian Deng, and Caroline Rocha Travassos Colbert, "One China Policy: Origins and Implications for the Current US Taiwan Policy," *Mural Internacional* 9, no. 1 (2018): 8–20.

12. Richard Bush, *One-China Policy Primer* (Washington, DC: Brookings Institution, 2017).
13. Joint communique between the United States and China, February, 28, 1972, Wilson Center, Washington, DC, https://digitalarchive.wilsoncenter.org/document/121325.
14. The 1972 Shanghai Communiqué is notorious for its controversy. For more information and nuanced analyses, see Stephen Hartnett, *A World of Turmoil* (East Lansing: Michigan State University Press, 2021).
15. Bush, *One-China Policy*, 20, 17.
16. Chris Horton, "Taiwan's President, Defying Xi Jinping, Calls Unification Offer 'Impossible,'" *New York Times*, January 5, 2019. In 2019, Xi equated the alleged "1992 Consensus" with its "one country, two systems" policy. See Derek Grossman. "Where Does China's 'One country, Two systems' Stand in 2020?," *The Diplomat*, February 13, 2020.
17. In 2018, several political scientists found from their survey that one-third of participants held an incorrect interpretation of the 1992 consensus and believed that it treated Taiwan and China as two separate countries. More than 75 percent favored supporting Taiwan and China as two separate countries. Only 5 percent accepted the PRC's definition of the consensus as aiming for reunification. Austin Wang, Charles Wu, Yao-Yuan Yeh, and Chen Fang-Yu, "What Does the 1992 Consensus Mean to Citizens in Taiwan?," *The Diplomat*, November 10, 2018.
18. Bush, *One-China Policy*.
19. Hsin-I Cheng, *Cultivating Membership in Taiwan and Beyond: Relational Citizenship* (London: Lexington Books, 2021), 1–27.
20. Dean P. Chen, "The Trump Administration's One-China Policy: Tilting Toward Taiwan in an Era of U.S.-PRC Rivalry?," *Asian Politics & Policy* 11, no. 2 (2019): 250–278.
21. Ian Rowen, "Inside Taiwan's Sunflower Movement: Twenty-Four Days in a Student-Occupied Parliament, and the Future of the Region," *The Journal of Asian Studies* 74, no. 1 (2015): 5–21.
22. See Hartnett, *A World of Turmoil*, chap. 5.
23. These internet nationalists are made up of both civilians and governmental personnel. Rongbin Han, "Defending the Authoritarian Regime Online: China's 'Voluntary Fifty-Cent Army,'" *China Quarterly* (London) 224 (2015): 1006–1025; Gary King, Jennifer Pan, and Margaret E. Roberts, "How the Chinese Government Fabricates Social Media Posts for

Strategic Distraction, Not Engaged Argument," *The American Political Science Review* 111, no. 3 (2017): 484–501; Li Yuan, "China Students Trapped Abroad by the Coronavirus Are Criticized at Home," *New York Times*, June, 2020.

24. Chen, "The Trump Administration's One-China Policy."
25. James C. Scott, *The Art of Not Being Governed: An Anarchist History of Upland Southeast Asia* (New Haven: Yale University Press, 2009), 31.
26. Neil Roberts, *Freedom as Marronage* (Chicago: University of Chicago Press, 2015), 141–172.
27. Ibid., 212–230, 11, 165. The uses of "land" here derive from Glissant's usage of *pays* to denote "the sum total of physical territories, spatial zones, diversity, collective expressions, and political strategies."
28. Ibid., 141–172, 226.
29. Jonathan Manthorpe, *Forbidden Nation: A History of Taiwan* (New York: Macmillan, 2008).
30. Esther Fitzpatrick and Kelly Freebody, "Battling the Neoliberal Beast: A Pedagogy of Piracy and a Place of Resistance," *International Journal of Critical Pedagogy* 10, no. 1 (2019): 176–191.
31. Hua-Lun Huang, "Who Are Sea Cutthroats? A Typological Analysis of Pirates," *Crime Law Soc Change* 53 (2010): 277–298; Peter Kang, "Koxinga and His Maritime Regime in the Popular Historical Writings of Post-Cold War Taiwan," in *Sea Rovers, Silver and Samurai: Maritime East Asia in Global History 1550–1700*, edited by Tonio Andrade, Xing Hang, Jerry Bentley, and Anand Yang, 335–352 (Honolulu: University of Hawai'i Press, 2016). Ben Blanchard, "Taiwan Scrambles Fighters as Chinese Jets again Fly Near Island," *Reuters*, September 19, 2020; Chris Buckley and Steven Lee Myers, "U.S. and China Enter Dangerous Territory Over Taiwan," *New York Times*, November 10, 2021; Chris Buckley and Amy Qin, *Taiwan: America's Next War?* (Fort Belvoir, VA: Defense Technical Information Center, 2021).
32. Roberts, *Freedom*, 10.
33. Bob Kurik, "Emerging Subjectivity in Protest," in *The SAGE Handbook of Resistance*, edited by David Courpasson and Steven Vallas (London: SAGE Publications, 2016), 59, 54.
34. Meryl Brodsky DeLaure, "Planting Seeds of Change: Ella Baker's Radical Rhetoric," *Women's Studies in Communication* 31, no. 1 (2008): 1–28.
35. Mohan J. Dutta, *Voices of Resistance: Communication and Social Change* (West Lafayette, IN: Purdue University Press, 2012).
36. Office of the President Office Republic of China (Taiwan), "President Tsai," December 18, 2020, https://english.president.gov.tw/Page/40.
37. Alan D. Romberg, "Tsai Ing-Wen Takes Office: A New Era in Cross-Strait Relations," *China*

Leadership Monitor 50 (2016): 1–13; Bonnie S. Glaser, "Prospects for Cross-Strait Relations as Tsai Ing-Wen Assumes the Presidency in Taiwan," *Center for Strategic & International Studies*, April 20, 2016, https://www.csis.org/analysis/prospects-cross-strait-relations-tsai-ing-wen-assumes-presidency-taiwan; Dafydd Fell, "Divergent Understandings of Taiwanese Democracy: Ma Ying-Jeou vs. Tsai Ing-Wen," *Taiwan Sentinel*, July 19, 2019; Mark Harrison, "Reading between the Lines of Tsai Ing-Wen's Inaugural Address," *East Asia: Economics, Politics and Public Policy in East Asia and the Pacific Forum*, May 30, 2016, https://www.eastasiaforum.org/2016/05/30/reading-between-the-lines-of-tsai-ing-wens-inaugural-address/; Wen-cheng Lin, "Taiwan Enters the Tsai Ing-Wen Era and the Impact on Cross-Strait Relations," *Milan: ISPI Analysis* 293, January 2016.

38. Sachi Sekimoto, "A Multimodal Approach to Identity: Theorizing the Self through Embodiment, Spatiality, and Temporality," *Journal of International and Intercultural Communication* 5, no. 3 (August 1, 2012): 229, 231–234.
39. A-chin Hsiau, "Epilogue," in *Cultural, Ethnic, and Nationalism in Contemporary Taiwan: Bentuhua*, edited by John Makeham and A-chin Hsiau (New York: Palgrave Macmillian, 2005), 262.
40. Cheng, *Cultivating Membership*.
41. Election Study Center, National Chengchi University, "Changes in the Taiwanese/Chinese Identity of Taiwanese as tracked in Surveys by the Election Study Center (1992~2022, 06)," https://esc.nccu.edu.tw/upload/44/doc/6960/People202206.jpg.
42. DeLaure, "Planting Seeds," 18.
43. Office of the President Office Republic of China (Taiwan), "President Tsai delivers 2020 National Day Address," October 10, 2020, https://english.president.gov.tw/NEWS/6051.
44. Roberts, *Freedom*, 116.
45. Office of the President Office Republic of China (Taiwan), "President Tsai delivers 2018 National Day Address," October 10, 2018, https://english.president.gov.tw/NEWS/6051.
46. Sonja Foss and Cindy Griffin, "Beyond Persuasion: A Proposal for an Invitational Rhetoric," *Communication Monograph* 62 (1995), 2–18, 5, 13.
47. Ruth Wodak, "Analyzing Meetings in Political and Business Contexts," in *Discourse Approaches to Politics, Society and Culture*, edited by Piotr Cap and Urszula Okulska, 187–221 (Amsterdam: John Benjamins Publishing Company, 2013).
48. John Wilson, "Political Discourse," in *The Handbook of Discourse Analysis*, edited by Deborah Hamilton Tannen, Deborah Heidi Schiffrin, 775–794 (Malden, MA: John Wiley & Sons, Inc., 2015).
49. Office of the President Office Republic of China (Taiwan), "President Tsai delivers 2017 National Day Address," October 10, 2017, https://english.president.gov.tw/NEWS/5231.

50. Hsin-I Cheng employed the concept of Manichean mechanism to describe how concepts are rhetorically arranged in a hierarchical order where each is mutually exclusive of the other. Hsin-I Cheng, "Space Making: Chinese Transnationalism on the U.S.-Mexican Borderlands," *Null* 1, no. 3 (2008): 244–263.
51. Foss and Griffin, "Beyond Persuasion," 9.
52. Office of the President Office Republic of China (Taiwan), "President Tsai deliver 2020 National Day Address," October 10, 2020, https://english.president.gov.tw/NEWS/6051.
53. Adam Hodges, "Intertextuality in Discourse," in *The Handbook of Discourse Analysis*, edited by Deborah Tanne, Heidi Hamilton, and Deborah Schiffrin (Malden: John Wiley & Sons, Inc., 2015), 44–45.
54. The number for those under forty years old was even as high as 84 percent. See Fung-yu Chen, "She me shi 'xian zhuang'? Taiwan ren shi zi ji shi Taiwan ren, bo shi Zhong guo ren" [What is "status quo"? Taiwanese identify as Taiwanese, not Chinese.], January 5, 2017, https://whogovernstw.org/2017/01/05/whogovernstw5/.
55. Hartnett, *World of Turmoil.*
56. Cheng, *Cultivating Membership.*
57. Roberts, *Freedom*, 163–164.
58. Liao Ting-hui "520 Jien shi Tsai Ing-wen—zhu zhai zheng tse pien" [520 on Tsai Ing-wen's housing policy], *The News Lens*, May 19, 2020.
59. Lindsey W. Ford and Ryan Hass, "Democracy in Asia," *Brookings*, January 22, 2021.
60. Scott, *Art of Not Being*, 8.
61. Office of the President Republic of China (Taiwan), "Inauguration of the 15th-term President and Vice President of the Republic of China (Taiwan)," May 20, 2020, https://english.president.gov.tw/Page/548.
62. Office of the President Republic of China (Taiwan), "President Tsai delivers 2020 National Day Address," October 10, 2020.
63. Cheng, *Cultivating Membership*, chap. 3.
64. For more information on this tragedy, see Shelly Shan, "Seven Dead, Hundreds Injured in Temblor," *Taipei Times*, February 8, 2020.
65. President Tsai started using this phrase in the 2020 National Day Address.
66. Roberts, *Freedom*, 166, 168.
67. In *Cultivating Taiwanese Membership: Relational Citizenship*, I illustrate ways that President Tsai's government anchors *qing* in its various types of relationship-building with citizens in Asian countries and those in the West, with the aim of advancing Taiwan's liberation from Beijing's imperialist oppression. In essence, President Tsai laid out an action plan for be(com)ing Taiwanese on the global stage. Cheng, *Cultivating*

Membership, 29–56.

68. Stephen J. Hartnett, "Alternative Modernities, Postcolonial Colonialism, and Contested Imaginings in and of Tibet," in *Imagining China: Rhetorics of nationalism in an age of globalization*, edited by Stephen Hartnett, Lisa Keränen, and Donovan Conley (East Lasing: Michigan State University Press, 2017), 91–138.
69. For Xi's chauvinistic nationalistic policy in Xinjiang, see Chris Buckley, "Brushing Off Criticism, China's Xi Calls Policies in Xinjiang 'Totally Correct,'" *New York Times*, June 8, 2021; Maya Wang, "China: Visiting Officials Occupy Homes in Muslim Region 'Becoming Family' Campaign Intensifies Repression in Xinjiang," *Human Rights Watch*, May 13, 2018.
70. Hsiau, "Epilogue," 273.
71. Cheng, *Cultivating Membership*, 6–20; Fen-Mei Luo, *Bei Niuqu de Taiwan Shi 1684–1972* [The distorted Taiwan history 1684–1972] (Taipei: Readingtimes, 2015).
72. Chang Maukuei, "The Movement to Indigenize the Social Sciences in Taiwan: Origin and Predicaments," in *Cultural, Ethnic, and Nationalism in Contemporary Taiwan: Bentuhua*, edited by John Makeham and A-chin Hsiau (New York: Palgrave Macmillan, 2005), 243.
73. Richard Bush, "Taiwan's Democracy and the China Challenge," *Brookings*, January 22, 2021.
74. Dongtao Qi and Shengqiao Lin, "Dividing without Conquering: Generation, Class, Ethnicity, and Nationalism in Taiwan's 2016 Presidential Election," *Issues & Studies: A Social Science Quarterly on China, Taiwan, and East Asian Affairs* 57, no. 3 (2021): 1–32.
75. "Taiwan Independence vs. Unification with the Mainland (1994/12~2020/12)," Election Study Center, NCCU, https://esc.nccu.edu.tw/PageDoc/Detail?fid=7800&id=6963.
76. Joanne P. Sharp, Paul Routledge, Chris Philo, and Ronan Paddison, eds., *Entanglements of Power: Geographies of Domination/Resistance* (London: Routledge, 2000).
77. The creator Yang Dazheng of the band wrote the song "Island Sunrise" and released the rights on March 29, Day of Youth in Taiwan, in 2014 to support the Sunflower Movement. In a short amount of time, young student artists created visual versions of this song and reached a wide audience both within and outside Taiwan. This theme song played a key role in what Wang calls "affective-politics" in the success of the Sunflower Movement. It further promoted the idea of "becoming brave" for Taiwan's nationalism. See Chih-ming Wang, "'The Future that Belongs to Us': Affective Politics, Neoliberalism and the Sunflower Movement," *International Journal of Cultural Studies* 20, no. 2 (March 1, 2017), 177–192.
78. Benedict Anderson, *Imagined Communities* (London: Verso Books, 2016).
79. Hsiau, "Epilogue," 264.
80. Tukumbi Lumumba-Kasongo, "China-Africa Relations: A Neo-Imperialism or a

Neo-Colonialism? A Reflection," *African and Asian Studies* 10 (2010): 236–266.

81. Here, I refer to the work of Chicana feminist Gloria Anzaldúa, who writes about how borderlands are empowering transcultural spaces for nurturing multi-tongued and multicultural individuals. See Gloria Anzaldúa, *Borderlands/La Frontera: The New Mestiza* (San Francisco: aunt lute, 1987); H-I Cheng, *Culturing Interface: Identity, Communication, and Chinese Transnationalism* (New York: Peter Lang, 2008).
82. However, it is important to note that the recent Comprehensive Agreement on Investment (CAI) signed between China and the European Union in 2020 may suggest a more friendly and collaborative relationship between these two powerful global polities. See Alexis Leggeri, "EU-China Investment Deal: Has China Revived its European Diplomacy?," *The Diplomat*, December 31, 2020.
83. Yang Guang-shuen, "Taiwan shi qi zi hai shi qi zi: mei guo zai liang an de he xin li yi shi she me?" [Is Taiwan a cher piece or an abandoned son? What is American's crucial interests in both sides of the Taiwan Strait?], *News Lens*, July 2 2018.
84. Roberts, *Freedom*, 166.

Beyond Critique and Conspiracy

COVID Memes as Reparative Practices in Digital Taiwan

Wen Liu

The COVID-19 pandemic has significantly rearranged our social relations and affective connections. In the midst of disinformation and virus origin conspiracy theories circulating across the social landscape, governmental responses to the pandemic have included various public health measures, such as lockdowns and mask mandates, and political measures, such as escalating geopolitical conflicts between the United States and China. Around the world, fear has been one of the most prominent affective responses to the pandemic, driven by disinformation practices, intensified geopolitics, and our raw psychic fear about the unknown. When the outbreak went global in March 2020, the director of the U.S. National Institute of Allergy and Infectious Diseases, Anthony Fauci, said: "If it looks like you're overreacting, you're probably doing the right thing."[1] Fauci is not an alarmist, but an informed scientist who meant the statement to communicate that Americans needed to take the virus seriously. Yet the remark also evinces the easy conflation of being cautiously and appropriately prepared and sliding into anxiety intertwined with other political and cultural implications, which I describe below as the state of paranoia.

Paranoia is not only a state driven by one's individual psychic anxiety, but also a collective coping mechanism in the face of global trauma. While many Western countries scrambled to develop a cohesive public health response to the rapidly evolving pandemic, Taiwan has been relatively successful in curbing the virus and its impact on the daily economic and social functioning of residents in the country. In March 2021, one year after the global spread of the virus, the *New York Times* published an article titled, "Covid? What Covid? Taiwan Thrives as a Bubble of Normality." The article praised the seemingly impossible low infection cases and deaths (fewer than one thousand cases, and only ten deaths as of March 2021) as well as the thriving domestic economy.[2] Portrayed by reporters as a "virus-free paradise," Taiwan appeared to be outside of the overall global mood of pessimism and devastation under the pandemic. The country went for more than 250 days without any locally transmitted COVID-19 cases before a local outbreak was found in quarantine hotels servicing airline staff in May 2021.[3] Taiwan's early successful virus control was driven by a certain kind of paranoia, as the early discoveries of "atypical pneumonia cases" from Wuhan, China, suggested an ominous resemblance to the Severe Acute Respiratory Syndrome (SARS) that killed more than seven hundred people in Asia between 2002 and 2003.[4] By early January 2020, Taiwan began to monitor all individuals who had travel histories to Wuhan and by the end of the month became one of the first countries to suspend all air travel to and from China. Taiwan has not been immune from the collective experience of paranoia surrounding the pandemic, however; in fact, it is precisely because of Taiwan's paranoia about a potentially contagious virus and distrust of the Chinese government that the country's early judgments and responses to the virus were so successful. As Taiwan's effective response to COVID illustrates, paranoia cannot be understood simply as a pathology to be eliminated. Instead, it is better understood as a multidirectional affect built with an inherent drive toward self-protection. As I demonstrate herein, Taiwan's COVID paranoia has led to form of healthy watchfulness and a sense of community-building as the residents are collectively bound by a high level of alertness.

Intensified political pressures during the "New Cold War" and continued exclusion from international governing bodies such as the World Health Organization (WHO) notwithstanding, Taiwan has shown considerable resilience in its pandemic management. Under President Tsai Ing-wen's leadership, the island nation has navigated a catastrophic global event with creative and reparative nation-making responses, in part by relying upon Taiwan's vibrant digital culture. The geopolitical conflicts between Taiwan, China, and the United States manifest through COVID-19 international governance as well as through the transnational digital media. These state actors have reiterated Cold War rhetoric vis-à-vis the pandemic to bolster their claims about freedom, privacy, democracy, authoritarianism, and what constitutes good governance. Taiwan has participated in this international political rivalry, but also demonstrated a unique case of affective and informational practice in which the relationship between the state and civil society has grown closer, rather than more distant, throughout this catastrophe. This unique response warrants analysis of Taiwan's popular internet memes, which helped the nation steer its way through COVID with a sense of playful resilience. To pursue this thesis, I begin the chapter by discussing Eve Sedgwick's reparative reading of paranoia as a queer intervention that transcends right-wing conspiracies and anti-state "leftist" renditions of this affect.[5] Secondly, by examining the reparative functions of internet memes that have circulated in and beyond Taiwan during the pandemic, I offer a queer reading of memes, arguing that they portray the reparative forms of collective belonging and agency that have emerged in the seams between biopolitics and geopolitics. Specifically, I argue that memes in Taiwan's digital culture have used humor, a postcolonial sense of Taiwanese nationalism, and a commitment to resilience to produce new forms of community bonding.

Queer Paranoia and Multiple Pandemics

If SARS is the collective traumatic memory of pandemics in Asian societies, AIDS would be the analog in many Western societies prior to COVID-19. In her seminal essay "Paranoid Reading and Reparative Reading, Or You're So Paranoid, You Probably Think This Essay Is about You," Eve Sedgwick points out the affinity between critical theory in general and queer theory in particular with a methodology centered around paranoia. Sedgwick argues that queer theory has formed around a distinctively paranoid epistemology of antihomophobic analysis and truth-seeking, a literary and interpretative style that approaches texts with a skepticism borne out of a Foucauldian poststructuralism and the "hermeneutics of suspicion."[6] In other words, queer theory has developed an analytical method of "revealing hidden structures of power" that treats any conceptual assertion, identity, or category as potentially suspect and rife with the disciplinary power of normality. Such skepticism is particularly allergic to state interventions and assistance as queer theorists and activists tend to view them as forms of normalizing power. Far from a purely academic development, this antagonism arises out of the AIDS epidemic in the

1980s, when queer communities in the United States were treated as scapegoats for the spreading of HIV via state-produced disinformation. Strategically, AIDS activism shows that the queer demands for health access and state assistance were the means of exposing the interconnected apparatus of power including but not limited to public health policy, pharmaceutical industries, immigration control, scientific research, and the legal definition of "family." David Halperin argues that the queer approach to AIDS activism embodied the Foucauldian concept of biopower, which understands power as diffused rather than concentrated in the state.[7] Since the 1980s, the ethics and spirit of queer activism has predominately been challenging the normative power that the state has established through various institutions, instead of seeking state recognition and incorporation, which means that the politics of skepticism, at least in the variants discussed here, has tended to lean toward an anti-state cynicism, indeed, even nihilism.

For marginalized subjects who are continually betrayed and excluded by authorities in times of crisis, paranoia becomes a reactive shield against the unknown. Sedgwick articulates what has become an almost reactive habit of analytical style in queer theory: "You can never be paranoid enough."[8] The paranoid genre of knowledge production has been productive in teasing apart hidden structures of heteronormative power as evident in the success of queer studies as a discipline. Nonetheless, Sedgwick, among other queer theorists, including but not limited to Heather Love and Lauren Berlant,[9] have warned that the paranoid mode of analysis often traffics in rigid binaries of the repressive and the emancipatory, effectively leaving no middle room for negotiation or space to unpack the "local, contingent relations" between the articulated piece of knowledge and its utility for the knowledge teller or seeker.[10]

Privileging the hermeneutics of suspicion in queer theory frequently leads to an anti-hegemonic queer position trapped in a theoretical idealism that attempts to prevent what Sedgwick calls "bad surprises," the slipping in of normative power.[11] For instance, Sedgwick points to Judith Butler's vigilant demonstrations in *Gender Trouble* that there is no moment prior to the hegemonic institutionalization of gender difference—that gender does not come from biological sex because sex is *always already* gendered.[12] By stating a queer analysis of gender this way, Butler avoids "bad surprises" by locating gender in a specific paranoid temporality where "no time could be too early for one's having-already-known, for its having-already been inevitable, that something bad would happen."[13] Nonetheless, this theoretical position can be counterproductive to efforts to further the goals of marginalized communities, particularly when activists must negotiate power relations with the state by pursuing a tangible and achievable demand. From this perspective, the fact that power is *always already* in formation does not change the imperative to intervene in social life while searching for pragmatic improvements—yet the radical skepticism discussed herein lends itself not so much to pragmatic compromise as to extremism.

For example, I have argued elsewhere how the importing of U.S.-based queer studies in the Taiwanese context can potentially lead to falsely dichotomized positions in the LGBTQ movement.[14] During the heated debates over same-sex marriage legislation around 2015, a milieu of the "anti-marriage queer left" emerged, arguing that marriage as an institutional form is inherently capitalistic and patriarchal, and thus not reformable and must be fully rejected. The self-proclaimed anti-capitalist and leftist queer groups pushed against same-sex marriage legislative reform and called for "abolishing family and marriage," which incidentally and ironically resonated with the anti-queer, conservative discourses against same-sex marriage.

The queer left's paranoia was produced by their fear that the same-sex marriage legislation would allow the Taiwanese state institution to reinforce heteronormative values on queer communities and thus assimilate them into the traditional values of marriage and family. By distancing themselves from such reformist efforts, the queer left could avoid "bad surprises." However, this paranoid framing of the issue often neglects the "good surprises" of how queer people have the capacity to transform the marriage and family institutions to some extent, such as by the increasing call to loosen restrictions on assisted reproductive technology for both queer families and single parents.[15] If the paranoid critique is incapable of either directing the movement toward other actionable demands or facilitating an examination of the multidimensional goals and debates within the movement, then the more hopeful "good surprises" version offers attempts to work toward reframing the contested relations between queer activists and the Taiwanese state.

For Sedgwick, paranoia-driven queer theory is inevitably a "strong theory" that preemptively sets up defenses to anticipate every possible attack.[16] To articulate a different vision for queer theory, one that seeks to maximize positive affects and orients toward unexpected possibilities, she draws on what psychologist Silvan Tomkins calls "weak theory."[17] For Tomkins, theories must remain weak to be effective, as they can better account for the near-experiential phenomenon and multiple directionalities of any given affect. Put another way, whereas strong theory tends to be *decryptive*, revealing structures of power, weak theory is *descriptive*, approaching the object of study with curiosity and hope.[18]

During a time of global crisis, it is imperative that scholars engaged in cultural critique revisit the multiple affective capacities of paranoia in driving our work beyond warning against negative outcomes to seeking new forms of sociality that have emerged out of the pandemic. As Sedgwick argues, a reparative approach to understanding the social issues at hand is not only helpful but indeed necessary if we hope to welcome the possibility that "the future may be different from the present."[19] A reparative practice does not seek to reject paranoia, but instead, turn it in a direction that opens up to curiosity and the unknown. In this sense, the knowledge we seek via reparative practice can take us to the speculative and the imaginative, where the becoming of history can extend along alternative paths.

Disinformation and Conspiracy

One of the dominant features of paranoia during the pandemic has been the proliferation of conspiracy theories that have permeated national boundaries. Taiwan, as a nation that is rightfully paranoid about China's constant annexation threats and disinformation attacks, has also become a hub where conspiracies about COVID-19 have found audience. As Stephen Hartnett and Chiaoning Su point out, China's cyber campaigns into Taiwan through disinformation practices that aimed to disturb regional peace and democratic processes were the most expansive and visible between 2018–2020, coinciding with Taiwan's presidential election.[20] These attacks have also instigated a wave of Taiwanese citizen-led initiatives of fact-checking practices that have largely boosted media literacy in the country. However, China's sophisticated disinformation campaigns have normalized the presence of a "post-truth" communication ecosystem in the country, where political persuasion and reasonable debates have been replaced by "chaos" and the "noise" of the attention economy.[21]

On the global stage of the "post-truth" world, more than three years after the initial outbreak in Wuhan, China, the international communities thus far have not ceased the divisive debate on the origin of the virus, using it to wage a proxy battle in the U.S.–China geopolitical conflict. Caught between U.S.–China rivalries, Taiwan was one of the places most immediately impacted by viral paranoia.

Conspiracies around the virology of COVID-19 were rampant in Taiwanese media, social networks, and even academic fields before the spread of the pandemic was known to the Western world. Images of wildlife trading in the Huanan Seafood Market that make explicit inferences between the outbreak and China's unsanitary food practices saturated Taiwanese news.[22] In February 2020, an epidemiologist at National Taiwan University, Chi-Tai Fang, claimed that COVID-19 could have been a human-made, synthetic virus leaked from the Wuhan Institute of Virology.[23] The lab-leak theory served as an affective holder for Taiwanese peoples' paranoia as we faced a catastrophic and uncertain event. More specifically, Taiwanese paranoia over COVID-19 came, at least in part, from accumulated feelings of distrust toward the Chinese government, especially surrounding their practice of withholding information and pattern of undermining Taiwan's sovereignty through unpredictable means. In other words, many Taiwanese found ourselves transformed into the traumatized subjects of Sedgwick's essay: as Taiwan is concerned regarding China, *we can never be paranoid enough.*

On the global stage, the "lab-leak theory" was initially disregarded as conspiratorial by the WHO and deemed "extremely unlikely" by the scientific community.[24] This conspiracy was largely rejected by Western liberals, as it resonated deeply with Donald Trump's right-wing milieus, such as the Republican China hawks and conspiracy-generating figures like Steve Bannon.[25] The lab-leak theory, however, went mainstream in May 2021, with scientists, the U.S. intelligence community, and even President Joe Biden demanding further investigation into the origins of COVID-19.[26] In February 2022, the updated scientific reports have zeroed in on the Huanan Seafood Wholesale Market in Wuhan as the more likely sources of the outbreak, again, countering the popular lab-leak theory.[27] As the question over the origin of the virus gets further entangled with the politics in Washington and Beijing, on one hand, it seems that no hard evidence will be able to dissolve the already paranoid sphere of the heated geopolitical contestations. On the other hand, the COVID-19 origins debate exposes the unproductiveness of labeling an event as simply "conspiracy" or "not conspiracy." The world's reality often demands that we more closely examine the affective capacities of why certain ideas become popular and under in context, rather than make a quick judgment on their veracity or falsity, liberalism or illiberalism.[28]

Conspiratorial thinking targeted against China was popular in Taiwan, and as the outbreak spread internationally, Sinophobic images of China as a bat-eating, disease-ridden country went rampant and circulated globally.[29] A video clip showing a Chinese woman enjoying cooked bat soup provoked mass outrage on the internet during the early phase of the pandemic, but was later found to be filmed for a travel show in 2016 in Palau, not China.[30] Through our collective paranoia, conspiracy has become the fabric of life under COVID-19, generating false claims that allow people to cast their fear of the unknown onto an embodied figure of blame. U.S. president Donald Trump infamously named COVID-19 the "Chinese virus" amid a heated trade war between the United States and China, effectively stirring up anti-China sentiments globally.[31]

China, however, is not an innocent actor in this disinformation war. As early as January 2020, China launched disinformation campaigns about COVID in Taiwan. An expert researcher on disinformation, Puma Shen, has identified at least four distinct patterns of disinformation from China, which include the discourses that (1) COVID-19 is just a flu, (2) the pandemic is more serious in Taiwan than the media is reporting, (3) the virus originated in the United States, and (4) China is actively helping the world curb the spread of the virus.[32] Disinformation claiming that COVID-19 is not more deadly than influenza was found to be very effective not only in Taiwan but also across international social media platforms. In Taiwan, the government's preemptive caution against disinformation from China—coupled with proactive public communication of correct information via social media—has minimized the negative effects of these disinformation campaigns.[33] In the United States, however, a lack of centralized massaging on COVID-19 has allowed for pandemic disinformation to divide people across the political spectrum and threatened the country's democratic process. A Brookings Institute study by Jonathan Rothwell and Sonal Desai found that in early September 2020, 41 percent of Republicans believed that influenza caused more deaths than COVID-19, compared to 13 percent of Democrats.[34] The distrust of the U.S. government has led to the right-leaning mobilization of "anti-maskers" and "anti-vaxxers" who believe that the pandemic is a hoax and refuse to comply with public health measures such as self-quarantining and social distancing.[35]

The scientific community has responded to the impact of conspiracy and disinformation on public health outcomes by stressing the need to deliver evidence-based health information and to correct flows of misinformation.[36] Ironically, the critique of empiricism is often fruitless to conspiracy believers as their conspiracies are confirmed by the same desire to seek knowledge through a form of embodied empiricism bound by their specific and partial experience. As in the case of climate-change denialism, Kath Weston points out that conspiracy believers' thinking operates off a similar form of scientific empiricism, although they often reject how their sense-experiences ("It's not getting hotter here because I'm not sweating") are partial and limited.[37] Conspiracy theorists' defense against scientific evidence that is incongruent with their claims is always: "I did the research."[38] Interestingly, people who believed that COVID-19 is a "hoax" were in fact not disinterested or unconcerned about the pandemic, but were found to exhibit more "self-centered prepping behaviors" such as hoarding goods, withdrawing cash, and stocking up on petrol oil.[39] This paradoxical behavioral evidence shows that those who believe in COVID-19 conspiracies were, in fact, equally if not more anxious about the consequences of the pandemic. Yet their paranoid drive pushes them toward a series of confirmation biases: the more evidence they select, the stronger they believe in the conspiracy.

The Paranoid Critic

In this sense, the framing of conspiracy as a mere individual pathology that can be dismissed or repaired by better empiricism ignores what Richard Hofstadter calls a "paranoid style" of politics at the structural heart of liberal democracy and is "always present in some considerable minority of the population."[40] Drawing from Sedgwick's conceptualization of paranoia as a *style* or *genre* of analysis rather than an irrational feeling,[41] we may reconsider the rampant circulation of conspiracy as a warning sign that is less about the psychological health of conspiracy believers and more about the instability of political structures and overall ineffective democratic governance.

Mark Fenster has pointed out that conspiracy is certainly not just a right-wing phenomenon, as progressive critics and the left have utilized the same style of paranoid politics to generate knowledge and attract audiences.[42] Fenster articulates that the difference between the right and the left lies in how the latter insists on "the analysis of power, the gathering of information about covert power, and properly progressive political activism."[43] In other words, rather than fixating on the critique of a group of elites or "evil" individuals as in right-leaning conspiratorial thinking, the left primarily focuses on the structural mechanisms and conditions that have created the present crises. It is significant to note that "the left" is certainly not monolithic but divergent in its traditions and approaches. The anti-capitalist left, undoubtedly, has made critical interventions into the pandemic by linking the emergence of the virus to the disastrous structures of capitalism. Mike Davis's book *The Monster Enters: COVID-19 and the Plagues of Capitalism* describes in details how the interlocking conditions of deforestation by agricultural businesses, class exploitation, and the poor living conditions of the urban proletariat in China, as well as the deterioration of the U.S. health system by pharmaceutical industries have created the devastating pandemic today.[44] Such critique has generated valuable insights into where political actions can take place—toward an intersectional anti-capitalist analysis of ecology, urban working conditions, and the healthcare system. While the critique is still paranoid in its *style*, it is capable of creating new social relations and curiosity about alternative possibilities. In Sedgwick's word, a critique performs a *reparative* function insofar as it is not closed off from different surprises but rather generates desire for new forms of sociality through social movements.

However, during the pandemic, there has emerged a distinct kind of Foucauldian, paranoid cultural critique mostly situated within the academia that sees any state intervention as a repressive form of biopolitics. As COVID-19 spread to Europe, Italy, as the first Western country that reported a spike in infected cases and deaths, initiated a first provincial lockdown in February 2020 and later a national lockdown and quarantine on March 9, 2020. Giorgio Agamben, a well-known Italian intellectual, criticized how the Italian state invoked the "state of emergency" to justify a disproportionate reaction that "produces an authentic militarization" for "something not too different from the normal flus."[45] Drawing on Foucault,[46] Agamben reads any governmental measures that limit individual freedom—including quarantine and contact tracing—as an exercise of exceptional forms of biopolitical power and thus must be opposed. Far from a policy that ensures public safety, his comments suggest that social distancing has been utilized by Italy's politicians as a way of suppressing spontaneous protests.[47] His concerns about state biopolitical control were warranted, for instance, regarding Beijing's efforts to use the pandemic as an excuse to curb and eventually crush Hong Kong's prodemocracy protests between 2019 and 2020.[48]

These cultural critiques, nonetheless, discharged the responsibility of state institutions to exercise public health regulation. They signify a common leftist and critical theory tendency to analyze the crisis using a hermeneutics of suspicion. While Agamben's theory of states of exception may be useful to reflect on the expansion of militarized state practices in the context of the "War on Terror,"[49] his critique of governmental public health measures during COVID-19 may have missed the mark. In fact, Agamben's discourse mirrors the Italian right-wing's anti-lockdown, "orange vests" movement, which is fueled by conspiracy theories similar to anti-mask mobilizations in the United States.[50] The anti-state position from both the left and the right can lead to the misconception that the successes of pandemic management in Asian countries such as China, Singapore, and South Korea are the result of swift and dominating measures based in authoritarianism that could never happen in Western democracies.

The Reparative Capacity of Memes

On the contrary to the leftist critique, Taiwan's relatively effective response to COVID-19 in the early stages of the pandemic has shown that democratic governance as well as transparent and open communication are in fact the key to managing the pandemic crisis without incurring immeasurable civic, economic, and social damage.[51] Even under pressures to contain a community outbreak since May 2021, Taiwan raised a nationwide level 3 alert and restricted certain sizes of gathering without a full lockdown completely banning people's movements.[52] By adding targeted testing sites at the "hot zones" of community infections, utilizing a secure contact tracing system via SMS, and emphasizing non-pharmaceutical measures such as facemask wearing, the government has kept the outbreak at a manageable level while buying time to implement its vaccination plans.

In the midst of a global crisis, geopolitical conflicts, and a national emergency, I have found internet memes in Taiwan to be a site of humorous relief from the paranoid atmosphere. Some of the memes, indeed, go beyond a pleasurable moment, but are specifically crafted to be a reparative critique. For example, a "is this a pigeon" meme that was popular on Taiwan Twitter mocks the Orientalist bias of authoritarian Asian governance from both the Western left and right.[53] The original meme shows a newly trained android, an Asian-looking male figure with a scholarly appearance holding an encyclopedia, who misidentifies various things around him, such as pointing at a butterfly and asking: "is this a pigeon?"[54] The meme has been utilized to make fun of moments of misidentification in which the speaker is utterly confused and ignorant in various contexts. To counter stereotypes around Asian authoritarianism and Confucianism, the meme on Taiwan Twitter illustrates the android pointing at the butterfly with the text "Western countries are messing up / East Asian countries are doing something right" and falsely naming asking "is this

Confucianism?"[55] This alternation of the meme exemplifies the Orientalist bias of how the complex and nuanced differences between Asian and Western societies frequently come down to a dogmatic framework of Confucianism that is often linked to authority, hierarchy, and obedience.

While painting the successes of Asian societies in managing COVID-19 as rooted in culturally essentialist stereotypes of Confucianism or homogenous authoritarianism may not be the original drive of left-oriented, anti-state critique, the dismissal of the experiences and practices of non-Western democracies is ultimately counterproductive to solving the global crisis. The "is this a pigeon" meme intervenes in the global politics of the pandemic in the form of a "weak theory" by pointing out that there are explanations for why Asian societies managed COVID-19 better than the West beyond the hegemonic paradigm of Confucianism or the dichotomy between liberal democracy and authoritarianism, as both explanations have served as forms of "strong theory" in the cultural heuristics of Western academic criticism. While not making an explicit argument about "why" Asian societies were successful in epidemic prevention, the meme pushes the readers to think further and imagine otherwise about "good surprises" through its sarcastic humor.

Both the socially damaging circulation of disinformation and conspiracy as well as the anti-state leftist critique against COVID-19 management measures are driven by the affective capacities of paranoia. Paranoia has emerged out of our psychic inability to completely process the uncertain crisis at hand and thus leaves us to anticipate the worst outcomes. As Sedgwick argues, a paranoid style of interpretation and politics is a "strong theory" insofar as it rejects ambiguity and indulges in a proleptic recursion whereby the theorist preemptively confirms the very negative effect they anticipate.[56] In this sense, while conspiratorial thinking is suspicious of any role of authority, the practice of critical theory can often lead to a phobic relationship to power as all power is construed as susceptible to corruption and contamination. Both approaches are incapable of building collective resistance toward a resolution of the problems at hand.

If we subscribe to the idea that paranoia is not something that can be eliminated by simply *thinking rationally*, particularly in the midst of a global crisis, then it is imperative that we recover paranoia's reparative capacity. The proliferation of internet memes during the pandemic can be understood as a function of paranoia itself whereby we anxiously attempt to process the mass amount of information and uncertainty about the present crisis by viewing, producing, and sharing these memes. Guobin Yang's study on cyber activism and the internet memes draws on

James Carey's work and argues that communication is not just about information transmission but about establishing a ritual function in constructing a sense of community via shared values and symbols.[57] In this sense, memes are not necessarily tools built for ideological or social persuasion, but rather, a medium that generates spaces for exchanges and negotiation. Therefore, I argue that memes carry the reparative capacity of paranoia as a highly participatory and cathartic form of digital culture that builds social connections by rearticulating and reassembling small pieces of information. Different from the original analogy of memes as self-replicating genes by biologist Richard Dawkins based in evolutionary theory,[58] memes today are complex cultural practices that are a fundamental part of our digital experiences and are indicative of "deep social and cultural structures."[59] A meme shares similar affective structures with both conspiracy and critique insofar as memes are a form of paranoid knowing—a meme is diagnostic, reflexive and, in Sedgwick's words, "places its faith in *exposure*" (emphasis original).[60] Memes connect what is already known and circulatable within a given culture, revels in potential linkages, and thus produces different meanings and affective responses to an event. However, memes are also self-deprecating. They do not take the information they generate too seriously; after all, their goal is humorous or pleasurable release.

For instance, a "me explaining" meme that mocks conspiracy theorists by depicting how they generate complex yet nonfactual information to craft *a single narrative* about COVID-19 sums up the dynamics of their misdirected paranoid drive.[61] It even makes jokes about conspiracy theories through the format of conspiracy theory itself. The meme shows a white man in office attire in front of a wall filled with papers and connected lines, resembling the investigation board in a murder detective show, indicating a concentrated effort to unravel an elaborate crime. With bloodshot eyes and a cigarette in hand, the man appears to be saying something conspiratorial to another person in the frame. The texts on the meme state, "Me explaining to my grandchildren how a guy eating bat soup in China led to a toilet paper shortage in the US." In this conspiracy meme that jokes about conspiracy theory and its theorist, the man connects two divergent events—"eating bat soup in China" and "toilet paper shortage in the US"—together in this very historical moment of global pandemic. While the cause-and-effect connection between the two events is completely fabricated, the meme has signified a visceral anxiety of the public that is unprepared to deal with the drastic changes in their daily lives due to COVID-19 and the distrust of political elites to solve the crisis effectively. By linking the two conspiratorial events of "eating bat soup in China" and "toilet paper shortage in the US" on the fictional conspiracy theorist's graph, the meme reads these two events, originally deemed to be revelatory of "deeper meanings" about COVID-19, as absurd, if not foolish. Without making scientific arguments about the origin of the virus, or directly blaming the toilet paper hoarders as irrational, the meme has created a humorous opening for the audience to *sense* the absurdity of these theories themselves. This meme's the desired outcome—to expose these COVID-19 conspiracies as unsubstantiated—is relatable and identifiable. It manages to accurately identify people's inevitable paranoid thinking in the pandemic context, but simultaneously shift the blame onto a fictional conspiracist away from the audience, providing them with a moment of humorous introspection and cathartic relief.

Memes can be read as a genre of repetitive performative acts that consists of decoding and recoding signs to assemble new information in an imitated form for a new audience. According to Limor Shifman, memes can be analyzed along three dimensions: their content, form, and stance.[62] One can repeat the same form (the graphic portion) with different contents (the texts) to create new meanings (the stance) for circulation. The participatory aspects of memes, I argue, are what set them apart from the anti-social tendency often observed in paranoid knowing. Just like a virus, memes that do not spread will cease to exist. Berger and Milkman have asserted that successful memes are marked by high arousal of emotions that facilitates a desire to share the content.[63] Shifman further elaborates that successful memes are positive, simple, and humorous, with memes that feature ordinary people and flawed masculinity being the most successful. This attribute of content spreadability leads to the surprising finding that relatively unrefined memes are more popular than tones that have been over-interpreted or over-determined by existing meanings. Shifman observes that this finding is because "the ostensibly unfinished, unpolished, amateur-looking memes" appear to be more welcoming and inspire people "to fill in the gaps, address the puzzles, or mock its creator."[64]

The dimensions of memes that are open to interpretation and generative of positive affects, I argue, are what make them a genre of *reparative practices* when compared to the equally viral phenomena of conspiracy and critique. Memes create the in-between spaces for paranoia to temporarily land and reconcile with the uncertainty of the present crisis. While memes are certainly not a sufficient form of politics that can replace social movement interventions that have been crucial to changing the structural and material conditions of our societies, as scholars and critics we should look at memes as a common form of everyday political participation in today's digital sphere. During COVID-19, as mass populations of people have been quarantined at home and rely upon digital communication to receive information and form social relations, internet memes become even more central to the mundane practices of living.

In Taiwan, memes are not only ways in which Taiwanese netizens challenge the international exclusion of the country from global health dialogues and China's continuous annexation threats, but also tools of the government to combat disinformation about the virus. While "positive energy" (正能量) has been appropriated by China to uplift emotions that align with the value systems of the party-state under Xi Jinping's rule,[65] Taiwan provides a distinct case of communication practice that simultaneously generates identification with the state and critical intervention in governmental policy via the medium of internet memes. In what follows, I illustrate two fields of politics—the biopolitics of pandemic control and the geopolitics between Taiwan, China, and the WHO—in which internet memes have intervened by rearticulating meanings toward more reparative understandings of these situations and gesturing toward new social relations.

Building Democratic Biopolitics

According to the Foucauldian notion of biopolitics, the modern state exercises a specific form of power over life that governs and disciplines the behaviors of a collective population.[66] The framework has been immensely productive in analyzing how technological and medical innovations and health policies are normalized as a form of disciplinary power by the state to control the distribution of resources and life chances. Following the same theoretical milieu, Agamben's critique of the Italian government's pandemic policy, such as quarantine and school closure, as forms of excessive biopolitical control in a time of global public crisis seems to be out of touch and indeed paranoid. This critique often creates a false dichotomy of the state as either having absolute control over citizens or as implementing a neoliberal, hands-off approach of letting people die, such as the British prime minister Boris Johnson's initial response of "herd immunity." Both approaches—the left-leaning Agamben and the neoliberal Johnson—have proven ineffective, and hence a different kind of active engagement and negotiation between the state and the public to efficiently "flatten the curve" of infection and death rates is needed. In search of such a reparative approach to biopolitics in times of crisis,

I turn to Karsten Schubert's concept of *democratic biopolitics*, which recognizes not only the normalizing potential of biopolitical governmentality but also takes into account the constant negotiations between the state and different demands within civic communities.[67] Democratic biopolitics rejects a simplistic critique of state intervention and regulation that neglects those whose health are at stake and instead recognizes the agency of various actors who engage in biopolitical citizenship through democratic negotiation and open communication.

Amid scholarly debates around whether authoritarian or democratic governments deal with COVID-19 better, Taiwan stands out as a critical case that has implemented both a strong form of state governmentality and a flexible process of transparent democracy. In an invited speech with Ireland's Construction Industry Federation on October 1, 2020, Taiwan's digital minister, Audrey Tang, discussed "how digital innovation can fight pandemics and strengthen democracy."[68] Tang, particularly, emphasized how the Taiwanese government adopts a transparent communication approach built on the principles of "fast, fair, and fun" to combat the pandemic. The designated phone line for all questions related to COVID-19, the daily press conference hosted by the Central Epidemic Command Center (CECC), and a citizen-initiated interactive map about mask distribution were all central aspects of daily life during the height of the pandemic in Taiwan and created a collective bonding experience—communication as *ritual* in Carey's words[69]—among Taiwanese residents.

Rather than simply taking hegemonic control over information flows, the CECC has been responsive to public concerns and criticisms.[70] For instance, Tang highlighted the utilization of memes to correct misinformation and disinformation such as "Zongchai" (總柴), the Ministry of Health and Welfare's (MOHW) Shiba Inu mascot, which features in memes offering various suggestions about how to stay safe during the pandemic. These MOHW memes include the graphic below which portrays multiple "Zongchai" standing in a line to demonstrate social distancing standards both indoors and outdoors.[71]

Not merely an internet phenomenon, the MOHW's "Zongchai" Shiba Inu messages are now a common feature of multilingual public announcements in places such as government buildings, shopping malls, and convenience stores. The media has called the clever utilization of social media by state institutions "Governing by Memes" (迷因治國), which has been adopted by different government agencies to spread information during COVID-19. On a similar note, in an attempt to reduce toilet paper panic hoarding, the Ministry of Economic Affairs produced a meme

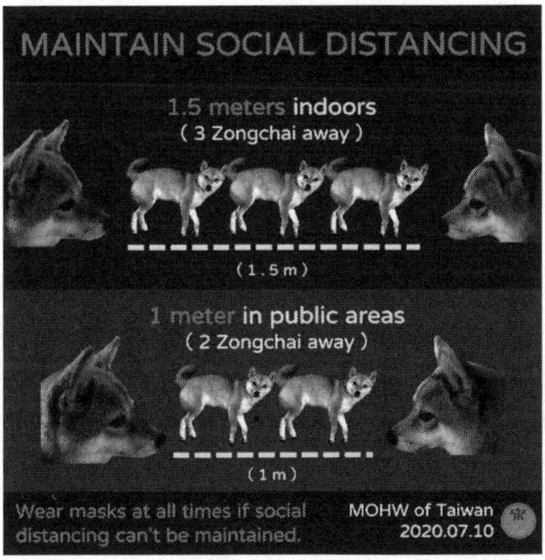

FIGURE 1. Maintain social distancing. Image by Ministry of Health and Welfare of Taiwan, July 10, 2020, https://twitter.com/MOHW_Taiwan/status/1281563042589716480/photo/1.

of a cartoon version of the Premier Su Tseng-chang shaking his buttocks with the text, "We only have one butt. Don't hoard. Don't trust rumors," which plays with the homophony between the pronunciation of "hoard" and "butt" in Mandarin.[72] Furthermore, as one of the few countries that hosted in-person classes during the 2021 spring semester, the Ministry of Education also created a series of iconic memes tailored toward college students in Taiwan. The memes imitate well-known Taiwanese astrologist Jesse Tang's weekly horoscope by featuring an astrologist figure that dresses in the same way as Tang alongside twelve horoscope forecasts that playfully address how people of different astrological signs must pay attention to epidemic prevention. For example, the meme reminds Pisces to remember "washing hands after holding hands with others" and warns Leos that "wearing face masks even if lining up to buying the masks may easily agitate you."[73]

Instead of sending dry statistics on toilet paper usage and storage or the risks of going to in-person classes, these memes utilize humor to raise public awareness and spread coherent messages about epidemic prevention. These memes turn state institutions into figures that ordinary citizens can relate to and localize their content to fit into Taiwanese popular culture preferences for cute animal characters and astrology. The discourses of warning and risk that are often associated with public health measures are transformed via memes into forms of cultural communication that spark interest and dialogue in and beyond the digital sphere. In the era characterized by a scarcity of attention, memetic communication effectively attracts attention in its fast circulation cycles. The highly specified content that requires complex "meme literacy" of a given subculture also enhances its bonding experience in a country facing challenges over its national status. The unspoken yet shared national consciousness of Taiwan is embodied in the practice of ritual communication, which continues to realize and articulate Taiwan's existence. While strong theories of governmentality from figures such as Foucault and Agamben may immediately render state measures as suspect in an attempt to build analytical defenses against any "pandemic nationalism," a weak theory attends to the middle ground of the affective capacity and creative performativity of these memes in terms of how they carry messages between divergent actors within a society. Certainly, weak theory is at risk of failing to provide a robust critique of state power, but it nevertheless recognizes the intermediate space of interconnection as a necessary condition for more explicitly political ends. To put it simply, weak theory rejects the all-or-nothingness presumed in strong theory cultural criticism.

Memes, as ordinary, mediocre, and politically messy objects may not be perfect ideological exemplars or cultural signifiers, but nonetheless, the positive affects they elicit cannot be ignored in building effective communication methods between the state and civil society. In *The World Made Meme*, Ryan Milner points out how memes have given new shapes and textures to public conversations.[74] They change our interactions with the state and with each other. The influence of memetic logic exceeds individual examples, as we have seen in the past few years, as the Taiwanese government's public relations have grown more and more "memefied." Different branches of government agencies have adopted memetic communication on social media to engage with Taiwanese netizens. In the context of COVID-19, these memes also provide a space for ordinary citizens to provide quick feedback to health management institutions about whether a given policy if effective. For instance, complaints around people waiting in long lines to purchase face masks pushed the CECC to implement an online registration method to reduce waiting times. While these issues, at first glance, seem mundane and minor, I see them as necessary practices of democratic biopolitical governance that calls the state into accountability and treats the public as communicative agents rather than mere objects of state control.

Reshaping China-Centric Geopolitics

The pandemic has exacerbated existing geopolitical conflicts, specifically the issue of engaging with China since its rise as a global power. While China is at fault for withholding information about COVID-19 in a way that led to the virus's drastic impact across the world, it has also portrayed itself as the victim of Sinophobia and Orientalism in the face of racist discourses about COVID-19 targeted against the Chinese state and its citizens. By conflating the Chinese state with its people, China has infamously attempted to divert and deny international criticism against its violent treatment of Hong Kong and Xinjiang by condemning the United States for promoting anti-Asian violence against "Chinese-looking people" through their "tough on China" policy.

In the midst of these geopolitical conflicts, Taiwan is situated in a critical yet delicate position. On one hand, the distrust and fear of China that arises out of Taiwan's unique political history can be easily interpreted as "Sinophobic" and feeding into U.S. Cold War aggression against China; on the other hand, there is a lack of official communication routes for Taiwan to publicly issue its demands for international recognition and accuse China of repeated annexation threats against Taiwan's ambiguous statehood. Within this perpetual dilemma, memes have developed as a low stakes yet highly contagious mode of political participation that can respond to and renegotiate the easily dichotomizing stance of "pro-China vs. pro-United States" Cold War discourses. For Taiwanese, memes also function as a cathartic practice that unites communities in a non-threatening and playful way beyond the Cold War binary.

While Taiwan is one of the few countries that effectively managed COVID-19 prior to the wide usage of vaccines by wealthy Western nations to contain the virus, it continues to be excluded from the WHO, which follows the United Nation's "One-China Policy" and is put under continuous pressure from one of its biggest partners, China, in relation to vaccine access.[75] The early warning from Taiwan's Centers for Disease Control to the WHO on December 31, 2019, about possible human-to-human transmission was dismissed. Taiwan's continuous efforts to participate in COVID-19-related meetings at the WHO were also ignored. This repeated marginalization of Taiwan in the global public health community can also be seen in how the WHO refuses to address Taiwan by its national name and instead changes Taiwan's name in official reports: first as "Taiwan, China," then "Taipei Municipality," and finally,

"Taipei and Environs" on February 6, 2020.[76] An "expanding brain" meme mocks the ironic progression of the WHO's refusal to name Taiwan by generating various proximal terms until reaching the most absurd designation, "Taipei and Environs."[77] The term not only trivializes the active democratic governance of the country but also minimalizes the agency and existence of twenty-three million Taiwanese residents as nothing but abstract and empty "environs."

In March 2020, a Hong Kong journalist named Yvonne Tong interviewed WHO assistant director-general Bruce Aylward via an online video communication platform. When Tong posed a question to Aylward about Taiwan's epidemic control and whether the WHO will consider granting Taiwan organizational membership, Aylward responded with silence, pretending that he could not hear the question and then allegedly hanging up on Tong shortly thereafter. The level of absurdity and awkwardness in how the WHO, the leading global public health organization, is implicated in the political drama of Taiwan's status and its utter lack of professionalism in dealing with questions about Taiwan has left Taiwanese people with a sense of frustration and powerlessness. In another contentious episode with the WHO in April 2020, Director-General Tedros Adhanom Ghebreyesus called a press conference and suddenly accused Taiwan of sending him racist slurs and attacks online: "[There are] personal attacks that have been going on for more than two, three months. Abuses, or racist comments, giving me names, black or Negro . . . Three months ago, this attack came from Taiwan."[78] Taiwan's Ministry of Foreign Affairs promptly released a statement rejecting Tedros's charges and stressing that these attacks were "baseless."

In response to the accumulation of tensions with the WHO, Taiwanese netizens initiated a social media hashtag campaign turned viral meme called #ThisAttackComesFromTaiwan, which involved posting photos of Taiwan's famous street food, bubble milk tea, and landscape scenery alongside messages about the lack of COVID-19 local transmissions in an effort to elevate the beauty of daily life in Taiwan, which has generally been ignored by the international world. Using the format of a photo from Taiwan alongside the #ThisAttackComesFromTaiwan hashtag, netizens created a viral memetic effect through similar visual content spread with the same hashtag.[79] This netizen-initiated campaign then raised around USD $330,000 to place a full-page advertisement in the *New York Times*. The advertisement-crowdfunding campaign was initially meant to center on writing a letter to refute Tedros's accusations of racist attacks from Taiwan, but contributors raised concerns that the hashtag #ThisAttackComesFromTaiwan may seem petty to a global audience and so the organizers changed the message in their *New York Times* advert to #TaiwanCanHelp and #TaiwanIsHelping, which is the official slogan promoted by Taiwan's Ministry of Foreign Affairs, in an attempt to center Taiwan's desire to be incorporated into the global public health community.[80]

The campaign became an example of when memetic, viral responses online become a form of citizens' political participation, influencing the government's diplomatic efforts and vice versa. From sporadic memes that deflect the WHO's trivialization and false accusations to a netizen campaign that gestures toward global recognition, Taiwanese netizens are engaging in a new form of digital politics where contributors can in fact engage in productive dialogues and negotiate between different interests and priorities. Here, the "nation" not only consists of institutions and bureaucracies but also active exchanges between the government and civil society. Furthermore, by not directly engaging with the question of China or Taiwan's legal status directly, the parodic quality of memes leveraged by Taiwanese netizens has transformed the WHO's dismissive acts into a humorous and unifying campaign that signifies solidarity within and beyond the boundaries of Taiwan. As the crowdfunded advertisement in the *New York Times* says: "In a time of isolation, we choose solidarity."[81]

A similar logic of reshaping Western- and Chinese-centric geopolitical framings can also be seen in the popular emergence of the #MilkTeaAlliance hashtag, which has created an online space of cross-national alliance among netizens involved in radical social movements in Taiwan, Hong Kong, Thailand, Myanmar, India, and the Philippines. By adopting milk tea as an object of solidarity across these diverse locations and their distinct milk tea practices and cultures, #MilkTeaAlliance—which initially started as an internet fight against "little pink" (小粉紅) Chinese nationalist trolls around the politics of Taiwan and Hong Kong statehood—has now turned into a bourgeoning platform where activists share tactics and analyses from their respective movements, all of which center on the principle of anti-authoritarianism.[82] One of the most popular #MilkTeaAlliance meme is a map that illustrates a coalition of different Asian countries, linked by their diverse forms of milk tea—for instance, Boba Tea in Taiwan, silk stocking tea in Hong Kong, and cha nom yen in Thailand—enclosing and seizing the center of China, whose regional imperial domination has become especially pronounced within the last decade.[83] The map meme cleverly mocks the imperialist project of China's Belt and Road Initiative, which began in 2013 with the expressed purpose of exerting the Chinese state's influence by initiating infrastructure building projects across Southeast Asia,

South Asia, the Middle East, and Africa vis-à-vis debt financing and other economic means. By illustrating each country's respective yet distinct struggle in the symbol of milk tea and isolating China visually, #MilkTeaAlliance radically reshapes the China-centric discourses of Asian geopolitics and defies the Orientalist view of Asia as both homogenous and submissive.

It is not my intention to erase the right-wing and ethnocentric side of memes—as the lens of strong theory would have addressed—that are also popular in Taiwan by highlighting memes as a reparative genre. Strong theory's sole focus on critique may erase the middle levels of resistance, where memes circulate and open up the potential to be amplified into larger waves of activism. In the midst of global chaos and crisis, from the standpoint of weak theory, I argue that we cannot ignore how memes have built new forms of sociality and solidarity. The "weakness" of memes as a flexible form of politics, in a sense, also allows them to rapidly change and adapt to new social conditions. The intervention of weak theory resides in its ability to reorient our conversations to the moment, despite not knowing where the future will land and knowing that there will be more critiques ahead.

Building New Sociality in the Time of the Pandemic

Driven by a potentially traumatizing affect of paranoia, the epistemologies of conspiracy and critique have emphasized an anticipation of harms and injuries in a time of crisis. From the angle of critical scholarship, we cannot deny that the mode of paranoid knowing through a hermeneutics of suspicion is imperative to challenging any potentially emergent hegemonic power, such as when the state's biopolitical control bypasses necessary thresholds of privacy, or when nationalistic sentiments become exclusionary and dismissive of democratic critique. However, the COVID-19 pandemic has shown that by conceptualizing the state as either "evil" in concealing information or having alternative motives (as in conspiracy theory), or absolutely "antagonistic" of its citizens' interests (as in leftist critique), we may be left with no options other than building networks of care by ourselves. While this idealized vision of democratic practices from below will certainly appeal to proponents of anti-statist critique, in the face of global crisis, we cannot afford to *not* work with state actors. The digital culture and sociality of Taiwan, as I have demonstrated in the two examples above, have created spaces for generating what Sedgwick terms a reparative practice based in "weak theory." In contrast to strong theory, weak theory rejects the paranoid mode of analysis that tends toward universality and prodromal diagnosis.

Practicing weak theory means opening oneself up to both possibilities and vulnerabilities. It pushes the scholar to get closer to the descriptive moment and the thickness of the field and move just a little ahead to examine the phenomenon at hand without making a universal or over-determined judgement. Like memes, weak theory aims to produce surprises and joys through circulation. Writing reparatively about Taiwan's state governance during COVID-19 itself, in fact, places me, a critical theory scholar, in an exposed position that is vulnerable to criticism as well. The local virus outbreak that occurred in mid-May 2021, for instance, stirred up many critiques of Taiwan's epidemic control methods both domestically and internationally. On June 7, 2021, at the peak of the local outbreak, the *Guardian* bluntly described Taiwan as "a victim of its own success."[84] One year and three months after the global outbreak, as wealthy Western nations were announcing the end of lockdown measures and resuming normal life, the news cycle seemed eager to portray the "poster child" for COVID-19 prevention as ultimately failing due to insufficient vaccine supplies and testing capacity.

This circle of paranoid criticism and search for "I told you so" defensive moments elicit an impulse to produce yet another strong theory of Western dominance, such as, for example, how the United States may have been right all along to place all of its hope into vaccine developments. However, no success can erase the hundreds of thousands of lives lost due to the lack of prevention measures in the United States or the millions of deaths globally. As another COVID-19 variant resurfaces and infection cases rise again two years after the initial outbreak, it is also too soon to conclude that Taiwan's epidemic control practices have been a total failure. Taiwan's democratic governance, information transparence, and robust civil society have shown to still be positive factors in stabilizing the COVID-19 outbreak and minimizing its damages despite divergent political opinions over governmental measures. Taiwan's face mask aids to Lithuania and Slovakia in 2020, countries with which Taiwan has no formal diplomatic ties, have turned out to be another set of "good surprises," as both countries decided to donate vaccines to Taiwan as not only a reciprocal move but also—especially for Lithuania—an anti-Beijing geopolitical move in 2021.[85] Whereas the paranoid affect drives us toward diagnostic judgment and critique, weak theory rejects predetermined universality and captures the thick phenomenological experience of a given moment and pries open its immanent possibilities for changing global social relations.

I have proposed how, as a vibrant and popular form of digital culture, the genre of memes can be read as a reparative practice of weak theory that rejects binary categorization between "conservative" and "progressive" politics. Memes construct an epistemology of knowing that pays attention to multidirectional, localized opportunities of resistance, such as how Taiwanese netizens have responded to continuous international isolation during the pandemic through meme-making. Taiwan's malleable diplomatic approach, undetermined yet resilient national existence, and pleasure-oriented communication are the unique characteristics of the nation's *queer* aesthetics and politics. While certainly numerous kinds of memes bend toward conspiracy theory and right-wing politics, the inherent characteristics of memes, which reject a singular narrative or interpretation of any given event, allow them to invite critiques via repeated circulation and mutation. Most importantly, taking memes as a *style* of interpretation propels us as critical theory scholars to produce knowledge not just through paranoia but through *pleasure*, as only humorous, fun, and pleasurable kinds of memes will survive and spread.

As the COVID-19 virus quickly transmits and mutates across national boundaries and populations, memes in the digital sphere display a parallel process of contagion, constantly taking new shape and affecting social discourse in novel ways. While memes are certainly not capable of replacing carefully crafted scholarship and cautious criticism, they must be understood as an emergent form of sociality that have resulted in political shifts and consequences on the ground. At its best, the meme genre has shown its potential to forge reparative and pleasurable forms of sociality: from the democratic biopolitical community against viral pandemic proliferation to the imagined digital community against rising authoritarianism.

Acknowledgments

I would like to thank the editors, Dr. Hsin-I Cheng and Dr. Sydney Yueh, for their productive comments on this chapter, as well as Daniel Yo-Ling's help in copyediting multiple revisions of the manuscript.

NOTES

1. Zack Burdryk, "Fauci: 'If It Looks Like You're Overreacting, You're Probably Doing the Right Thing,'" *The Hill*, March 15, 2020, https://thehill.com/homenews/sunday-talk-shows/487639-fauci-if-it-looks-like-youre-overreacting-youre-probably-doing-the.
2. Amy Qin and Amy Chang Chien, "Covid? What Covid? Taiwan Thrives as a Bubble of Normality," *New York Times*, March 13, 2021.
3. "Is Taiwan's COVID Success Story in Jeopardy?," *DW*, May 18, 2021, https://www.dw.com/en/is-taiwans-covid-success-story-in-jeopardy/a-57567374.
4. Louise Watt, "Taiwan Says It Tried to Warn the World about Coronavirus: Here's What It Really Knew and When," *Time Magazine*, May 19, 2020.
5. Eve K. Sedgwick, "Paranoid Reading and Reparative Reading; Or, You're So Paranoid, You Probably Think This Essay Is About You," in *Touching Feeling: Affect, Pedagogy, Performativity* (Durham: Duke University Press, 2003), 123–151.
6. The methodology of "hermeneutics of suspicion" is most associated with Peter Sloterdijk's work *Critique of Cynical Reason*, trans. Michael Eldred (Minneapolis: University of Minnesota Press, 1987). See also Sedgwick, "Paranoid Reading," 124.
7. David M. Halperin, *Saint Foucault: Towards a Gay Hagiography* (Oxford: Oxford Paperbacks, 1997), 28–29.
8. Ibid., 127.
9. Heather Love, "Truth and Consequences: On Paranoid Reading and Reparative Reading," *Criticism* 52, no. 2 (2010): 235–241. See also Lauren Berlant, "Preface: Reading Sedgwick, Then and Now," in *Reading Sedgwick*, edited by Lauren Berlant, 1–5 (Durham: Duke University Press, 2019).
10. Sedgwick, "Paranoid Reading," 124.
11. Ibid., 130.
12. Judith Butler, *Gender Trouble* (New York: Routledge, 1990).
13. Sedgwick, "Paranoid Reading," 130–131.
14. Wen Liu, "The Queer Paranoia of Homonormativity and Reparative Reading of the Taiwanese LGBT Movement," *Applied Ethics Review*, no. 58 (2015): 101–128.
15. Rik Glauert, "Taiwan Emerges as New Market for LGBT+ Surrogacy after Gay Marriage Law," *Reuters*, December 23, 2019, https://www.reuters.com/article/us-taiwan-lgbt-familyplanning-feature-tr-idUSKBN1YR02P.
16. Sedgwick, "Paranoid Reading," 131.
17. Silvan Tomkins, *Affect Imagery Consciousness*, vol. 2, *The Negative Affects* (New York: Springer, 1963).
18. Paul Saint-Amour, "Weak Theory, Weak Modernism," *Modernism/Modernity* 3, no. 3

(2018), https://modernismmodernity.org/articles/weak-theory-weak-modernism.

19. Sedgwick, "Paranoid Reading," 146.
20. Stephen J. Hartnett and Chiaoning Su, "Hacking, Debating, and Renewing Democracy in Taiwan in the Age of 'Post-Truth' Communication," *Taiwan Journal of Democracy* 17, no. 1 (2021): 21–43.
21. Hartnett and Su, "Hacking, Debating, and Renewing Democracy," 26.
22. AFP Shanghai, "Wildlife Trade Enhances Risks of Viral Outbreaks," *Taipei Times*, January 27, 2020, http://www.taipeitimes.com/News/world/archives/2020/01/27/2003729919.
23. Frank Chen, "Covid-19 May Be Man-made, Claims Taiwan Scholar," *Asia Times*, February 25, 2020, https://asiatimes.com/2020/02/covid-19-may-be-man-made-claims-taiwan-scholar/.
24. Smriti Mallapaty, "After the WHO Report: What's Next in the Search for COVID's Origins," *Nature* 592, no. 7854 (April 2021): 337–338.
25. Peter Knight, "COVID-19: Why Lab-Leak Theory Is Back Despite Little New Evidence," *The Conversation*, June 22, 2021, https://theconversation.com/covid-19-why-lab-leak-theory-is-back-despite-little-new-evidence-162215.
26. Glenn Kessler, "Timeline: How the Wuhan Lab-Leak Theory Suddenly Became Credible," *Washington Post*, May 25, 2021, https://www.washingtonpost.com/politics/2021/05/25/timeline-how-wuhan-lab-leak-theory-suddenly-became-credible/.
27. Carl Zimmer and Benjamin Mueller, "New Research Points to Wuhan Market as Pandemic Origin," *New York Times*, February 27, 2022, https://www.nytimes.com/interactive/2022/02/26/science/covid-virus-wuhan-origins.html.
28. See Nathan Crick, *The Rhetoric of Fascism* (Tuscaloosa: University of Alabama Press), in which he argues that fascism thrives globally today precisely because it is not a cohesive ideological unit, but a set of persuasive strategies that can be adopted to different contexts and events.
29. Fatemeh Tahmasbi et al., "'Go Eat a Bat, Chang!': An Early Look on the Emergence of Sinophobic Behavior on Web Communities in the Face of COVID-19" (paper presented at the 30th The Web Conference, online, April 20, 2021), https://arxiv.org/abs/2004.04046.
30. BBC Monitoring, "China Coronavirus: Misinformation Spreads Online about Origin and Scale," *BBC News*, January 30, 2020, https://www.bbc.com/news/blogs-trending-51271037.
31. Jérôme Viala-Gaudefroy and Dana Lindaman, "Donald Trump's 'Chinese virus': The Politics of Naming," *The Conversation*, April 21, 2020, https://theconversation.com/donald-trumps-chinese-virus-the-politics-of-naming-136796.
32. Yen-zhi Peng and Puma Shen, "China's Disinformation Campaign in Taiwan about COVID-19," The National Bureau of Asian Research, July 24, 2020, https://www.nbr.org/

publication/chinas-disinformation-campaign-in-taiwan-about-covid-19/.

33. Ching-fu Lin, Chien-huei Wu, and Chuan-feng Wu, "Reimagining the Administrative State in Times of Global Health Crisis: An Anatomy of Taiwan's Regulatory Actions in Response to the COVID-19 Pandemic," *European Journal of Risk Regulation* 11, no. 2 (2020): 256–272.
34. Jonathan Rothwell and Sonal Desai, "How Misinformation is Distorting COVID Policies and Behaviors," *Brookings Institute*, December 22, 2020, https://www.brookings.edu/research/how-misinformation-is-distorting-covid-policies-and-behaviors/.
35. Emily Stewart, "Anti-maskers Explain Themselves," *Vox*, August 7, 2020, https://www.vox.com/the-goods/2020/8/7/21357400/anti-mask-protest-rallies-donald-trump-covid-19.
36. Kim et al., "Effects of COVID-19 Misinformation on Information Seeking, Avoidance, and Processing: A Multicountry Comparative Study," *Science Communication* 42, no. 5 (2020): 586–615.
37. Kath Weston, "Climate Change, Slippery on the Skin," in *Animate Planet: Making Visceral Sense of Living in a High-Tech Ecologically Damaged World*, 105–134 (Durham: Duke University Press, 2017).
38. Jason Read, "Reduction to Ignorance: Spinoza in the Age of Conspiracy Theories," *Unemployed Negativity*, February 24, 2021, http://www.unemployednegativity.com/2021/02/reduction-to-ignorance-spinoza-in-age.html.
39. Roland Imhoff and Pia Lamberty, "A Bioweapon or a Hoax? The Link Between Distinct Conspiracy Beliefs About the Coronavirus Disease (COVID-19) Outbreak and Pandemic Behavior," *Social Psychological and Personality Science* 11, no. 8 (2020): 1110–1118.
40. Richard Hofstadter, "The Paranoid Style in American Politics," in *The Paranoid Style in American Politics and Other Essays* (Cambridge, MA: Harvard University Press, 1996), 39.
41. Sedgwick, "Paranoid Reading," 142.
42. Mark Fenster, *Conspiracy Theories: Secrecy and Power in American Culture*, 2nd ed. (Minneapolis: University of Minnesota Press, 2008).
43. Fenster, *Conspiracy Theories*, 45.
44. Mike Davis, *The Monster Enters: COVID-19, Avian Flu and the Plagues of Capitalism* (New York: OR Books, 2020).
45. Giorgio Agamben, "The Invention of an Epidemic," *European Journal of Psychoanalysis*, February 26, 2020, https://www.journal-psychoanalysis.eu/coronavirus-and-philosophers/.
46. Michel Foucault, *Discipline and Punish: The Birth of the Prison*, trans. Alan Sheridan (New York: Pantheon, 1977).
47. Christopher Caldwell, "Meet the Philosopher Who Is Trying to Explain the Pandemic,"

New York Times, August 21, 2020, https://www.nytimes.com/2020/08/21/opinion/sunday/giorgio-agamben-philosophy-coronavirus.html.

48. Marc A. Thiessen, "Opinion: China Is Using Covid-19 to Throttle Hong Kong's Pro-Democracy Movement," *Washington Post*, May 21, 2020, https://www.washingtonpost.com/opinions/2020/05/21/china-is-using-covid-19-throttle-hong-kongs-pro-democracy-movement/.
49. Giorgio Agamben, *State of Exception*, trans. Kevin Attell (Chicago: University of Chicago Press, 2005).
50. Philip Willan, "Leaders of Italy's 'Orange Vests' Inspires Far-Right and Coronavirus Conspiracy Theorists," *Times*, June 2, 2020, https://www.thetimes.co.uk/article/leader-of-italys-orange-vests-inspires-far-right-and-coronavirus-conspiracy-theorists-kxrf705v7.
51. Ilan Alon, Matthew Farrell, and Shaomin Li, "Regime Type of COVID-19 Response," *FIIB Business Review* 9, no. 3 (2020): 152–160.
52. Chingfang Wu, "NTU Expert: Taiwan Doesn't Need Lockdowns," *Common Wealth Magazine*, May 27, 2021, https://english.cw.com.tw/article/article.action?id=2995.
53. Katharin Tai (@katharintai), "Most Western Analyses of East Asian #Covid19 Responses in One Meme (thx @lnachman32)," Twitter, April 21, 2020, 12:43 a.m., https://twitter.com/katharintai/status/1252276632414498816.
54. Aja Romano, "'Is This a Meme?': The Confused Anime Guy and His Butterfly, Explained," *Vox*, May 15, 2018, https://www.vox.com/2018/5/15/17351806/is-this-a-pigeon-anime-butterfly-meme-explained.
55. Tai, "Most Western Analyses."
56. Sedgwick, "Paranoid Reading," 131.
57. Xiaoan Guo and Shaoting Yang, "Memetic Communication and Consensus Mobilization in the Cyber Nationalist Movement," in *From Cyber-Nationalism to Fandom Nationalism*, edited by Hailong Liu, 72–92 (New York: Routledge, 2019). Also see James W. Carey, *Communication as Culture: Essays on Media and Society* (Boston: Hyman, 1989).
58. Richard Dawkins, *The Selfish Gene* (Oxford: Oxford University Press, 1976).
59. Limor Shifman, *Memes in Digital Culture* (Cambridge, MA: MIT Press, 2014).
60. Sedgwick, "Paranoid Reading," 130.
61. "Me explaining to my grandchildren how a guy eating bat soup in China led to a toilet paper shortage in the US," Image by u/it_hurts_when_IP, March 16, 2020, Reddit, https://www.reddit.com/r/memes/comments/fj6yic/me_explaining_to_my_grandchildren_how_a_guy/. The "me explaining" me is also known as the "Pepe Silvia" meme, which originally comes from a famous scene out of the TV series, *It's Always Sunny in Philadelphia*, where the character Charlie frantically explains his conspiracy

about how a person named "Pepe Silvia" does not exist in real life. See "Pepe Silvia," *Know Your Meme*, https://knowyourmeme.com/memes/pepe-silvia.

62. Shifman, *Memes*, 39–40.
63. Jonah Berger and Katherine L. Milkman, "Social Transmission, Emotion, and the Virality of Online Content," *Marketing Science Institute Working Paper Series*, Report No. 10–114 (2010): 1–38.
64. Shifman, *Memes*, 87.
65. Yang Peidong and Tang Lijun, "'Positive Energy': Hegemonic Intervention and Online Media Discourse in China's Xi Jinping Era," *China: An International Journal* 16, no. 1 (2018): 1–22.
66. Foucault, *Discipline and Punish.*
67. Karsten Schubert, "The Democratic Biopolitics of PrEP," in *Biopolitiken–Regierungen des Lebens heute*, edited by Helene Gerhards and Katharin Braun, 121–153 (Wiesebaden: Springer VS, 2019).
68. Audrey Tang and Ivan Yates, "How Digital Innovation Can Fight Pandemics and Strengthen Democracy," YouTube video, 27:12, from the Construction Industry Federation annual conference on October 1, 2020, posted by "Taipei Representative Office in Ireland," October 7, 2020, https://www.youtube.com/watch?v=nPtm-7ukcaI.
69. Carey, *Communication as Culture.*
70. Lin, Wu, and Wu, "Reimagining the Administrative State."
71. MOHW of Taiwan (@MOHW_Taiwan), "Maintain social distancing," image by Ministry of Health and Welfare, July 10, 2020, Twitter, https://twitter.com/MOHW_Taiwan/status/1281563042589716480. The image is used under the Creative Commons "Attribution-NonCommercial-ShareAlike" license guideline with the permission of MOHW of Taiwan.
72. Amber Wang, "Virus Outbreak: Mascots Embraced for Virus Prevention Campaign," *Taipei Times*, February 18, 2020, https://www.taipeitimes.com/News/taiwan/archives/2020/02/18/2003731193.
73. The Ministry of Education, Taiwan, "唐揚姬3/2–3/8星座運勢週報 (Jesse Tang's 3/2–3/8 Weekly Astrology Reports)," Facebook, March 2, 2020, https://www.facebook.com/www.edu.tw/posts/1482813591893257.
74. Ryan M. Milner, *The World Made Meme: Public Conversations and Participatory Media* (Cambridge, MA: MIT Press, 2018).
75. Helen Davidson, "Taiwan Accuses China of Interfering with Covid Vaccine Deals," *Guardian*, May 27, 2021, https://www.theguardian.com/world/2021/may/27/taiwan-president-accuses-china-interfering-covid-vaccine-deals.

76. 外交部 Ministry of Foreign Affairs, Taiwan (@MOFA_Taiwan), ".@WHO, what's wrong with you?," Twitter, February 6, 2020, 11:36 a.m., https://twitter.com/MOFA_Taiwan/status/1225261907084361728?s=20.
77. Taiwan Scene, "WHO Refers to Taiwan as 'Taipei and Environs' in Latest Coronavirus Report," *Taiwan Scene: Formosa Tourism Journal*, February 7, 2020, https://taiwan-scene.com/who-refers-to-taiwan-as-taipei-and-environs-in-latest-coronavirus-report/.
78. Will Feuer, "WHO Chief Addresses Death Threats, Racist Insults: 'I Don't Give a Damn,'" *CNBC*, April 8, 2020, https://www.cnbc.com/2020/04/08/who-chief-addresses-death-threats-racist-insults-i-dont-give-a-damn.html.
79. Dimitrios Kotsakos, Panos Sakkos, Ioannis Katakis, and Dimitrios Gunopulos, "# tag: Meme or Event?" *2014 IEEE/ACM International Conference on Advances in Social Networks Analysis and Mining (ASONAM 2014)*, 391–394 (Piscataway, NJ: Institute of Electrical and Electronics Engineers, 2014), https://dl.acm.org/doi/pdf/10.5555/3191835.3191913.
80. Ministry of Foreign Affairs, Republic of China (Taiwan), "Taiwan Can Help, and Taiwan Is Helping!" https://en.mofa.gov.tw/cp.aspx?n=2318. Nicholas Haggerty and Daphne K. Lee, "The Story Behind the 'Taiwan Can Help' Ad on *New York Times*," *The News Lens International*, April 15, 2020, https://international.thenewslens.com/article/133864.
81. Aaron Nieh et al., "Taiwan Can Help," Taiwan Can Help, https://taiwancanhelp.us/.
82. Adam K. Dedman and Autumn Lai, "Digitally Dismantling Asian Authoritarianism: Activist Reflections from the #MilkTeaAlliance," *Contention* 9, no. 1 (2021): 1–36.
83. "Milk Tea Alliance Map," image from Twitter, reproduced in the *News Lens*, April 28, 2020, https://www.thenewslens.com/article/134348.
84. Helen Davidson, "A Victim of Its Own Success: How Taiwan Failed to Plan For a Major COVID Outbreak," *Guardian*, June 7, 2021, https://www.theguardian.com/world/2021/jun/07/a-victim-of-its-own-success-how-taiwan-failed-to-plan-for-a-major-covid-outbreak.
85. David Hutt, "EU Left Behind as US Pushes 'Vaccine Diplomacy' in Southeast Asia," *DW*, July 15, 2021, https://www.dw.com/en/eu-left-behind-as-us-pushes-vaccine-diplomacy-in-southeast-asia/a-58279954.

Excavating Truth

Assessing Citizen-Led Fact-Checking Practices in Taiwan

Chiaoning Su and Wei-Ping Li

From sophisticated disinformation campaigns to patriotic trolling and clickbait, the flood of mis/disinformation has become a global phenomenon.[1] While "fake news" has always existed, modern technology has exacerbated the problem. To combat mis/disinformation, numerous fact-checking organizations have emerged around the world in the past five years. According to the Duke Reporters' Lab, a research center studying global fact-checking efforts, forty-four such centers existed in 2014; by 2019, 226 were in operation in seventy-three countries.[2] Collectively, they serve as a "vital defense in response to falsehoods, hyperboles and half-truths targeting democracy, health, economy and national security."[3] Yet, fact-checking is not a monolith with universal values and histories.[4] Therefore, it is crucial to examine fact-checking organizations through a local lens to fully capture their historical roots, evolution, and future opportunities and challenges.

The recent growth of fact-checking initiatives in Taiwan is a result of both internal and external factors. Taiwan remains one of the few countries that enjoys press freedom in Asia—a region where journalistic practitioners are often threatened by "totalitarian propaganda, censorship, intimidation, physical violence and cyber-harassment."[5] In April 2017, Reporters Without Borders selected Taiwan as the location for its Asian headquarters because of its high level of press freedom.[6] Nevertheless, intensifying sensationalism and partisanship have eroded public trust in local journalism, which hit a new low in 2020, when only 24 percent of surveyed respondents expressed confidence in local news outlets.[7] Furthermore, the open and free press that accompanies a democratic society makes Taiwan an easy target for disinformation and misinformation. Studies have shown that Taiwan's young democracy ranks as one of the countries most exposed to misleading viewpoints or false information disseminated by foreign forces—especially from China.[8] Often these campaigns aim to demonize high-profile Taiwanese politicians, divide Taiwanese society, and promote the unification of China and Taiwan.[9] Sometimes such campaigns also aim to steer Taiwan away from anti-China policies or international alliances, notably with the United States.

In recent years, Taiwanese citizens have initiated several projects to battle false information. As one of the earliest endeavors, MyGoPen (麥擱騙) was established in 2015 to help users verify internet rumors per request via LINE, the most popular messaging app in Taiwan.[10] Inspired by MyGoPen, Cofacts (真的假的) was founded in 2017 and offered a collaborative model of fact-checking. This pioneering platform integrated a hoax database, LINE automated chat bots, and a group of volunteers to debunk online false information.[11] Finally, Taiwan FactCheck Center (台灣事實查核中心, TFC) launched its website in July 2018, with the aim of applying journalistically informed methods to verify dubious claims with the potential for negative societal impact. This latest initiative aims to improve the local information ecosystem.[12] Despite different fact-checking practices and orientations, these three civic organizations produced a synergized, collaborative network to foster media literacy among Taiwanese citizens. As TFC founder Hu Yuan-hui noted, fact-checking and media literacy in Taiwan is a "social movement about participation in . . . democracy."[13] In November 2021, Google donated USD$1 million to the Taiwan Media Literacy Cultivation Initiative, a project led by TFC, MyGoPen, and several other groups. The funding finances six hundred workshops and seven hundred trainers to help highly vulnerable groups in Taiwan, such as the elderly, Aboriginal communities, and newly naturalized citizens, become better equipped to debunk misinformation and stop the weaponization of disinformation.

Building upon this work, this chapter first reviews the journalistic literature on global fact checking movements with an emphasis on their contexts, practices, collaborations, and challenges. The focus then shifts to historically contextualizing these dis/misinformation issues in Taiwan. The subsequent section is based on in-depth interviews with eight informants from MyGoPen, Cofacts, and TFC and identifies different fact-checking approaches as shaped by unique motivations, verification practices, target audiences, and institutional biases. Unlike most Western fact-checking enterprises, which are connected to media companies and guided by journalistic norms, Taiwan's fact-checking platforms tend to be led by either veteran journalists or engineers who are savvy with computer coding and new media applications. Their concerns include accountability in journalism and information transparency as well as protecting democracy through civic technologies.

This case study contributes to journalism scholarship by improving our understanding of fact-checking as a set of practices shaped by both journalistic ideals and technological advancement, and as a response to both the history and future needs of a particular society. As geopolitical conflicts have intensified, Taiwan stands on the frontlines against China's Russian-inspired disinformation strategies.[14] As such, Taiwan illuminates Beijing's sharp power and forecasts the impending clash between global democracy and authoritarianism as embodied in recent U.S.–China tensions.[15]

Fact-Checking in Taiwan—Past, Present, and Future

Increasingly used in popular discourse, the term "fact-checking" indicates a wide range of information verification behaviors, from line-by-line reading to an analysis of competing narratives. In journalistic circles, fact-checking refers to "a deliberate critique of conventional reporting and its practice of objectivity." While traditional news outlets typically cover claims made by public figures as *simply* claims, fact-checkers investigate and verify these claims and publish their results. As Lucas Graves notes, fact-checking in the United States represents an effort to "revitalize the 'truth-seeking' tradition in journalism by holding public figures to account for the things they say."[16]

The Origins of Fact-Checking Initiatives in the United States and Beyond

The United States is often considered the epicenter of the modern fact-checking movement.[17] Early examples of fact-checking operations first attracted notice during the 1990s when several mainstream television news channels, such as ABC, CNN, and NBC, began to verify claims in political campaign commercials in their "adwatch" reports.[18] The widespread adoption of the internet, which flooded American households with false information, led to several fact-checking sites around the turn of the millennium. While some of them focused on debunking online hoaxes and urban legends (e.g., Snopes.com), others concentrated on the factual accuracy of statements made by U.S. political figures (e.g., Spinsanity).[19]

FactCheck.org was established in 2003 to verify political information produced and disseminated during elections. As the first fact-checking organization in the United States staffed with experienced political journalists, FactCheck.org "aims to reduce the level of deception and confusion in U.S. politics."[20] Four years later, the *St. Petersburg Times* (now *Tampa Bay Times*) initiated another "election-year" project—PolitiFact, to check not only statements by politicians but also the discourse of media figures. Using an innovative "Truth-O-Meter" method to rate the accuracy of political claims on a six-point scale, PolitiFact cemented itself as a database of verdicts that users can search by topics, ratings, and speakers.[21]

Finally, Fact Checker joined the landscape in September 2007. Unlike the previous two organizations, which operate as independent ventures, Fact Checker developed out of a column in the *Washington Post* intended to check the claims of presidential candidates. The feature column later developed into a full-fledged fact-checking team and website to "explain difficult issues, provide missing context and offer analysis and explanation of various 'code words' used by politicians, diplomats and others to obscure or shade the truth."[22] Together, these three dedicated American outlets set the tone for many fact-checking initiatives across the world.

In countries with insufficient press freedoms, fact-checking often merges with political activism to push for social change or to protect against foreign propaganda. As Michelle Amazeen notes, "Severe social disequilibrium or political crisis where current frameworks fail" are critical factors that give rise to fact-checking efforts.[23] In Ukraine, a group of students and professors at Kyiv Mohyla School of Journalism founded StopFake in 2014. Disturbed by Russian disinformation campaigns targeting Ukraine and Russia's military invasion of Crimea, StopFake worked as a "counter-propaganda site" to dispel fake news and increase the public's media literacy.[24] During Russia's invasion of Ukraine in 2022, StopFake has also played an important role to counter Russia's rampant disinformation attack.[25] In the case of Turkey, Ukraine's neighbor to the south, the independent fact-checking website Doğruluk Payı (Turkish for "grain of truth") grew out of the response to the Gezi

Park protests in 2013, which were rooted in disputes over urban development and quickly expanded into broader concerns involving freedom of press, free expression, and Turkey's secularism. Doğruluk Payı endeavored to verify politicians' statements and has since become a full-fledged fact-checking organization.[26] Despite the nuances among the fact-checking practices in these countries, they are united in their journalistically grounded and politically focused approach.

The Fact-Checkers' Role-Perceptions and Practices

Given their varied sociocultural contexts, practitioners in the field of fact-checking tend to see their roles through different lenses. Based on in-depth interviews in eight European countries, Lucas Graves and Federica Cherubini found fact-checkers adopting three common identities—reporter, reformer, and expert. Each contributes differently to traditional forms of journalism.[27]

To see themselves as reporters is to understand the practice of fact-checking through a journalistic approach. Practitioners who adopt this identity describe their primary mission as informing society through explanatory, data-driven, and investigative reporting.[28] Furthermore, they strive to maintain a critical non-partisan stance in assessing political discourses, and to go beyond "false balance," or "he said, she said" reporting, to factually challenge official claims.[29] In this way, their collective efforts can be seen as a much-needed "field repair" of journalism—a critical response to restore credibility to an industry under a constant barrage of public disappointment and critique.[30]

Other practitioners see themselves more as reformers than reporters. Often operating in contexts where mainstream media are controlled by powerful political or economic forces, these fact-checkers position themselves as activists monitoring both political actors and media outlets. They see fact-checking as a blueprint for social reform that is rendering information into action. To this end, practitioners in this group typically couple fact-checking with social advocacy and include citizens in the process of verifying political claims, as seen in the work of FactCheck Ukraine.[31] By doing so, these activists expand journalistic fact-checking into political education and so encourage active citizenship.[32]

A smaller but still notable percentage of fact-checkers approach their task as authoritative experts, especially on public policy. Branding their fact-checking platform as a "think tank," practitioners with an expert outlook typically specialize in a single domain of knowledge, such as politics, public health, or economics.[33] Whereas journalistic and activist fact-checkers stop at verification and action respectively, expert fact-checkers pursue explicit correction of problematic sources. For example, the British fact-checking organization Full Fact is known for its success in pushing media outlets and high-profile politicians to correct the record; these include the prime minister David Cameron rescinding his claim about the number of schools operating at full or over capacity in 2016. Through this strategy, expert fact-checkers attempt to improve the output of journalism by strengthening the quality of sources.[34]

Despite their various self-perceptions, fact-checking practices across the world have become increasingly institutionalized, and are seen as "a fact-centered activity that borrows basic elements from the scientific method."[35] According to Graves, they proceed through a five-step process: (1) Identification: Fact-checkers are trained to identify politically significant claims, especially those that are practically checkable; (2) Contact: Once a claim is made, the fact-checkers reach out to claimants to instill fairness into the investigative reporting that backs their claims; (3) Tracing: Fact-checkers use digital software and databases to trace the origin and dissemination of specific claims; (4) Collaborating: Fact-checkers also rely on authoritative organizations and figures to interpret obtained data; and (5) Publishing: A published report typically details the steps taken to complete a fact-check to achieve transparency and objectivity. This process is mainly based on journalistic principles, such as using credible sources to verify and vet information from different statements. In some fact-checking projects, practitioners even go further to provide material contexts and deliberate over "factual coherence."[36] However, no matter how divergent fact-checking practices may be, these initiatives aim to rebuild trust in civil society and "foster a culture of accuracy."[37]

Opportunities and Threats to a Global Fact-Checking Network

As fact-checking becomes a global movement, collaboration among practitioners, which Lucas Graves and Magda Konieczna term "news sharing,"[38] has become frequent. Whereas mainstream journalists actively compete against each other to break the story, fact-checkers work as "a kind of fraternity."[39] Cooperation replaces rivalry as fact-checkers routinely acknowledge each other's work and seek replication rather than fresh angles in their verifications of claims. As documented in an editor's letter at PolitiFact, "It's much more satisfying when the major fact-checking organizations agree, because we know we've reached the same conclusions independently."[40]

Even at the global scale, collaboration among fact-checkers has been evident, especially in recent months as the COVID-19 pandemic has shifted into an "infodemic."[41] For example, according to Poyu Tseng and Puma Shen, several widespread rumors in Taiwan during the COVID-19 pandemic alleged that the virus originated in the United States and even assigned culpability to the U.S. government. By reframing the narratives about the origins of the virus, these rumors tried to shift the public's blame from China to stoke anger toward the United States.[42] Led and coordinated by International Fact-Checking Network (IFCN), the CoronaVirusFacts Alliance became the largest ever global fact-checking initiative, with more than seven thousand fact-checkers from seventy countries. Since the first article published by TFC in Taiwan on February 12, 2020, this alliance has published more than thirty-five hundred fact-checking stories and weekly reports to date, pinpointing the volume and trends of COVID-19 hoaxes around the world and in different locations.[43] Such large collaborative efforts legitimize fact-checking as a new approach to resist shallow "horse race" journalism and as a potential solution to the spread of mis/disinformation.

Despite these ideals, the practice of fact-checking faces constant scrutiny and opposition in the present "post-truth" world. Studies have shown a clear "partisan divide" in terms of users' reception and sharing of information verified by fact-checking sites in the United States.[44] Conservative partisans tend to accuse fact-checks of being illegitimate or biased, while some even use derogatory terms such as "prostitute" to describe practitioners in this field.[45] Another example is a Ukraine news outlet criticizing Ukraine's StopFake as being far-right, especially when dealing with information relating to national identity.[46] A critical step toward increasing the psychological efficacy of debunking messages is that fact-checkers disentangle information reception from political ideologies, offer detailed explanations and evidence that enhance correcting messages, and engage the audience in the process of verification.[47]

This review of evolving global fact-checking practices reveals the origins, practitioners and norms, and complications of fact-checking. The review also shows that fact-checking sites and actors in the West dominate the scholarship addressing fact-checking. Sakari Nieminen and Lauri Rapeli found that thirty-seven out of forty-eight articles published between 2013 and 2018 on the topic of fact-checking targeted the U.S. context in that "participants were US citizens or the analytical focus was solely on US-based actors."[48] Analyzing fact-checking platforms in Taiwan thus affords a reexamination of the journalistic and Western epistemology adopted by most fact-checking literature, while adding missing perspectives and an Asian context.

Contextualizing Fact-Checking Practices in Taiwan

The phenomenon of "fake news" has deep roots in Taiwan. From 1895 to 1945, Taiwan was a Japanese colony. In post–World War II Taiwan, politicians and media skillfully manipulated information for both political and economic purposes. At this time, Taiwan existed in a period of authoritarian rule under the Kuomintang (KMT), which replaced Japan as an occupying force following KMT's retreat from mainland China. Taiwan remained under martial law until 1987, when the island nation established itself as a democracy. For four decades (1949–1987), the KMT used both legal concepts, such as martial law and the Publication Act, and the acquisition of news organizations to fully control the media landscape in Taiwan.[49] Indeed, local media served as an instrument for the KMT to legitimize its political interests while demonizing its opponents. To fight against authoritarian rule and media censorship, several "dangwai" (outside the KMT party) magazines were published between the 1970s and 1980s to advocate for democracy and press freedom.[50] As Gary Rawnsley notes, these publications "were at the forefront of the first attempt to create a credible alternative to the KMT."[51]

The end of martial law in 1987 and the passage of the Cable Television Act in 1993 propelled Taiwan into a new era in which the media landscape was gradually privatized and driven by corporate profits. The exponential growth in media companies resulted in fierce competition and sometimes led to the unwitting use of fabricated content to drive viewership, as seen in the notorious "Meals for the Dead incident" (腳尾飯事件). In June 2005, Yu-chen Wang, a Taipei City councilor and television show host, sent a videotape to several news outlets, suggesting restaurants recycled the meals left by the feet of corpses—a religious act meant to prepare the deceased for the long journey to the afterlife—and made them into dishes for customers. TVBS-N, one of the earliest nationwide twenty-four-hour news channels, was the first to broadcast the story while others quickly followed; public anxiety on food safety ensued. Although the original video was soon proven to be scripted and fabricated, this incident illuminated the insufficient internal fact-checking in local newsrooms. The Satellite Television Broadcasting Association (STBA) was founded later that year to establish better professional protocols for the TV news industry.[52]

China's influence on Taiwan's media landscape has become more visible since the 2000s. Eager to secure investments and profit from the Chinese market, Taiwanese media companies either complied with Beijing's mandated mass communication policies or produced flattering content about China.[53] Some even turned themselves into explicit mouthpieces to implement China's playbook, such as Eng-meng Tsai's Want Want China Times Media Group. Tsai initially developed a food production business but began to acquire local Taiwanese media in 2008. Tsai has since faced allegations that his Taiwanese business acquisitions and operations are backed by Chinese subsidies.[54] Currently, he owns three TV channels, three newspapers, three news magazines, and eight news sites in Taiwan.[55] The acquisitions by Eng-meng Tsai significantly altered topic selection and editorial practices in the newsroom. Investigative reporting from the *Financial Times* shows that the managerial team would "take instructions directly from the Taiwan Affairs Office, the body in the Chinese government that handles Taiwan issues."[56] This new chain of command explains why *China Times* decreased its coverage of human rights issues in China by two thirds in 2015.[57] In May 2019, Tsai led seventy Taiwanese media representatives to attend the fourth Cross-Strait Media People Summit in Beijing—a conference aimed to promote cross-strait reunification and Chinese domination of Taiwan.[58] As Chui-cheng Chiu, Deputy Minister of the Mainland Affairs Council, concluded: "China has stretched its hands into our democratic politics and into the heart of it, our media."[59]

Technology diffusion in Taiwan further complicates the phenomenon of fake news. According to Facebook Asia Pacific vice-president Dan Neary, Taiwan has "the world's highest per capita Facebook penetration rate at 15 million active users per month."[60] Meanwhile, 91 percent of Taiwanese aged twelve to sixty-five years old use LINE, a messaging app, to share information via closed individual or group conversations.[61] The penetration of these social media platforms results partly from the important political function they serve for election campaigns.[62] This function drives traffic and bolsters these platforms as an information source competing with legacy media, but also provides a hotbed for disseminating and amplifying dis/misinformation. In the era of broadcast media, those wishing to spread dis/misinformation had to first draw the attention of a trained journalist and then convince them to run a false story. However, digital technology can bypass this filter, allowing online falsehoods to be created and spread by anyone with a vested interest. Taiwan's internet readiness and social media engagement offered the Chinese regime another platform to interfere in its domestic politics. A huge number of government-hired netizens, widely known as members of the "50c party" (五毛黨), regularly "engage in 'hand-to-hand' verbal combat, making specific, directed arguments that support the [Chinese] government, its leaders, and their policies, and opposing arguments to the contrary" in the digital space.[63] These strategic, pro-China messages sew confusion and division in Taiwanese society.

The flow of disinformation from China to Taiwan is often enabled through cross-strait collusion, as shown in the case of Su Chii-cherng. In September 2018, thousands of travelers were stranded at Kansai airport in Japan because of Typhoon Jebi. In the midst of the chaos, a pseudonymous post appeared on PTT (批踢踢), a Reddit-like message board widely used among Taiwanese youth, to call for help. This post emphasized that Taiwanese travelers had to rely on evacuation buses arranged by the Chinese consulate. Without rigorous verification, local media and political commentators quickly picked up the narrative to criticize the Taiwanese government's slow and inadequate disaster relief efforts. The intense criticism allegedly led to the suicide of Su Chii-cherng, the head of the Taipei Economic and Cultural Office in Osaka. Later, several studies found striking similarities between content from a Chinese content farm and the first post on PTT, revealing a trajectory of disinformation flowing from China to Taiwan. Local news media further legitimized this manipulative political astroturfing while social media and closed communication apps augmented it.[64]

Facing the disinformation attack from China, Taiwan's legislature passed the Anti-Infiltration Act in January 2020, which aims to prevent foreign states, especially China, from attacking Taiwan's democracy. The law forbids hostile foreign entities from making illicit financial contributions to politicians, media, and other campaign efforts in Taiwan.[65] The government also plans to introduce media literacy into Taiwan's twelve-year mandatory education to cultivate the next generation of critical thinkers.[66] Meanwhile, several civic initiatives, mostly in the format of fact-checking, have been undertaken to answer the questions of news consumers regarding online falsehoods and to prompt further verification. Among them, MyGoPen, Cofacts, and TFC are the most active platforms that have gained attention from mainstream media for their work and established partnerships with social media to combat dis/misinformation.

TABLE 1. Interviewee List

ORGANIZATION	NAME	ROLE	INTERVIEW DATE AND FORMAT
MyGoPen	Charles Yeh	Founder and principal fact-checker	July 10, 2019 (In person) September 11, 2020 (Google Meet)
Cofacts	Billion	Cofounder	August 8, 2019 (In person group interview)
	Johnson	Cofounder	
	B. L.	Programmer	
TFC	Yuan-hui Hu	Founder	June 27, 2019 (In person)
	Chao-hwei Huang	Former editor-in-chief	June 28, 2019 (In person)
	Summer Chen	Editor-in-chief	September 13, 2020 (Google Meet)
	R	Fact-checker	June 28, 2019 (In person)

Interviewing Fact-Checkers in Taiwan

Currently, there are four active citizen-initiated fact-checking organizations in Taiwan. This analysis draws on interviews with practitioners from three of them: MyGoPen, Cofacts, and TFC. The fourth organization, Rumor & Truth (蘭姆酒吐司), declined to participate. The study (IRB Protocol #: 1450582, 1467145-1) was conducted from June 2019 to September 2020. Interviewees were recruited through snowball sampling, namely "the process of accumulation as each located subject suggests other subjects."[67] The authors interviewed one representative from MyGoPen, three from Cofacts, and four from TFC (Table 1). This small sample size reflected the scale of these organizations. For example, MyGoPen was a one-person operation when first interviewed by the authors in June 2019. These practitioners' experiences offer a good representation of the field of fact-checking in Taiwan.

Most interviews were conducted one-on-one in a face-to-face format and lasted approximately 1.5 hours. Each time, a semistructured questionnaire facilitated the interview conversation while allowing flexibility for new ideas to emerge. Three exceptions to this arrangement were a group interview with the three Cofacts representatives (per their request), a follow-up Google Meet interview with the MyGoPen founder, and a Google Meet interview with the last TFC member due to COVID-19. Cofacts's request for a group interview reflects the decentralized and inclusive character of that platform, which encourages all members to partake in decision-making.

All interviews were recorded, transcribed, and analyzed through a three-step process. First, the authors independently read all transcripts to develop a broad sense of fact-checking practices in Taiwan. After initial readings, high-level concepts were jointly identified through line-by-line analysis to break the raw data into discrete examples embodying thematic patterns, including each platform's objective, audience, technology, and organizational values.[68] Furthermore, through constant comparisons and contrasts, the authors mapped the intersections among these patterns and identified their convergences—collaborative fact-checking practices—and divergence. As all interviews were conducted in Mandarin, the quotations presented in the analysis below are translations that the authors have verified as accurate.

The Objectives and Audiences of Fact-Checking Platforms in Taiwan

Established in 2015, MyGoPen, which means "Don't fool me again" in Taiwanese, was one of the earliest local fact-checking projects. Operated first in a blog format to help the founder's mother-in-law identify and debunk scams, MyGoPen has gradually gained popularity among senior citizens and evolved into a full-fledged website that also provides a one-on-one fact-checking service through LINE. In 2020, MyGoPen had more than three hundred thousand LINE subscribers and received about two thousand queries per day. Currently, MyGoPen operates as a for-profit company funded by collaborative partnerships (e.g., Facebook), content authorization (Yahoo!), and reader donations. MyGoPen has three full-time and three part-time staff. The founder is the principal fact-checker, a programmer writes and maintains LINE bot programs, and other employees respond to one-on-one queries via LINE.

MyGoPen did not categorize itself as a news organization immediately. As the founder Charles Yeh said, "I was originally an engineer . . . just an ordinary person who didn't know much about journalism. I didn't even know the phrase 'media literacy' until I got to know Professor Hu, the co-founder of TFC . . . I haven't thought about how to label us." Yet, in 2020, MyGoPen earned certification with IFCN and became the second fact-checking organization (after TFC) to collaborate with Facebook. These developments forced MyGoPen to become increasingly aware of its social responsibilities to the Taiwanese people, especially those most vulnerable to dis/misinformation. For example, MyGoPen has collaborated with Google to hold public events to promote media literacy. In 2020, it also recruited an editor with a journalism background to reinforce its fact-checking process.

Started in 2017, Cofacts was sponsored by a Civic Tech Prototype Grant and built by a group of computer programmers from gov, a "decentralized civic tech community" that advocates for information transparency and digital activism.[69] Inspired by MyGoPen's rumor-debunking service, these programmers went a step further to integrate a LINE chatbot with a hoax database. Once it receives a dubious message submitted by LINE users, the Cofacts bot will check against its database and provide an automated response indicating the veracity of the information. For queries not included in the database, a Cofacts volunteer will fact-check each submission manually and add it to the database. In other words, Cofacts is a collaborative fact-checking project enabled by big data, crowdsourcing, and technology diffusion.

Three to five core members keep Cofacts operating. Every two months, these key personnel hold a gathering to develop offline connections with volunteers. These in-person meetings provide an opportunity to connect online information–verifying behaviors with real-life identities and prevent the platform being "hijacked by rogue editors."[70] Meanwhile, guided by the concepts of open data, Cofacts publishes its source code, LINE bot analytics, and data set of verified messages for public use. In fact, Aunt Meiyu, another popular LINE chatbot created in 2018, provides fact-checking information built upon Cofacts's open source coding and a combined database of Cofacts, TFC, and MyGoPen.[71]

Among the three fact-checking initiatives in this study, TFC was the only one established and run by fact-checkers with journalistic training. In 2018, two nonprofit organizations, Taiwan Media Watch and the Association for Quality Journalism Taiwan, initiated the center using donations from philanthropic foundations. TFC aims "to conduct fact checks on information relevant to public affairs as well as to improve the information ecology and news quality of Taiwan."[72] More than just an organization, founder Yuan-hui Hu has described TFC as a movement: "We want to raise awareness about the importance of accurate information for a democracy and the harms of false information to a society like Taiwan, which is in a unique situation . . . I promote it [fact-checking] as a movement to raise awareness in our civil society."[73] Thus, TFC views fact-checking as an act of resistance working toward a larger cultural shift in society's relationship to information. TFC is interested in reshaping citizens' mindsets about the role of information in democratic societies, and raising awareness of what is at stake when information quality is undermined.

TFC devotes itself primarily to two lines of activity: producing fact-checking reports and participating in media literacy events. Currently, TFC has eight full-time employees, including the editor-in-chief, six fact-checkers, and one graphic designer. Together, they produce around thirty to forty articles per month, including original content, translation, and event coverage. "Our goal is not to pursue quantity but quality . . . especially being such a young organization, the most important thing for us is to establish credibility through the quality of our work," said Summer Chen, editor-in-chief of TFC. Because of its persistence in rigor and accountability, TFC first earned IFCN certification in 2018 and then won a highly competitive Coronavirus Fact-Checking Grant (USD$50,000) in 2020 to "combat COVID-19 misinformation through multimedia."[74] Meanwhile, IFCN selected TFC's 2019 publication entitled "a Chinese spy named Wang Liqiang" as one of the best fact-checking reports of the decade.[75] TFC also became a leader in media literacy education in Taiwan and is heavily involved in seminars to exchange ideas with experts and in workshops to promote fact-checking practices to the public.

Despite their shared concerns with dis/misinformation, these fact-checking organizations represent three identities with different objectives and audiences. Founded by journalists and journalism scholars, TFC represents the reporter identity, which is focused on news production, and working to eliminate falsehoods from published news stories. That is, through their rigorous reports, they hold local media accountable. Positioning itself as a user-friendly tool to investigate suspicious claims, MyGoPen does not fit neatly into any of the three existing identities. It seeks to resolve the dis/misinformation problem by addressing audience reception, especially among digitally illiterate senior citizens. That said, MyGoPen is transitioning toward the reporter identity by hiring a new staff member with journalistic training. Cofacts, with its crowdsourced and technological approach, is the most difficult to classify. Cofacts believes that everyone, regardless of background, experience, or expertise, can act as a fact-checker. Simply engaging in fact-checking thus becomes more important than the results of that fact-checking. Thus, Cofacts may demand a new identity category, perhaps best expressed as coordinator. The differences among the three organizations shape their choice of topics and verification methods (Table 2).

TABLE 2. Three Fact-Checking Platforms' Practices

	MYGOPEN	COFACTS	TAIWAN FACTCHECK CENTER
Topic Selection	Suggested by LINE users and chosen by fact-checkers at MyGoPen.	Suggested by LINE users and chosen by online volunteer editors who routinely cull topics from the hoax database.	Chosen by fact-checkers at TFC who routinely cull topics from both mainstream media coverage and social media conversation.
Verification Norms	Unclear; Leaning toward journalistic norms.	Guided by crowdsourcing and data transparency.	Guided by journalistic norms.
Sources Used for Verification	Online sources (Primary) Offline sources: Experts	Online sources (Primary)	Offline sources: Experts (Primary) Online sources
True/False Rating System	True Misleading Partially false False Rumor	True False Uncheckable Opinion	True False Fact clarification Unproven
Report Dissemination	Website & LINE (Primary) Facebook page	LINE (Primary) Website	Website (Primary) Facebook page LINE

Convergence and Divergence among Taiwan's Three Fact-Checking Platforms

Choosing claims to check is the first step in the process of fact-checking. As Graves notes, this decision typically "involves considerations of newsworthiness, meaning political significances as well as utility or interest for the imagined audience."[76] MyGoPen focuses primarily on fact-checking information concerning the daily lives of senior citizens, such as public health–related scams and rumors. The queries MyGoPen receives via LINE are another mechanism for gauging their target audiences' suspicions regarding specific messages. Once a topic is selected, the fact-checker at MyGoPen employs mostly online tools, such as Google and Yandex or InVID image reverse search, to evaluate the veracity of the associated message. Asked if this heavy reliance on internet resources could compromise fact-check quality, MyGoPen founder Yeh explained: "We tend to use online information that has already been verified by other organizations or statements made by experts." Contacting governmental officials or experts happens only when online information is insufficient to reach a conclusion.

Having senior citizens as its target audience guides the way MyGoPen presents verified information. There are three established rules: multiple visuals, large font, and straightforward language. Using the story entitled "False Don't tell police you are sick when a car accident occurs? Misleading rumor regarding insurance" as an example, it starts with background information in yellow, then follows with the dis/misinformation portion in red, including a brief description of the rumor and three visuals demonstrating its online presence. Finally, the conclusion takes the form of a short fact-checking report in blue. The use of color coding is especially helpful in guiding senior citizens through the report and helping them quickly distinguish non-trustworthy from trustworthy information. The sources used for the fact-checking are listed as hyperlinks at the end of the report.[77]

Like PoltiFact's Truth-O-Meter, MyGoPen uses various labels to indicate the degree of truth in each fact-checking report: true, misleading, partially false, false, and rumor. Furthermore, MyGoPen cares more about media literacy than establishing itself as a singular authority. According to Yeh, "When giving a presentation, we would constantly tell the audience: 'you don't have to believe us. You should look for the information you need [to verify the dubious message] and make decisions for yourself. Or you can learn fact-checking skills from us and do fact-checking yourself. Even we sometimes make mistakes in our fact-checking.'" MyGoPen encourages skepticism even of themselves and acknowledges that fact-checking is an imperfect process.

Rather than curating topics, Cofacts takes a responsive approach that involves addressing topics submitted via a LINE chatbot and uses crowd-verification and collective-editing for fact-checking. "We do not restrict who can contribute. As long as you are willing, you are welcome to participate," said cofounder Billion.[78] Although core members use bimonthly in-person gatherings to provide one-on-one tutoring, volunteers often follow their own methods and writing styles to compose verification responses. Cofacts thus serves as an open forum responding to suspicious information rather than a platform offering singular answers. The only consistency among these fact-checks is the labeling system, whereby the veracity of individual submitted messages is indicated using the labels "true," "false," "uncheckable," and "opinion."

As a decentralized platform that believes in transparency, Cofacts does not remove any verified responses, even those that seem problematic. According to Billion: "We can only respect everyone's freedom of speech and leave all the comments here [on the platform] and let readers evaluate or assess their veracity. We present all the information. We have no right to delete anyone's messages [on the platform]."[79] Nevertheless, the decision by Cofacts to present unfiltered fact-checking results might open the door to malicious volunteers attempting to manipulate public opinion. While no perfect solution exists, a core member stated that when responses containing possible misinformation are spotted, they quickly add another fact-check to show multiple perspectives. "For example, if someone thinks a response on the platform is unfair, that person can provide a new response. The new response will be shown at the top of the list, and together with other previous responses," said Johnson, cofounder of Cofacts. This model explains why multiple entries sometimes appear for a single dubious story, such as one on the danger of ractopamine in U.S. pork.[80]

TFC relies on three criteria to identify topics for fact-checking: social impact, checkability, and the scale of a story's distribution. Guided by journalistic norms, fact-checkers at TFC are instructed to use at least two primary sources to investigate a selected topic. As editor-in-chief Chen noted, "this [expert interview] requirement is intended to help our fact-checkers think like a reporter and establish their connections with the most authoritative voices in the field." Digital tools, such as image reverse search and Google Maps, are also employed to enrich fact-checks. Once completed, the report is read and discussed by all fact-checkers, and then edited by the editor-in-chief to ensure accuracy and clarity.

TFC adopts a standardized presentation format for its fact-checking report. Each report begins with a headline accompanied by a rating—namely, true, partially false, false, fact clarification, or unproven. The main body consists of a news lead summarizing the verified result, background information, controversies relating to the claim, and the conclusion. While colors and visuals are used to increase readability, the primary sources add depth and credibility to these investigations. For instance, a report on an online rumor regarding the dangers of mask-wearing debunked the misinformation using quotes from two doctors and a government official from the Taiwan Center for Disease Control.[81] Furthermore, the limitations of the verification process are sometimes discussed to achieve sufficient transparency to allow readers to evaluate the validity of the result on their own.

Despite their commitment to improving Taiwan's information ecosystem, TFC fact-checkers do not self-describe as the "the ultimate arbiters of truth."[82] According to editor-in-chief Chen, "What we offer is verification or clarification of information, not necessarily the truth . . . Society is eager to have the truth, and sometimes people seem to think that fact-checks equal truth, but in fact they are different. Truth is a big puzzle; we can only offer a small piece at a time, and that piece may or may not complete the picture." While its fact-checking approach mostly closely approaches the idea of a platform offering a singular answer, TFC qualifies this model by distinguishing fact from truth, with the former as its focus. In other words, TFC sees its capacity as more limited in scope—small protective acts to defend democracy and improve journalism. In keeping with the interviewee's metaphor, their aim is to study a single puzzle piece in isolation from the puzzle into which it fits. While fact is objectively verifiable, truth can only be reached through public discourse.

Disagreements can also be found, mostly regarding service effectiveness and fact-check quality. In an interview with *Rappler*, Cofacts cofounder Johnson voiced his concerns about positioning independent fact-checking as the most crucial method for debunking dis/misinformation. He suggested that "the reach and influence of the media and educational institutions can't compete with that of hugely popular chat apps like LINE."[83] In other words, Cofacts seems to prioritize technical efficiency and reach, a vision shared by those who advocate for "automated fact-checking" initiatives—computer scrapping and matching transcripts with factual claims.[84]

At the other end of the spectrum, TFC emphasizes the importance of human fact-checkers, journalistic training, and expert sources to ensure high-quality verification. Accordingly, TFC occasionally has concerns regarding some of Cofacts's crowdsourced fact-checking results. In the words of a TFC fact-checker who sees Cofacts more as a false information database than a fact-checking platform, "They [Cofacts volunteers] don't follow journalistic principles . . . sometimes they even use information from content farms as their sources for verification." From a journalistic perspective, fact-checking should not simply offer a superficial "true or false" answer. Instead, practitioners should present an in-depth analysis that traces the flow of false information and provides expert clarification. Only this rigorous approach can initiate true dialogue with local media on information integrity and with the public on media literacy.

The collaboration among these diverse fact-checking bodies is more visible than their disagreements. Because of their direct interactions with LINE users, both Cofacts and MyGoPen serve as effective channels to discern the patterns and cycles of online falsehoods. From time to time, TFC uses Cofacts's database to identify potential fact-checking topics. Conversely, TFC shares its verification report with Cofacts and other platforms such as Aunt Meiyu to update and bolster its responses to LINE subscribers. These platforms also exchange their observations about alarming trends of disinformation. This synergy goes beyond the fact-checking circle. "We [MyGoPen] receive a massive amount of inquiries from LINE users," said founder Yeh, "We share our observations with other units [research institutions and governmental officials who study cyber warfare and information security] so that they are in the know regarding the most popular rumors and can start working on responses." This data-sharing is particularly crucial during election seasons when malign actors attempt to disrupt Taiwan's domestic politics through disinformation campaigns. *Detecting Digital Fingerprints,* a recent report produced through the collaboration of international research groups and local fact-checking organizations, documents the Chinese Communist Party's political disinformation operations in Taiwan, specifically its meddling in the 2018 local elections.[85] As this report demonstrates, these fact-checking practices cultivate a synergy among and beyond themselves—a collaborative safety net—working to shield Taiwan's unique information space and vulnerable democracy.

Impacts and Challenges Facing These Fact-Checking Organizations

As a burgeoning movement, it is too early to evaluate the true impact of fact-checking practices on Taiwan's media ecosystem and public awareness of dis/misinformation. That said, some positive signs have already emerged. For example, TFC began working with National Education Radio in early 2019 to launch the program *What is Fake News* (誰是假新聞).[86] TFC's fact-checkers are regularly invited to this radio show to discuss a currently circulating false rumor and the verification process they have used to confirm its falsity. Later in 2019, Chinese Television System (CTS), a television station in Taiwan, also announced its collaboration with TFC to produce *Fake News Fighters* (打假特攻隊), a special news segment devoted to debunking rumors and false information.[87]

Media reform can be achieved through both positive influence and necessary pressure. As IFCN certified fact-checking organizations, both TFC and MyGoPen are empowered to flag and report questionable content on partnered social media platforms (i.e., Facebook), thus demoting the content's visibility. Visibility will be restored when the media in question make an appropriate correction. As editor-in-chief of TFC reflected,

> we were completely ignored by mainstream media in the past. Like two parallel lines, we did our fact-checks, they did their news reporting. Now that Facebook have made us an authority, they are very polite to us and revise their stories immediately after being flagged . . . Some of them even have their staff follow our work. Every time a new fact-check is published, they use it to examine their news coverage to see if there are any mistakes needing correction.

Through this mechanism, local news media are encouraged to engage in more rigorous internal verification processes before publishing their coverage.

Like their global counterparts, all three fact-checking organizations have faced allegations of political bias. Because of its connection with Audrey Tang, Taiwan's Digital Minister, Cofacts has been labeled a "spy app" through which the government monitors and controls public opinion.[88] Others accuse TFC of being "an affiliate of the ruling party" that helps the government restrict free speech.[89] In January 2020, a few KMT representatives even held a press conference to vilify MyGoPen as a "digital sting operation" the government would use to arrest citizens it deemed political opponents.[90] Ironically, all three organizations have fallen victim to fake news. Facing baseless allegations and hostile social media trolls, fact-checkers in Taiwan initially steered away from verifying political information, thus following a different path to the Western fact-checking tradition. Interviewees from both Cofacts and MyGoPen commented that the difficulty of separating opinion and fact makes political claims too difficult to verify. While TFC is willing to take a political route, it purposefully focuses on claims about policy—a realm that can be assessed through objective facts—not politics or politicians.

Recently, seeing more and more misinformation circulating regarding both domestic and international politics, Taiwan's fact-checking initiatives have realized they must engage in political fact-checking. They took several measures to remain neutral and fair in an increasingly politicized environment. For example, MyGoPen states on its website that "we are not affiliated with any political parties. . . . and apply the same standard when verifying information regardless of the political party involved. We request that our team members refrain from involvement in or attendance at political campaigns. Violators will be asked to resign."[91] MyGoPen's commitment to political neutrality attempts to bolster the credibility of the information the organization provides.

Similarly, TFC establishes its political neutrality through a strict policy limiting funding and collaboration opportunities with government and political groups. TFC founder Hu emphasized that TFC rejects donations from the government, political parties, and politicians. Fact-checkers in the center are also very cautious about which news sources they interview. As editor-in-chief Chen reiterated, TFC has no relationship with the government and no interest in furthering a governmental agenda. Independence and following the facts wherever they may lead are the top priority, and consequently it explicitly prohibits use of government press releases as sources for its fact-checking reports. "I check information just as a journalist would," said Chen, by which she meant skeptically and thoroughly.

Nevertheless, these fact-checking organizations are open about political fact-checking in other national contexts, especially in the United States. In November 2020, TFC published sixteen stories debunking false information regarding U.S. presidential election fraud while MyGoPen produced nine reports. Interestingly, a significant percentage of these online rumors were written in simplified rather than traditional Chinese characters, suggesting an origin in China—where simplified characters are standard. Their investigations demonstrate: first, there is a concerning pattern of China's state-backed disinformation operation aimed to delegitimize Western authority; and second, these fact-checking organizations are becoming bolder in their defense against these Chinese disinformation efforts in other political systems.

Conclusion

The three studied organizations—MyGoPen, Cofacts, and TFC—are innovative citizen-led initiatives intended to improve the deteriorating information ecosystem. Interviews with key members of these organizations reveal that fact-checking in

Taiwan is an evolving concept shaped by each platform's objectives, target audience, verification methods, and technology usage. MyGoPen approaches fact-checking through user-centered practices that aim to protect citizens from all forms of deception, including online rumors and digital scams. Cofacts, understanding facts to be the product of public deliberation, advocates for a user-involved fact-checking process whereby online users decide what is true. Finally, TFC, which prioritizes facts with social impact, views facts as information that needs to be uncovered and practices fact-checking guided by journalistic principles and rigorous research. Together, with their diverse fact-checking practices and the range of disinformation they cover, these organizations form a collaborative safety net to shield Taiwan's unique information space and vulnerable democracy.

Studying fact-checking initiatives in Taiwan illuminates both global trends and a unique local terrain. The differences between technology-driven Cofacts and human-centered TFC reflect the current scholarly debate about best fact-checking practices. Computer scientists believe that "machine learning, natural language processing, and database query techniques" can eventually build an end-to-end automated verification solution, such as ClaimBuster, to optimize fact-checking efficiency.[92] Journalism scholars, on the other hand, emphasize the importance of human fact-checkers excavating truth from complex and intricate rhetoric.[93] Nevertheless, both agree that the best current course is to build automated fact-checking tools to assist human practitioners to identify and verify claims and report accordingly. Support from the scholarly community, traditional media, and platform companies will be necessary to realize such an approach.

Meanwhile, the late development of the fact-checking movement in Taiwan and its focus on nonpolitical issues also reflect Taiwan's unique situation. In recent decades, Taiwanese citizens often called for newspaper boycotts or participated in "turn-off your TV" campaigns to express their distrust of news media.[94] In other words, civil society sought to improve news quality by *rejecting the fake* rather than *deliberating over the truth*. Furthermore, Taiwan differs from Western countries in lacking a mainstream political fact-checking culture. As shown in one study, out of 487 fact-checks produced by TFC in twenty-two months, only one directly verified political claims made by politicians.[95] Two factors might explain this deficiency. First, in-depth political fact-checking requires years of experience and institutional knowledge, and exceeds the capabilities of Taiwan's current group of young and inexperienced fact-checkers. Recruiting senior reporters to staff fact-checking organizations could improve the future quality of fact-checks. Furthermore, this deficiency can be read as a legacy of Taiwan's authoritarian past. Having long existed in a controlled media environment, Taiwanese are still learning how to challenge political authority through deliberative voices and reasoned argument. Improving political fact-checking can help Taiwan cultivate a healthy and resilient democracy.

Taiwan's fact-checking practices offer a timely and fitting lesson as China becomes increasingly bold in its cyber intrusions. While Taiwan may be the training ground for Beijing to exercise its sharp power, the ultimate target is the United States, in an effort to destabilize the postwar international order. For example, the COVID-19 pandemic became an avenue for an onslaught of pro-China disinformation campaigns directed at widening social divisions in the United States.[96] Taiwan's fact-checking practices offer an illustrative case for other vulnerable democracies that need to bolster their media literacy. It is therefore critical that we learn from Taiwan before it is too late.

NOTES

1. Over the past years, researchers have categorized different types of false information. The key distinction between misinformation and disinformation is intention. Most generally agree that misinformation is produced or spread without the intention to cause harm, while disinformation is purposefully created for achieve certain aims. Deen Freelon and Chris Wells, "Disinformation as Political Communication," *Political Communication* 37, no. 2 (2020):145–156; Claire Wardle and Hossein Derakhshan, *Information Disorder: Toward an Interdisciplinary Framework for Research And Policy Making* (Strasbourg, France: Council of Europe, 2017), https://rm.coe.int/information-disorder-toward-an-interdisciplinary-framework-for-researc/168076277c.
2. Mark Stencel and Joel Luther, "U.S. Fact-Checkers Gear up for 2020 Campaign," Duke Reporters' Lab, November 25, 2019, https://reporterslab.org/u-s-fact-checkers-gear-up-for-2020-campaign/.
3. Bass Connections, "Fact Checking and Democracy," Duke University, https://bassconnections.duke.edu/virtual-showcase/fact-checking-and-democracy.
4. Lucas Graves, "Boundaries Not Drawn," *Journalism Studies* 19, no. 5 (2018): 613–631, https://doi.org/10.1080/1461670X.2016.1196602.
5. Reporters Without Borders, "2019 RSF Index: Asia-Pacific Press Freedom Impacted by Political Change," Reporters Without Borders, April 17, 2019, https://rsf.org/en/2019-rsf-index-asia-pacific-press-freedom-impacted-political-change.
6. Judy Lin, "Reporters Without Borders Opens First Asia Office in Taipei," *Taiwan News*,

April 7, 2017, https://www.taiwannews.com.tw/en/news/3135403.

7. Nic Newman et al., *Reuters Institute Digital News Report 2020* (Oxford: Reuters Institute for the Study of Journalism, 2020).
8. Valeriya Mechkova et al., "Digital Society Project Working Paper #1—Measuring Internet Politics: Introducing the Digital Society Project" (working paper, Digital Society Project, 2019), http://digitalsocietyproject.org/wp-content/uploads/2019/05/DSP_WP_01-Introducing-the-Digital-Society-Project.pdf.
9. Ying Yu Lin, "China's Hybrid Warfare and Taiwan," *The Diplomat*, January 13, 2018, https://thediplomat.com/2018/01/chinas-hybrid-warfare-and-taiwan.
10. Jason Liu, Hao-hsiang Ko, and Chia-yu Hsu, "Taiwan's Elderly Love Messaging App LINE. But So Do Health Scammers and Propagandists from China," *Taiwan Gazette*, March 10, 2019, https://www.taiwangazette.org/news/2020/3/9/content-farm-empire-part-1-meet-the-fact-checkers-helping-taiwanese-aunties-learn-about-fake-news.
11. Gary Schmitt and Michael Mazza, "Blinding the Enemy: CCP Interference in Taiwan's Democracy," Global Taiwan Institute, October 2019, http://globaltaiwan.org/wp-content/uploads/2019/10/GTI-CCP-Interference-Taiwan-Democracy-Oct-2019-final.pdf.
12. Keoni Everington, "Taiwan's First Fact-Checking Center Launches to Battle Fake News," *Taiwan News*, August 2, 2018, https://www.taiwannews.com.tw/en/news/3497482.
13. Staff Writer, "Google Endows Fact Check Hub," *Taipei Times*, November 8, 2021, https://www.taipeitimes.com/News/biz/archives/2021/11/08/2003767495.
14. During the revision of this chapter, Russia invaded Ukraine and weaponized disinformation as part of its larger war strategy. Greg Myre and Jenna McLaughlin, "The Russian Disinformation War Is Underway," NPR, February 23, 2022, https://www.npr.org/2022/02/23/1082622849/the-russian-disinformation-war-is-underway.
15. Christopher Walker, "What Is 'Sharp Power'?," *Journal of Democracy* 29, no. 3 (2018): 9–23.
16. Lucas Graves, *Deciding What's True: The Rise of Political Fact-Checking in American Journalism* (New York: Columbia University Press, 2016), 6, 9.
17. Michelle A. Amazeen, "Journalistic Interventions: The Structural Factors Affecting the Global Emergence of Fact-Checking," *Journalism* 21, no. 1 (2020): 95–111, https://doi.org/10.1177/1464884917730217.
18. Graves, "Boundaries Not Drawn."
19. Graves, *Deciding What's True.*
20. "Our Mission," *FactCheck.Org* (blog), June 27, 2009, https://www.factcheck.org/about/our-mission/.
21. Graves, *Deciding What's True.*

22. Glenn Kessler, "About the Fact Checker," *Washington Post*, January 1, 2017, https://www.washingtonpost.com/politics/2019/01/07/about-fact-checker/.
23. Amazeen, "Journalistic Interventions," 104.
24. Lucas Graves and Federica Cherubini, *The Rise of Fact-Checking Sites in Europe* (Oxford: Reuters Institute for the Study of Journalism, 2016), 11, https://reutersinstitute.politics.ox.ac.uk/sites/default/files/research/files/The%2520Rise%2520of%2520Fact-Checking%2520Sites%2520in%2520Europe.pdf.
25. Liam Scott, "Battle Is Intense Against Disinformation on Russia's War in Ukraine," VOA, https://www.voanews.com/a/battle-is-intense-against-disinformation-on-russia-s-war-in-ukraine-/6479748.html.
26. Zia Weise, "Fact-Checkers Seek out Grain of Truth in Turkey's Fake-News Onslaught," Politico, December 21, 2018, https://www.politico.eu/article/turkey-fact-checkers/.
27. Graves and Cherubini, *Rise of Fact-Checking Sites*, 12.
28. Ibid., 13.
29. Graves, *Deciding What's True*, 37.
30. Lucas Graves and Magda Konieczna, "Sharing the News: Journalistic Collaboration as Field Repair," *International Journal of Communication* 9 (2015): 1966–1984.
31. Graves and Cherubini, *Rise of Fact-Checking Sites*, 14, 16.
32. Chris Atton and James F. Hamilton, *Alternative Journalism* (Los Angeles: Sage, 2008).
33. Graves and Cherubini, *Rise of Fact-Checking Sites*, 17.
34. Full Fact, "The Full Fact Report 2020: Fighting the Causes and Consequences of Bad Information," *Full Fact*, April 2020, 18, https://fullfact.org/media/uploads/fullfactreport2020.pdf.
35. Glenn Kessler, "Fact-Checking Organizations around the Globe Embrace Code of Principles," *Washington Post*, September 15, 2016, https://www.washingtonpost.com/news/fact-checker/wp/2016/09/15/fact-checking-organizations-around-the-globe-embrace-code-of-principles/; Angie Drobnic Holan, "PolitiFact—What Do Fact-Checkers around the World Have in Common?" PolitiFact, June 28, 2016, https://www.politifact.com/article/2016/jun/28/what-do-fact-checkers-around-world-have-common/. Paul Mena, "Principles and Boundaries of Fact-Checking: Journalists' Perceptions," *Journalism Practice* 13, no. 6 (2019): 659, https://doi.org/10.1080/17512786.2018.1547655.
36. Lucas Graves, "Anatomy of a Fact Check: Objective Practice and the Contested Epistemology of Fact Checking," *Communication, Culture and Critique* 10, no. 3 (2017): 518–537, 518, 530, https://doi.org/10.1111/cccr.12163.
37. Graves, "Boundaries Not Drawn," 623.
38. Graves and Konieczna, "Sharing the News," 1966.

39. Graves, *Deciding What's True*, 36.
40. Graves and Konieczna, "Sharing the News," 1975–1976.
41. World Health Organization (WHO), "Immunizing the Public against Misinformation," August 25, 2020, https://www.who.int/news-room/feature-stories/detail/immunizing-the-public-against-misinformation.
42. Poyu Tseng and Puma Shen, "The Chinese Infodemic in Taiwan: A Preliminary Study on the Dissemination Model of Disinformation, Taking COVID-19 as an Example," Doublethink Lab, July 26, 2020, https://medium.com/doublethinklab/the-chinese-infodemic-in-taiwan-25e9ac3d941e.
43. International Fact-Checking Network, "CoronaVirusFacts Alliance," Poynter, 2020, https://www.poynter.org/coronavirusfactsalliance/.
44. Bill Adair and Rebecca Iannucci, "Heroes or Hacks: The Partisan Divide over Fact-Checking," Duke Reporters' Lab, June 7, 2017, https://reporterslab.org/heroes-hacks-partisan-divide-fact-checking/; Jieun Shin and Kjerstin Thorson, "Partisan Selective Sharing: The Biased Diffusion of Fact-Checking Messages on Social Media," *Journal of Communication* 67, no. 2 (2017): 233–255, https://doi.org/10.1111/jcom.12284.
45. Adair and Iannucci, "Heroes or Hacks."
46. Anton Troianovski, "Fighting False News in Ukraine, Facebook Fact Checkers Tread a Blurry Line," *New York Times*, July 26, 2020, https://www.nytimes.com/2020/07/26/world/europe/ukraine-facebook-fake-news.html.
47. Man-pui Sally Chan et al., "Debunking: A Meta-Analysis of the Psychological Efficacy of Messages Countering Misinformation," *Psychological Science* 28, no. 11 (2017): 1531–1546, https://doi.org/10.1177/0956797617714579.
48. Sakari Nieminen and Lauri Rapeli, "Fighting Misperceptions and Doubting Journalists' Objectivity: A Review of Fact-Checking Literature," *Political Studies Review* 17, no. 3 (2019): 306, https://doi.org/10.1177/1478929918786852.
49. Jaw-nian Huang, *The Political Economy of Press Freedom: The Paradox of Taiwan versus China* (New York: Routledge, 2020), 28, https://www.routledge.com/The-Political-Economy-of-Press-Freedom-The-Paradox-of-Taiwan-versus-China/Huang/p/book/9781138599482.
50. Stephen J. Hartnett, *A World of Turmoil: The United States, China and Taiwan in the Long Cold War* (East Lansing: Michigan State University Press, 2021); June Yip, *Envisioning Taiwan: Fiction, Cinema, and the Nation in the Cultural Imaginary* (Durham: Duke University Press, 2004).
51. Gary D. Rawnsley, "The Media and Popular Protest in Pre-Democratic Taiwan," *Historical Journal of Film, Radio, and Television* 20, no. 4 (2000): 569.

52. Lihyun Lin, "Taiwan," in *Information Disorder in Asia* (Hong Kong: Journalism and Media Studies Center, University of Hong Kong, 2018), 49.
53. Huang, *Political Economy of Press Freedom*, 89.
54. Apple Daily, "11年財報揭露　旺旺集團收中國政府153億補助金," April 22, 2019, https://tw.appledaily.com/property/20190422/YTECGJ7QUM7XWY6ASZOYJBNKE4/.
55. Reporters Without Borders, "China's Pursuit of a New World Media Order," Reporters Without Borders, October 22, 2019, https://rsf.org/en/rsf-report-chinas-pursuit-new-world-media-order.
56. Kathrin Hille, "Taiwan Primaries Highlight Fears over China's Political Influence," *Financial Times*, July 16, 2019, https://www.ft.com/content/036b609a-a768-11e9-984c-fac8325aaa04.
57. Chia Ai Li, "China Impact and Dictatorship in the News Production: A Case Study of Taiwanese Media Group," Tsing Hua National University, 2015, https://ndltd.ncl.edu.tw/cgi-bin/gs32/gsweb.cgi?o=dnclcdr&s=id=%22103NTHU5208019%22.&searchmode=basic.
58. Gary Schmitt and Michael Mazza, *Blinding the Enemy: CCP Interference in Taiwan's Democracy*, (Washington, DC: Global Taiwan Institute, 2019), http://globaltaiwan.org/wp-content/uploads/2019/10/GTI-CCP-Interference-Taiwan-Democracy-Oct-2019-final.pdf.
59. Hille, "Taiwan Primaries Highlight Fears."
60. Ralph Jennings, "Facebook Says It Already Has 97% of Taiwan's Internet Users, and Now It's Targeting Businesses," *Forbes*, October 11, 2018, https://www.forbes.com/sites/ralphjennings/2018/10/11/facebook-says-it-already-has-97-of-taiwans-internet-users-and-now-its-targeting-businesses/.
61. Rebecca Ping Yu, "Use of Messaging Apps and Social Network Sites among Older Adults: A Mixed-Method Study," *International Journal of Communication*, no. 14 (2020): 4453–4473.
62. Michael Chan, Hsuan-Ting Chen, and Francis L. F. Lee, "Examining the Roles of Mobile and Social Media in Political Participation," *New Media & Society* 19 (2017): 2003–2021.
63. Gary King, Jennifer Pan, and Margaret E. Roberts, "How the Chinese Government Fabricates Social Media Posts for Strategic Distraction, Not Engaged Argument," *American Political Science Review* 111, no. 3 (2017): 485.
64. Stephen J. Hartnett and Chiaoning Su, "Hacking, Debating, and Renewing Democracy in Taiwan in the Age of "Post-Truth" Communication," *Taiwan Journal of Democracy* 17, no. 1 (2021): 21–43.
65. Nick Aspinwall, "Taiwan Passes Anti-Infiltration Act Ahead of Election Amid Opposition Protests," *The Diplomat*, January 3, 2020, https://thediplomat.com/2020/01/

taiwan-passes-anti-infiltration-act-ahead-of-election-amid-opposition-protests/.

66. Nicola Smith, "Taiwan Is Leading the Way in Tackling Fake News," *Time Magazine*, April 7, 2017, https://time.com/4730440/taiwan-fake-news-education/.
67. Earl Babbie, *The Practice of Social Research*, 10th ed. (Belmote: Cangage Learning, 2004), 184, /c/the-practice-of-social-research-15e-babbie/9780357360767.
68. Juliet Corbin and Anselm Strauss, *Basics of Qualitative Research: Techniques and Procedures for Developing Grounded Theory* (Thousand Oaks, CA: Sage, 1998).
69. g0v, "G0v.Asia," 2020, https://g0v.asia/.
70. Kirsten Han Splice, "Taiwanese Cofacts Fact-Checks Information on LINE," International Journalists' Network, August 29, 2018, https://ijnet.org/en/story/taiwanese-cofacts-fact-checks-information-line.
71. Joyu Wang and Chuin-wei Yap, "Know-It-All Robot Shuts Down Dubious Family Texts," *Wall Street Journal*, February 28, 2019, https://www.wsj.com/articles/know-it-all-robot-shuts-down-dubious-family-texts-11551370040.
72. TFC, "Mission statement," Taiwan FactCheck Center, July 19, 2018, https://tfc-taiwan.org.tw/about/purpose.
73. Yuan-hui Hu, interview with the authors, June 27, 2019.
74. Cristina Tardáguila, "IFCN and Facebook Distribute Another $300k through the Coronavirus Fact-Checking Grants and Will Support 8 Projects," Poynter, April 30, 2020, https://www.poynter.org/fact-checking/2020/ifcn-and-facebook-distribute-another-300k-through-the-coronavirus-fact-checking-grants-and-will-support-8-projects/.
75. Cristina Tardáguila, "Fact-Checkers Say These Are the Best Fact-Checks They Did during This Decade," Poynter, December 31, 2019, https://www.poynter.org/fact-checking/2019/fact-checkers-say-these-are-the-best-fact-checks-they-did-during-this-decade/.
76. Lucas Graves, "Anatomy of a Fact Check: Objective Practice and the Contested Epistemology of Fact Checking," *Communication, Culture and Critique* 10, no. 3 (2017): 524, https://doi.org/10.1111/cccr.12163.
77. MyGoPen, "【錯誤】發生交通意外不能跟警方說生病？誤導保險謠言," *MyGoPen* (blog), October 26, 2020, https://www.mygopen.com/2020/10/car-accident.html.
78. Billion, interview with the authors, August 8, 2019.
79. Billion, Interview with the authors, August 8, 2019.
80. MrOrz and Ann, "最新查核," Cofacts, October 22, 2020, https://cofacts.g0v.tw/replies.
81. TFC, "【錯誤】網傳訊息指稱「平常沒事口罩不要戴，戴了血液酸化造成心血管病，然後肺炎細菌叢生超高」？," 台灣事實查核中心, November 3, 2020, https://tfc-taiwan.org.tw/articles/4670.
82. Petter Bae Brandtzaeg, Asbjørn Følstad, and María Ángeles Chaparro Domínguez, "How

Journalists and Social Media Users Perceive Online Fact-Checking and Verification Services," *Journalism Practice* 12, no. 9 (2018): 1122, https://doi.org/10.1080/17512786.2017.1363657.

83. Nithin Coca, "Disinformation from China Floods Taiwan's Most Popular Messaging App," Rappler, October 12, 2020, https://www.rappler.com/technology/features/disinformation-from-china-floods-taiwan-line-app-coda-story.
84. Julia Sittmann and Andrew Tompkins, "The Strengths and Weaknesses of Automated Fact-Checking Tools," DW.COM, July 17, 2020, https://www.dw.com/en/the-strengths-and-weaknesses-of-automated-fact-checking-tools/a-53956958.
85. Nick Monaco, Melanie Smith, and Amy Studdart, *Detecting Digital Fingerprints: Tracing Chinese Disinformation in Taiwan* (Palo Alto, CA: Institute for the Future's Digital Intelligence Lab, 2020).
86. TFC, "Now you can listen to TFC's fact-checks," Taiwan FactCheck Center, January 24, 2019, https://tfc-taiwan.org.tw/articles/367.
87. Lian Pei-bei and Dai Rong-xian, "Fake News Fighter Aims to Debunk False Information and Rumors," Chinese Network System, April 3, 2019, https://news.cts.com.tw/cts/general/201904/201904031956757.html.
88. 王大師, "真的假的？ 唐鳳在搞輿論勞改？ 訾," *Viewpoint Taiwan* (blog), February 3, 2017.
89. Liu Li-ren, "「台灣事實查核中心」是民進黨附隨組織？ 胡元輝：喝水差點噴出來—政治," *Liberty Times*, June 12, 2018, https://news.ltn.com.tw/news/politics/breakingnews/2455987.
90. Zhao Wan-chun, Zhou Yu-shiang, and Lin Tzu-han, "綠色恐怖又一樁？！ 轉傳立委質詢竟被約談 藍批蔡政府文字獄," *China Times*, January 1, 2020, https://www.chinatimes.com/realtimenews/20200101002267-260407?chdtv.
91. MyGoPen, "Code of Conduct," *MyGoPen* (blog), 2020, https://www.mygopen.com/p/blog-page_84.html.
92. Naeemul Hassan, Gensheng Zhang, Fatma Arslan, Josue Caraballo, Damian Jimenez, Siddhant Gawsane, Shohedul Hasan, Minumol Joseph, Aaditya Kulkarni, Anil Kumar Nayak, Vikas Sable, Chengkai Li and Mark Tremayne, "ClaimBuster: The First-Ever End-to-End Fact-Checking System," Proceedings of the VLDB Endowment 10, no. 12 (2017): 1945–1948, https://dl.acm.org/doi/10.14778/3137765.3137815.
93. Lucas Graves, "Understanding the Promise and Limits of Automated Fact-Checking," Reuters Institute for the Study of Journalism, February 2018, https://reutersinstitute.politics.ox.ac.uk/our-research/understanding-promise-and-limits-automated-fact-checking.

94. Yuan-hui Hu, "Independent Media, Social Movements, and the Traditional News Media in Taiwan," in *Digital Technology and Journalism: An International Comparative Perspective*, ed. Jingrong Tong and Shih-Hung Lo (New York: Palgrave Macmillan, 2017), 219.
95. Yuan-hui Hu, "事實是正確報導的礎石：台灣事實查核中心的經驗與反思," *NCC NEWS* 14, no. 4 (2020): 1–22.
96. Zachary Cohen, "Pro-China Misinformation Operation Attempting to Exploit US Covid Divisions, Report Says," *CNN*, September 8, 2021, https://www.cnn.com/2021/09/08/politics/pro-chinese-disinformation-operation-coronavirus-pandemic-protests/index.html.

Vernacular Collaboration

In Search of a New Taiwanese Identity through "Worshipping Japan" and Resisting China

Hsin-i Sydney Yueh

Taiwan is a young democratic nation-state with a long colonial history. Taiwan is also a PRC-claimed territory, making it "the most dangerous place on earth," despite protection provided by the United States.[1] Within this context, nostalgia for Taiwan's colonial past and the lived experience of daily threats from China constitute two key aspects of Taiwan's developing identity. By studying everyday communication discourse, this chapter offers a partial record of that identity struggle. I focus on two seemingly irrelevant terms that capture some of the nuances of identity in Taiwanese people's daily conversations. One of the terms is "*hari*" (哈日, meaning "Japan-worshipping" or "Japan-mania") in Taiwan's anime, comic, and gaming (ACG) community.[2] The other term is "*tienzhong*" (舔中, "kissing China's ass"), which frequently appears in the *hari* discussion. I argue that the meanings of these two terms and the competing discourses in the ACG community can be used to explore the formation of Taiwanese identity, which hinges in part on a nostalgic longing for Japan and a rising sense of resistance to China.

These two terms circulate among ACG netizens as vernacular expressions; the latter is even too vulgar to be used in formal writing. Here, I follow Kent Ono and John Sloop's definition of "vernacular" as the voice of the oppressed.[3] Extending from their concepts, online communities often constitute vernacular discourse that is unofficial, informal, and dialectical. However, these neologisms, or so-called vernacular words, hold cultural significance.[4] In recent cultural studies scholarship, scholars have used such vernacular terms to understand "the propensities of its participants" in particular social, economic, and political moments.[5] Importantly for this research, it is now more than twenty years since the term *hari* was invented; and although Taiwanese people continue to worship Japanese culture, the meaning of the term has changed. It seems that *hari* and *tienzhong* have formed an antagonistic relationship in the ACG discourse. If all political belief systems are partially about creating a sense of longing and identification with a positive self, which is then countered by a sense of disassociation from and even hostility toward some negative other, then *hari* and *tienzhong* work together, as opposite yet related terms driving Taiwan's emerging sense of national identity.

In the following sections, I offer the background for this communication phenomenon by tracing back the origins of Japan-mania and then tracking its changes. Second, I highlight resistance to the pro-Japan discourse and anxiety about the decline of a Chinese ideology that has been sustained by the long-term ruling party, the KMT. I then illustrate how my analysis intersects with the above context and explain how the term *hari* is associated with the vulgar term *tienzhong*. I argue that the competing discourses that appear in the online ACG forum epitomize the pro-Japan and pro-China identity struggle in current Taiwanese society. Finally, I explain how this specific case study is entangled in, and representative of, the recent conflicts in U.S.–China relations.

It should be noted that Japan-worshipping has little to do with the desire to become Japanese, and that the pro-China opinion does not mean that the Taiwanese want to unify with the PRC. According to Hsin-yen Yang, Taiwanese youth's Japan-mania allows a new cultural taste to grow, and these fans' creative use of Japanese popular cultural references facilitates the rediscovery of Taiwanese local culture.[6] On the other hand, although many Taiwanese people are proud of their Chinese cultural heritage and practice Chinese customs in Taiwan, a survey conducted in 2021 shows that only 1.4 percent of Taiwanese want to be unified with the PRC as soon as possible.[7] By focusing on the two terms in online debates, this chapter argues that the less formal and less noticeable phenomenon of "quotidian politics" illuminates evolving forms of resistance in Taiwan.[8] The vernacular discourse indicates a gradual, autonomous process regarding forming a national identity that stands with democracy and against an authoritarian Chinese regime.

The Rise and Changes of Japan-Mania in Taiwan

The term *hari* is vernacular; its origin is informal, and it reflects the voice of the populace. Moreover, this term combines Taiwan Hokkien and Taiwan Mandarin.[9] The first character, *ha*, is of Taiwan Hokkien origin, meaning "to desire," "to be infatuated with," or "to worship." The second character, *ri*, means "Japan" in Taiwan Mandarin. This neologism expresses the hybrid features of the term, which was invented by a popular Taiwanese author, Chen Guei-sing, in 1996. Chen used "Hari Kyoko" as her penname and coined the term *hari* to express her infatuation with Japanese culture. Since the 1990s, Taiwanese youth have been consuming Japanese cultural products and have developed a mania for everything from Japan. Chen was apparently one of them. After twenty-six years, Chen's love of Japan remains. She has published at least twenty-seven books about Japan, and now runs a website to continue promoting all things Japanese.[10] The highlights on her website include travel information, food, cultural commodity collections, and so forth. How could Japanese culture produce such a persistent fervor in Taiwan? In what follows, I introduce multiple dimensions of Japan-mania in different periods.

Although most research has identified the 1990s as the grand debut of Japan-mania, Lee I-yun argues that there has been an "underground" development period of modern Japanese popular culture in Taiwan. Before the end of WWII, Taiwan was a colony of Japan (1895–1945). Even after Taiwan was handed over to the nationalist government (known as Kuomintang, the KMT), Japanese culture did not disappear in Taiwan. In the 1950s, Japanese manga were still circulating and dominating in Taiwan. In the 1970s, unauthorized Japanese fashion magazines, cartoon animation, TV shows, and popular music were imported into Taiwan to satisfy market demands.[11] During this "underground" period, Taiwanese consumers might not have noticed the origin of these Japanese cultural products, because the import agencies would deliberately hide the Japanese elements by dubbing, reprinting, or disguising the original versions. These practices were common, especially after Japan terminated its diplomatic ties with the KMT government in 1972.[12] Nevertheless, this stealthy consumption of Japanese popular culture lay the foundations for the explosive growth of Japan-mania in the 1990s.[13]

Japanese TV dramas arguably triggered the first wave of Japan-mania in Taiwan. In 1992, STAR TV, the Chinese satellite channel began to broadcast the first so-called Japanese idol drama, *Tokyo Love Story*, to Taiwan. The mini-series became a mega-hit.[14] STAR TV was a foreign television service provider that broadcast its programs to Asia, including Taiwan. Technically, watching this TV drama in Taiwan was still illegal because the authorities did not lift the ban on Japanese programs and cable service until 1993 and 1997, respectively.[15] However, STAR TV's preemptive action on the eve of lifting the ban encouraged many TV networks in Taiwan to broadcast similar Japanese idol dramas, as well as other made-in-Japan TV programs. The popularity of *Tokyo Love Story* derived not only from its novelty, but also from its depiction of a modern, urban, and metropolitan lifestyle, which was something the Taiwanese audience longed for following the end of martial law.[16]

Since the term *hari* was created, many Taiwanese celebrities have embraced this identity of Japan-mania by sharing their love of Japanese fashion, experiences of traveling to Japan, and familiarity with Japanese singers and actors. Shuling Huang attributes the phenomenon of Japan-mania to the Taiwanese media's positive construction of Japanese culture. In the 1990s, major newspapers in Taiwan began to devote exclusive pages to Japanese entertainment and travel news. Popular writers and columnists, such as Hari Kyoko, helped to create a romantic image of Japan in their writings. Meanwhile, Taiwan's TV stations invited Japanese talent to Taiwan in hopes of securing high ratings. When these stars arrived at the airport, crowds of fans often made breaking news.[17] The frequent appearance of the term *hari* in headlines intensified another wave of Japan-mania.

In the 2000s, the Korean Wave shadowed Japan-mania in Taiwan, as Korean TV dramas successfully attracted a middle-aged female audience, whom Japanese dramas failed to reach in Taiwan.[18] Nevertheless, the craze for Japanese popular culture remained strong, and a generation of Taiwanese youth developed a tendency to follow Japanese trends. While the Korean Wave began sweeping the global music and film industries, Japan became dedicated to the "*otaku*" culture, which fostered a new type of tourism featuring anime, comics, and gaming.[19] Thus, the principal behaviors that define Japan-worshipping gradually transformed from watching Japanese TV shows, listening to Japanese pop music, and traveling to Japan,[20] to ACG-related activities. For example, the protagonist in the Japanese movie *Densha Otoko* (電車男 or *Train Man*) represents an *otaku*, who is shy and obsessed with the online world.[21] Although the movie was a blockbuster, it reinforced Taiwanese mainstream media's stereotypes of the ACG community, and generated some negative impressions of Japan-mania. A few common pejorative characterizations of ACG members include "socially awkward," "bad-looking," "bullied victims," and so forth.[22]

Scholars have attempted to explain why the Taiwanese have consumed Japanese popular culture so voraciously. One reason is globalization. After the lifting of martial law in 1987, Taiwan opened its market and allowed foreign cultural products to enter local shops. Koichi Iwabuchi argues that the dominant Japanese popular culture in East Asia established a transnational cultural empire that differed from the Western model in the 1990s, a salient example of which is how the export of Japanese culture successfully created Japan-mania via TV dramas in Taiwan.[23] On the other hand, from the postcolonial perspective, the infatuation with Japan in Taiwan is considered unusual, given that many previous Japanese colonies developed hatred toward the colonizers after they were emancipated at the end of WWII. What Leo Ching calls the "postcolonial colonization" explains why the local Taiwanese did not generate a deep hatred, but rather a sense of "intimacy" toward Japan, compared to neighboring countries that had been invaded and colonized by Japan.[24] In Taiwan's case, Ching believes, the dominant KMT party played the new colonizer after Japan left, meaning that Taiwan's emerging sense of postcolonial identity targeted the authoritarian KMT, and not the Japanese Empire, as the source of their anger.

Nevertheless, not all Taiwanese welcomed the trend; the Japan-worshipping craze worried KMT officials. The KMT had been one of the United States's anti-communist allies during the Cold War.[25] It was established in 1919, and its leadership later formed the nationalist government in mainland China, known as the Republic of China (ROC). The KMT witnessed the overthrow of the Qing Empire, conflicts among warlords, and the Japanese invasion of the Chinese mainland.[26] The KMT led and eventually won the war against Japan (1937–1945), and Taiwan was a Japanese colony during that time.[27] However, after the KMT took over post-war Taiwan, the transition did not proceed smoothly. In 1947, the KMT military suppressed protesters and caused death or injury to numerous people in an event known as the "228 Incident."[28] In 1949, the KMT lost the Chinese Civil War to the Communist Party of China (CPC), and KMT leader Chiang Kai-shek and his followers retreated to Taiwan.[29] While the new CPC government proclaimed the establishment of the New China, the KMT continued to govern Taiwan and several offshore islands under the name of the ROC. To legitimize its Sinicization project on the island, the KMT government eradicated the Japanese legacy.[30] To many local Taiwanese, the KMT rule was even harsher and crueler than that of the former colonizer.[31] Throughout this period, feeling nostalgic for Japan's colonial legacy—represented as efficient and modernizing—served as a protest against the KMT government, which has been regarded as monstrously inefficient, economically backward, and politically brutal.[32] Tracing this historical context enables us to understand the identity struggles within Taiwan's Japan-mania discourse.

With the support of the United States, the KMT cast Taiwan as the representative of "Free China," and became the only ruling party in Taiwan for fifty years.[33] However, the U.S. government began to recognize the PRC as the legitimate sovereign state of China in the 1970s, and officially terminated diplomatic relations with the ROC in 1979.[34] The ROC was no longer the representative of China, and Taiwan was denied an identity as a country in the world. Nevertheless, today in Taiwan, the KMT still insists on a Chinese orthodoxy in its national imagination, and the KMT-promoted China-centric historical narrative still influences the Taiwanese general public in identifying who they are.[35] The victory in the war against Japan and the retrocession of Taiwan back to the ROC are significant parts of the KMT's historical narrative. However, local Taiwanese people might have interpreted these two historical incidents differently.[36]

One example of the struggle between Chinese consciousness and Taiwanese consciousness is the 1997 dispute around the edition of junior high school textbooks. Under the main title *Getting to Know Taiwan*, each of the three textbooks had a subtitle to highlight its content: "History," "Geography," and "Society." This was the first set of textbooks to introduce basic knowledge of Taiwan to junior high school students in public education.[37] Before 1997, less than 5 percent of content in the previous edition of the national history and geography textbooks concerned Taiwan; such books were almost entirely devoted to KMT-ruled China before 1949.[38] Such a China-centric paradigm was built on the collective memory of the immigrants who followed the defeated KMT troops from the mainland to Taiwan after the Chinese Civil War. On the other hand, editors of old textbooks denied and suppressed the social memory of local Taiwanese who grew up in the Japanese colonial period.

The KMT's vehement resistance to revising the textbooks was concurrent with the high-point of Japan-mania in Taiwan. In April 1997, a major Taiwanese magazine, *The Journalist*, launched a special issue titled "Beware! Your Kids are Becoming Japanese,"[39] a sensational declaration that reflected anxieties about the prevalence of Japan-mania in the political discourse.[40] For a long time, in the KMT government's official narrative, Japan was depicted as an enemy and an invader of the ROC during WWII. Thus, KMT authorities and supporters found it difficult to accept that the youth in Taiwan had started to worship the former colonizer. Furthermore, glorifying Japanese culture seemed to lead to an independent Taiwanese consciousness,[41] which became a slap in the face to the KMT's insistence on reunification with China. Japan-mania signaled how easily censorship and information control in an authoritarian regime could collapse after society was forced open.

When the issues of Taiwan's independence or unification with China were brought to the fore and the China-centric narrative was challenged in the political discourse, the old guards blamed the Japan-worshipping craze for the decline of Chinese traditions and the alleged moral decadence in Taiwan.[42] To resist the growth of a Taiwanese consciousness or the proposal for Taiwan's independence, the KMT often cast these ideas as an act of "flattering Japan" (媚日, or *meiri*),[43] a term with negative and humiliating connotations that describes fans of Japanese popular culture. Such harsh criticism reflected the sense of loss KMT elites felt when they saw the decline of Chinese identity. These conflicting memories about China and Japan constitute ethnic and political divisions in Taiwan. Indeed, as an island caught between more powerful nation-states—with Japan to the northeast, China to the west, Russia to the northwest, and America to the east—Taiwan is perpetually *in-between*, negotiating identities.[44] Within this sense of liminal danger and possibility, cultural perceptions of Japan have become a salient identity marker. The Japan-mania phenomenon is thus a by-product of ongoing identity struggles and reflects the complicated process of forming a Taiwanese consensus.

Locating the Terms in Vernacular Discourse

Because ACG-related activities become a primary manifestation of Japan-worshipping, I choose one of Taiwan's largest online ACG communities, Bahamut (巴哈姆特), as my research site. In this entertainment ACG community, I examine controversial discourses about the ongoing identity struggle and explore why the term *hari* has become a trigger word for political controversy among members. I investigate the following questions: How does this controversy relate to the above-mentioned grand history and memory construction in Taiwan? What can we learn about Taiwanese identity from the vernacular discourse and quotidian politics in this unofficial, informal, and dialectical space? Finally, how can this understanding contribute to a reexamination of U.S.–China–Taiwan relations?

Bahamut was established in 1996, originally in the form of a bulletin board system (BBS) for members to exchange ACG product information. The forum function was launched in 2003, allowing users to discuss hundreds of anime works and general ACG-related topics. According to a consumer profile report in 2016, 68.6 percent of Bahamut users were male. In terms of age distribution, 86.1 percent were under forty-four years old, 46.3 percent of whom were under twenty-five.[45] Since 2018, I have had a registered account on Bahamut, and conduct a keyword search for posts containing the term *hari* every one or two months. I copied and pasted the discussion threads that used the term *hari* as an identity. As of August 2020, I collected 152 discussion threads in total (including over two thousand individual posts and reposts). Forum webpages that contained thirty posts usually had one to three political posts. However, when there were specific political incidents, such as elections, social movements, or threatening messages from China, reposts or responses to political posts would increase. Albeit a small number, the collected posts are useful resources for observing how memories of China and Japan influence these ACG community members' identification.

My analysis started with the term *hari*, and focused on how ACG community members have used it to communicate their identities and make sense of Japan-mania since 2018. Although it is apparent that the majority of ACG works are originally from Japan, and Japan-worshipping is supposed to be the default characteristic of the Bahamut members, posts that contain the term "Japan worshipping" often seek to provoke conflict. Thus, I paid particular attention to such posts in terms of their contexts, conflicting points, and responses. Then, I discovered that another term, *tienzhong*, frequently appeared in these controversial posts. Therefore, I analyzed these two terms in order to illuminate the relationship between "Japan worshipping" and "kissing China's ass" in this vernacular discourse. After identifying the conflict and divergence of the two terms, I considered how to interpret the identity struggle in the meaning-making process.

I view the Bahamut ACG community as a space that forms a vernacular discourse. Ono and Sloop propose the close examination of texts in vernacular discourse so as to understand how various communication forms help to construct the sense of community. The goal of critiquing vernacular discourse is to "upend essentialisms, undermine stereotypes, and eliminate narrow representation of culture."[46] They issue a call to treat "music, art, criticism, dance, and architecture of local communities" as analytical texts—indeed, as a way of revealing covert voices.[47] My attention to the use of two particular terms in the Bahamut ACG community presents another approach to studying vernacular discourse. In this case study, I particularly attend to one concept, "vernacular collaboration," the horizontal collaboration between minority voices.[48]

Most research that employs the concept of vernacular discourse is situated within the contexts or the borders of the United States.[49] Thus, to expand the theoretical application to a non-American, non-English-dominant context, I propose adding several concepts, including "vernacular collaboration," to the original model of the critique of vernacular discourse I have discussed in another paper. On many occasions, when scholars apply the theory of vernacular discourse, they focus on the vertical relations between dominance (mainstream and official) and opposition (non-mainstream and unofficial); however, they often neglect the horizontal interactions among minorities within the vernacular discourse.[50] In other words, I propose that we draw our attention to horizontal interactions, the "vernacular collaboration," in a vernacular discourse. While horizontal interactions offer rich analytical texts, they do not mean that "vernacular collaboration" guarantees no conflicts and contradictions among non-mainstream community members; in fact, resistance and confrontation are also common factors in this form of "collaboration." Such dialectical and controversial processes, I argue, will lead to a conclusion that incorporates members' divided opinions. In the case of Bahamut, we clearly see that such a vernacular collaboration facilitates the formation of a Taiwanese identity.

Similarly, Michael Hanchard's conceptualization of politics invites us to examine how a cultural activity, or quotidian practice, becomes political when situated in the context of power dynamics and political communities.[51] Moreover, this ephemeral, everyday activity reflects macro-politics, incorporating "the power of routine in shaping situations."[52] The seemingly fleeting, insignificant, and irrelevant activities, such as artistic and linguistic practices, have political signification because they enable a non-elite form of political continuity that interrogates the essence of politics. The discourse in the ACG community constitutes the characteristics of "quotidian politics" or "micropolitics," as all the posts risk being deleted, washed out, or blocked. Thus, its ephemeral nature makes this vernacular discourse an ideal site for analyzing how dialogic modes of interaction have formed a Taiwanese identity.

Consequently, I argue that these netizens' discussions reach a consensus through vernacular collaboration. In my opinion, all voices in the ACG community are vernacular and subordinate to official and mainstream expressions. I next present analysis and critique guided by the practices of vernacular collaboration through netizen politics.

Hari, Worshipping Japan, and Controversies

As mentioned, certain posts that contain the term *hari* aim to provoke conflict. The identity debate often starts with a controversial title, such as "Do those who like anime and comics in general flatter Japan?" (喜歡看動漫的是不是普遍媚日?).[53] Similar titles include "What's wrong with the Taiwanese to get so excited about the name for the era of the new Japanese Emperor?" (日本換年號干台灣p4?), "What's the reason why the Taiwanese hate Japan?" (在台灣仇日的人都是什麼原因仇日啊?), and "Who's the Japan-worshipping idiot?" (這哪個哈日智障?).[54] Such topics often generate heated discussion. Hence, I use the discussion thread generated from the first title as an example to outline a typical controversy, including the conversation sequence, the context in which the keywords appear, and the response details.

The post titled "Do those who like anime and comics in general flatter Japan?" appeared in the discussion board "Demon Slayer: Kimetsu no Yaiba" (鬼滅の刃) on May 26, 2020. *Demon Slayer: Kimetsu no Yaiba* is a popular Japanese manga serial by Gotoge Koyoharu; thus, many posts in this forum are related to the latest news about the work, and feature participants sharing their drawings of the characters. A particular question of mocking Japan-mania, posted on such a discussion board, appeared to be out of place. Therefore, the discussion board administrator removed the original post shortly after it was posted. I preserved the discussion thread, as it provides a typical example of an identity debate around Japan-worshipping in the online ACG community.

The author of the post chose the avatar of a male character in a popular anime. He claimed that he was from "China"; however, all his messages were written in traditional Chinese characters, which is unusual for that country. Currently, the Chinese characters that circulate globally follow PRC standards: simplified characters. Traditional Chinese characters are only used in Hong Kong and Taiwan, which casts doubt on his self-identification. Moreover, his personal profile and account had been banned because of his violation of the rules. Therefore, I was unable to confirm his alleged national and gender identity. Nevertheless, I was able to check the consistency of the other respondents' claimed identifications as long as their accounts were active. Before the post was removed, it had already accumulated fifteen responses, which in turn elicited 146 follow-up responses. Although the author might have used a fake identity, his post obviously provoked a genuine controversy among members. The following analysis provides a summary of how Taiwanese ACG lovers, and so-called Japan worshippers, negotiate their identity and make sense of Japan and China.

The author of the selected example wrote:

> Please do not overreact to the phrase *flatter Japan*. What I meant to say is that all the beautiful aspects of Japanese culture are originally from China. Many people are heavily influenced by anime and comics, and consider Japan to be the paradise of all good things. They talk about Japan all the time, and dream of becoming *subjects of the emperor*. Obviously, they know nothing about their cultural roots.[55]

In this paragraph, two phrases stand out. First, to say that someone "flatters Japan" (*meiri*, or 媚日) has a more negative connotation than referring to a person as "worshipping Japan" (*hari*, or 哈日). In the 1997 textbook controversy, KMT supporters used this phrase to criticize the reformists as "flattering Japan." Second, the phrase "subjects of the emperor" (*huangmin*, or 皇民) is an insulting term for referring to local Taiwanese who have been colonized by Japan.

In 2014, the retired KMT general, Hau Pei-tsun, a 1949 immigrant, used the term *huangmin* to refer to the then Taipei mayoral candidate, a descendent of a 228 Incident victim, in a TV interview during the election.[56] Hau's speech caused a huge disturbance and ethnic tensions in Taiwan. The divisive nature of Hau's language is not only reminiscent of issues raised in the 1997 textbook dispute, but also clearly manifests the latent symptoms of an unhealed historical trauma that still exists in the society. When the KMT took over Taiwan after WWII, its foremost mission was to expel all remnants of Japanese colonial rule. Based on a belief in the superiority of Chinese culture, the KMT strove to "reeducate" Taiwanese "subjects" and "reconfigure" their culture.[57] The use of *meiri* and *huangmin* in the post reflects that the author attempted to replicate such ethnic tensions and the discriminatory attitude toward the local Taiwanese in everyday communication.

I identify three tendencies in the responses to this malicious post: (1) attacking China by mentioning the evil deeds of Chinese people; (2) refusing the identity label of Japan-flatters or subjects of the emperor; and (3) denying Taiwan as an extension of China. For example, netizens responded retaliatorily to this post by mentioning "the Chinese Cultural Revolution," "Wuhan virus," and "product piracy," in an attempt to humiliate the author. Some blamed him for his deliberate intention to "provoke a war" in this forum: "Japan learned from others and made them a better country. Look at you! The only thing you do is disparage others by writing these bad words!" Moreover, for those young online users nowadays, the usage of *meiri* and *huangmin* has become an signpost of the PRC's perspective. One respondent pointed out, "it is common for Chinese people to criticize Taiwanese people as 'flattering Japan.' The common term used in Taiwan is 'worshipping Japan.'" This shows that the respondent recognized the difference between China and Taiwan, and corrected the inappropriate usage without denying the action of worshipping Japan.

In this specific discussion thread, the majority of the respondents defended their Japan-worshipping behavior and expressed a strong Taiwanese consciousness. For example, Yu-fong wrote: "Not only Taiwanese people love amine and comics, but also Europeans and Americans. Do they also flatter Japan? . . . China now claims that Japanese culture is all from China. In my opinion, you are just jealous and weird!" However, amid the heated debate, people might neglect a small detail. What the original post praised was "cultural China," the ancient Tang Empire that influenced Japanese culture. The author even mentioned the ROC, not the PRC, in one of his responses. Based on his interactions with others, it is highly possible that he was a Taiwanese with a strong belief in the KMT's Chinese narrative. However, no one noticed this nuance in the responses. Just as the author had interpreted worshipping Japan as a betrayal of one's cultural roots, the respondents associated praising cultural China with the obeisance to the PRC regime. It is unclear which responses the author would prefer to receive, but the actual results reflect the overall disapproval of this humiliating and confrontational discussion post about Japan-worshipping in the forum.

Tienzhong, Kissing China's Ass, and Criticism

It is hard to trace exactly when the term *tienzhong* became common in Taiwan, but it is undoubtedly a recent phenomenon, given how the media has frequently used this term and popularized it. One notorious controversy related to the term took place in 2016, when Huang An, a pro-China Taiwanese celebrity, who had moved to China a long time ago, accused a young Taiwanese singer, Chou Tzu-yu, of being a pro–Taiwanese independence dissident. Chou, a sixteen-year-old girl, went to Korea to develop her K-pop music career, and gradually attracted international fans, including Chinese nationalists. Huang's report on her waving a Taiwan flag caused angry Chinese netizens to leave cursing messages on Chou's social media and forced her to respond with an abject videotaped apology.[58] Since then, Taiwan's media has labeled the "whistleblower" Huang as a celebrity that "kisses China's ass."

Just like Huang, increasing numbers of Taiwanese talent or business brands have been denounced on Taiwan's media as "kissing China's ass" because they have publicly admitted their loyalty to China. Moreover, they must express that they are anti–Taiwanese independence "Chinese" people if they want to do business in the PRC.[59] To prevent Taiwanese independence, the PRC has intensified its warning to Taiwan, and one of its common coercions is to place pressure on Taiwanese talent and companies. However, how effective this threatening strategy is remains dubious. For example, Chou's heartbreaking apology for expressing her Taiwanese identity appeared online the day before Taiwan's 2016 presidential election. Many experts believe that Chou's video helped trigger Taiwanese nationalist emotion and increased the pro-Taiwan Democratic Progressive Party's (DPP) votes by 1 or 2 percent, enabling it to win the election.[60]

Situated in the larger political context, the use of the term *tienzhong* in the ACG community also reflects the antipathy toward Chinese authorities in Taiwan. Furthermore, I found that this term often appeared in posts that defended the behavior of Japan-worshipping as a counter-concept. Here, I use a separate discussion thread derived from the above discussion to illustrate what meanings about *teinzhong* these netizens generated in this particular online vernacular discourse. Within twenty-four hours, a netizen named Ken opened a new discussion thread in response to the original post. He imitated how the original author had criticized Japan-worshipping by replacing the term "flattering Japan" with "kissing China's ass" as a parody. In this way, Ken used the term "kissing China's ass" as a counterargument for worshipping Japan. His post reads as follows:

> Please do not overreact to the phrase *kissing China's ass*. What I meant to say is that many people are heavily influenced by Chinese TV dramas and consider China to be the paradise of all good things. They talk about China all the time, and dream of becoming subjects of the Chinese empire. Obviously, they know nothing about how rotten China has become now.[61]

Clearly, Ken's message was directed at the author of the original post. Ken expressed his disagreement with the author's opinion that consuming Japanese popular culture meant flattering Japan. He did not defend the action of worshipping Japan or flattering Japan, but questioned the author for neglecting the current problems in China; reminiscing about China's glorious past did not justify contempt for Japanese innovation in popular culture. He associated the author's attack against Japanese culture with the term "kissing China's ass," and criticized those who excessively praise China and Chinese culture.

Interestingly, a Taiwanese netizen nicknamed "Pig Head" fought against Ken's viewpoint and generated a long debate under Ken's post. Pig Head's main arguments include: (1) China is a strong force ("that's why all the countries learn from China and praise China's strong power!"); (2) Taiwanese people cannot tolerate any good words about China ("it's become politically incorrect to praise China nowadays. I will be criticized as if I 'kiss China's ass' . . . , but I don't care! China is strong and rich!"); and (3) Taiwan is declining and losing power ("I mourn for Taiwan for giving up the Chinese tradition and cultural heritage of China, and even though we gave up the name of the ROC, we couldn't enter WHO in the name of Taiwan!"). Again, we see the pro-China elements in an anti–Japan worshipping comment. Pig Head lamented the loss of Chinese cultural heritage in Taiwan. Facing a rising China ruled by the PRC regime, Pig Head voiced concern that the Taiwanese have chosen to ignore the KMT-preserved Chinese cultural tradition in Taiwan; they also seem to have abandoned the KMT's long-lasting claim of being the successor to a Chinese orthodoxy.

Ken's discussion thread burgeoned as other netizens joined to argue against Pig Head. By then, the discussion had become more emotional and rifer with labeling. Several responses were aimed directly at Pig Head: "Do we have to be Chinese to appreciate Chinese culture?"; "Can Taiwanese be Taiwanese and establish our own country?"; "I love Japanese culture but I am not worshipping it. Do I have the freedom to dislike Chinese culture?"; "I suspect you are a traitor. You keep belittling your own country!"; "The KMT wants to go back to China, but not me!" Throughout the thread initiated by Ken, we can find a communication pattern in the online community. A controversial title with the implication of "worshipping Japan" will easily generate an identity debate that involves China, Taiwan, and Japan. Although the PRC, China, and the KMT represent different concepts, the respondents in this discussion thread seemed to use these terms interchangeably. On the other hand, worshipping Japan appeared to be associated with a Taiwanese identity.

Such an act of labeling is a form of naming. Naming is an expression and a negotiation of social identities; the act allows one to participate in "a historical flow of social relationships, struggles, and meanings."[62] Labeling in this online ACG community explicates how different camps make sense of their own identities and histories. In this case, "worshipping Japan" and "kissing China's ass" form two oppositional camps that attack each other by leaving acrimonious comments and provoking a sensation. In all the threads that mention the term *hari*, we have already identified that the ACG participants view *tienzhong* as a contrasting term. Moreover, the two terms, *meiri* (flattering Japan) and *huangmin* (subjects of the emperor), are used to intensify the attack on the actions of worshipping Japan. Participants use these terms to serve their communication purposes, such as name-calling, self-despising, and building connections with like minds.

Identity Struggles between Japan and China

Situated in Taiwan's historical context and in the process of social change, the term *hari* contains further meanings, other than simply worshipping Japanese culture. This term has been interwoven into Taiwan's identity negotiation and attitude toward its colonial history. It reveals a choice of identity, a perspective for interpreting Taiwanese history, and an attitude toward China—namely, whether to resist or not.

One critique of vernacular discourse is that the voice of the local communities is not always "counter-hegemonic"; it can also be "affirmative" of dominant ideologies.[63] In the American context, this critique reveals the interwovenness of the dominant white culture with the minority community's protest; thus, the minority community's vernacular discourse is not necessarily liberatory. What would the equivalent vernacular discourse construction look like in Taiwan? I argue that the dominant ideologies in Taiwan are not derived from Japan, or from locally driven Taiwanese values, but are still governed by the China-centric values promoted by the KMT party. The vernacular discourse in the ACG online community demonstrates how the discussion threads are counter-hegemonic, protesting, confrontational, but also occasionally affirmative of a pro-China ideology. For example, a common term, "allies of the Chinese Communist Party" (中共同路人, *zhonggong tongluren*), circulates in this ACG community.

Those pro-China members often use this phrase in their posts as a form of self-mockery; for instance: "Am I becoming an ally of the Chinese Communist Party if I conduct an act of . . . ?" They expect a "no" response to this rhetorical question, as an indirect way to defend the KMT's Chinese historical perspective and resist the rise of a Taiwanese consciousness. Such expressions reveal these members' realization that their claimed identity is not mainstream in this ACG community, but marginalized and alienated. In other words, they aim to affirm an alternative "Taiwanese" identity, which includes numerous "unpopular" Chinese elements and legacies.

For instance, the discussion thread about the Taiwanese horror movie *Detention* unexpectedly became a battlefield of just such an identity negotiation. Against the backdrop of 1962 Taiwan, when the KMT government imposed martial law in order to suppress political dissidents or so-called *feidie* (Communist spies, or 匪諜), *Detention* tells the story of a boy and a girl who are trapped at their high school, and their experience of encountering ghosts. A young netizen posted several questions concerning the history during that time, because his unfamiliarity with that period obscured some details in the movie.[64]

His questions prompted several enthusiastic history fans to share their study results, and some older netizens also narrated their lived experiences and childhood memories of this period. This discussion thread accidently became an outlet for people to tell their personal stories of suffering or their fear of being censored. One claimed,

> Any books that delivered uncensored thoughts or challenged the KMT's central values would be viewed as rebellious, or worse; they were labeled as propaganda for the Communists, which was treasonous behavior . . . Doesn't it sound like the government across the Taiwan Strait now? We used to be a dictatorship regime![65]

Similar posts associated the image of the KMT in the 1960s with that of the CPC nowadays. Just as a debate started in the print media allowed those local Taiwanese in the 1997 textbook dispute to talk about their memories of the 228 Incident, the online forum in the ACG community offers a space for the younger generation to witness a forgotten history, as reported by the senior members.

In these memory-sharing posts, however, the opposing voice also appeared, as represented by a netizen nicknamed "King of War" (引戰之王). He began to surface and bring Japan to the table. First, he criticized *Detention* as "nonsense," and "not a horror movie at all." Then, he blamed Japan for its colonization and emphasized the atrocities committed by Japan against the Chinese and Taiwanese.

Thus, his comments triggered another round of labeling with "worshipping Japan" and "kissing China's ass." While King of War expressed his dislike of Japan, other members found fault with his contradictory actions: "Look at how many Japanese characters you have used in your account name! You Japan worshipper!"; "Don't tell me that you never watch Japanese anime! Otherwise, why are you here?"; "If you don't like Japan, go kiss China's ass!" Eventually, King of War posed a comment: "Am I becoming an ally of the Chinese Communist Party if I do not like the movie *Detention*?"[66] By asking this rhetorical question, he denied his association with the CPC; yet, he resisted a Taiwan-centered historical narrative with which this discussion thread had begun. His interference in the middle of the nostalgic discussion about Taiwan's past demonstrated those pro-China members' identity contradiction and discontent.

As a consumer of Japanese cultural products, King of War visits Bahamut's forums frequently and is notorious for provoking arguments with other members. A parodic fandom website, "Bahapedia," even selects him to enter the "Hall of Fame."[67] His excessively controversial comments probably reflect the confusion around a Japan-worshipping Taiwanese who also believes in KMT-promoted Chinese values. His identity struggle and conflict with other members show how different historical memories in Taiwan repeatedly generate divided opinions concerning past Japanese rule and KMT rule. These online identity disputes echo Leo Ching's "postcolonial colonization" sentiments, and Fu-chang Wang's interpretations of separate historical memories by local Taiwanese and 1949 immigrants. Although Leo Ching distinguishes the desire for Japanese commodity mass culture in 1990s Taiwan from the desire for Japanese colonialism,[68] these two aspirations seem to converge just as the PRC is further pursuing its ambition to threaten Taiwan.

Conclusion

Bahamut, the online ACG community, is an entertaining and energetic platform for Taiwan's young generation to discuss their favorite ACG characters, games, and works. However, when someone posts a topic to mock Japan-mania, discussion threads often become malicious, and split participants into two salient identity groups who label each other as "worshipping Japan" and "kissing China's ass," respectively. These heated identity debates occasionally appear but eventually the forum returns to status quo. Nevertheless, such sensitivity and agitation indicate that there has been no true reconciliation or healing of the past traumas caused by colonialism and authoritarianism.[69] Even though Taiwan lifted martial law in 1987 and has become a democracy, its legacy of contrasting memories in Taiwan still impacts how netizens react to identity issues in everyday interactions.

Within this context, Taiwanese people's admiration of Japanese culture demonstrates a form of resistance to the dominant China-centric narrative; the Japanese cultural elements thus offer a resource for building a Taiwanese culture. Many discussion threads in the online community express such a direct impact of Japanese culture on Taiwan. For example, when Japanese brands and shops open new stores in Taiwan, Bahamut will announce the news immediately; these posts often receive significant attention and welcoming reception.[70] Moreover, members share their reflections on Japanese TV shows, animation, and movies.[71] Their teenage memories are intertwined with these Japanese media products. These examples show how Japanese cultural elements constitute Taiwanese youth's lived experience and cultural taste. The addition to the Japanese elements, in the process of creating Taiwanese popular cultural memories, facilitates the formation of a Taiwanese consciousness. On the other hand, China's growing global power and its ambition to annex Taiwan over the last two decades have pushed the Taiwanese people to take a defiant position against their neighbor.

The PRC has been expediting its agenda to annex Taiwan after its leader Xi Jinping seized power in 2013.[72] This unabashed ambition has put the KMT in an awkward predicament. On one hand, the majority of loyal KMT supporters are living in the nostalgia constructed by the KMT's Chinese historical narrative; however, they are getting old. My analysis of Bahamut's identity-related discussion threads have confirmed the unpopularity of a pro-China position among young Taiwanese netizens. Even though some Bahamut members attempt to defend the ROC, others automatically connect such comments with "kissing the PRC's ass." The distinction between the ROC and the PRC has become blurred for the young generations. On the other hand, facing an increasingly hostile threat from the PRC, the KMT cannot propose a China policy that convinces Taiwan's voters; their distrust of the KMT has resulted in the triumph of the opposition party, the DPP, in the 2016 and the 2020 elections.[73]

Many cultural outsiders may feel confused about the Taiwanese people's national identity. For instance: Why do Taiwanese people often switch their opinions in terms of their Chinese/Taiwanese identity? Do the Taiwanese want to be unified with China? Do the Taiwanese want to be independent from China?

Since the first direct presidential election took place in 1996, Taiwanese people have been enthusiastically participating in voting.[74] Thus, elections in Taiwan become a site for observing Taiwanese people's consensus on issues of Taiwan's sovereignty and its relations with the PRC. However, election results are not the only index for understanding the Taiwanese people's identity. This chapter adds another dimension to the discussion: the everyday discourse in a vernacular community. These debates in the ACG community do not aim to decide whether Taiwan should be unified with China, but to construct what kind of Taiwanese people they want to become, with what histories, memories, and futures. By investigating the use of vernacular collaboration, we can see that contradictions, confrontations, and even affirmations of the mainstream ideologies are common in a vernacular discourse, and that all the dialectical interactions help form a collective, albeit ephemeral, consensus.

By revealing Taiwanese people's complicated attitudes toward Japan and China, this chapter explains why Taiwanese people are not discussing which country should rule this island; rather, they are searching for the answer that will determine a new national identity. However, quotidian, local politics are always connected to the macro-political situation. Even though the identity debates could take place in every corner of Taiwan—at the congress, night-time TV talk shows, or online gaming communities—Taiwanese people seem to be always wary of such internal discussions because of China's threats to the civil society of Taiwan.[75] Recently, due to U.S.–China tensions, the Chinese government has intensified its coercion of Taiwan.

After Donald Trump became the forty-fifth president of the United States in 2017, the U.S.–China trade war triggered a series of conflicts between the PRC and the United States. In addition to economic decoupling, the U.S. government challenged the PRC's One-China principle by strengthening various U.S.–Taiwan collaborations, including passing the Taiwan Travel Act in 2018 and approving an unprecedented scale of weapons sales to Taiwan in 2020.[76] Taiwan was pushed to play a role in the ongoing U.S.–China trade dispute, and the Taiwan government chose to strengthen U.S.–Taiwan relations in order to check China's ambitions. The outbreak of COVID-19 in Wuhan, China, in 2020 created an opportunity for Taiwan to help the world fight the virus, as it proved a trustworthy ally, despite China's diplomatic suppression.[77]

While Taiwan eagerly seeks international recognition, the PRC has resorted to every conceivable means to stop such efforts. Moreover, as Chiaoning Su and

Weiping Li point out, the PRC has attempted to interfere in Taiwan's politics through disinformation campaigns. Pro-China propaganda and fake news have been harmful to a society in which citizens are communicating, debating, and choosing their national and cultural identities by following democratic procedure. If scholars are dedicated to global justice in international relations by promoting diversity and empowering subordinate voices, then it is imperative to listen to Taiwanese people's vernacular narratives, set against the aggressive and influential propaganda the PRC transmits to the world. Taiwan does not make itself the most dangerous place on earth, but its ambitious neighbor does.

NOTES

1. "The Most Dangerous Place on Earth," *The Economist*, May 1, 2021.
2. Both translations are used by scholars. I use these two translations interchangeably.
3. See Kent A. Ono and John M. Sloop, "The Critique of Vernacular Discourse," *Communication Monographs* 62, no. 1 (1995): 20.
4. Hsin-i Sydney Yueh, "From Japanese Otaku to Taiwanese Zhainan: Understanding Transcultural Masculinity through a Cultural Term in Taiwan," *Journal of International and Intercultural Communication* 12, no. 2 (2019): 111.
5. Chih-ming Wang, "'The Future that Belongs to Us': Affective Politics, Neoliberalism, and the Sunflower Movement," *International Journal of Cultural Studies* 20, no. 2 (2017): 180.
6. Hsin-yen Yang, "The Uncivic Pop Culture?," *Critical Discourse Studies* 12, no. 1 (2015): 108.
7. Changes in the unification-independence stances of Taiwanese as tracked in surveys (1994–2021), Election Study Center, NCCU, https://esc.nccu.edu.tw/PageDoc/Detail?fid=7801&id=6963.
8. Michael Hanchard, *Party/Politics: Horizons in Black Political Thought* (New York: Oxford University Press, 2006), 26.
9. The naming of the various languages spoken in Taiwan reveals political stances. I use the term "Taiwan Hokkien" to refer to the common language used in Taiwan. Other names for this language include "Taiwanese language," "Taiwanese dialect," "Southern Min," "Taigi," etc. Each name represents one political view. Accordingly, from a Taiwan-centered perspective, I pair the name for Taiwan's "Chinese" with "Taiwan Mandarin." This name highlights that this form of language has been localized and "creolized" since 1949, which makes it different from "Beijing Mandarin." One-soon Her, "Language and Group Identity: On Taiwan Mainlander's Mother Tongues and Taiwan Mandarin," *Language and Linguistics* 10, no. 2 (2009): 375–419.

10. Hari Kyoko, "About Me," Hari Kyoko Travelogue, https://kyoko.tw/.
11. I-yun Lee, "1990 年代台灣哈日風的基礎" [The foundation of Japan-mania in the 1990s Taiwan], *Taiwan Fongwu* 58, no. 2 (2008): 142, 143, 147.
12. Hui-wen Luo, "The Flow of Japanese Films and Television Programs in Taiwan 1945–1996" (master's thesis, National Chengchi University, 1995).
13. Lee, "Japan-mania," 149.
14. Shuling Huang, "Nation-branding and Transnational Consumption: Japan-mania and the Korean Wave in Taiwan," *Media, Culture & Society* 33, no. 1 (2011): 7.
15. Joseph Man Chan, "National Responses and Accessibility to STAR TV in Asia," *Journal of Communication* 44, no. 3 (1994): 112–131.
16. Hsin-i Sydney Yueh, *Identity Politics and Popular Culture in Taiwan: A Sajiao Generation* (Lanham, MD: Lexington Books, 2016), 120–122.
17. Huang, "Nation-branding," 10.
18. Fang-chi Irene Yang, "The Gentrification of 'Korean Drama' in Taiwan," *China Information* 22, no. 2 (2008): 277–304.
19. Takeshi Okamoto, "Otaku Tourism and the Anime Pilgrimage Phenomenon in Japan," *Japan Forum* 27 (2015): 12–36.
20. Yang, "Uncivic Pop Culture," 97.
21. This Japanese word refers to people with an obsessive interest in anime, manga, and games. Their consumption has formed a unique Japanese culture since the 1970s. More information can be found in Patrick W. Galbraith, "Akihabara: Conditioning a Public "Otaku" Image," *Mechademia* 5 (2010): 210–230.
22. Yueh, "Japanese Otaku," 118.
23. See Koichi Iwabuchi, *Recentering Globalization: Popular Culture and Japanese Transnationalism* (Durham: Duke University Press, 2002), 121–157.
24. Leo T. S. Ching, *Anti-Japan: The Politics of Sentiment in Postcolonial East Asia* (Durham: Duke University Press, 2019), 118.
25. Stephen J. Hartnett, *A World of Turmoil: The United States, China and Taiwan in the Long Cold War* (East Lansing: Michigan State University Press, 2021).
26. Qiang Zhang and Robert Weatherley, "Owning up to the Past: The KMT's Role in the War against Japan and the Impact on CCP Legitimacy," *The Pacific Review* 26, no. 3 (2013): 222–223.
27. Yoshihisa Amae, "Pro-colonial or Postcolonial? Appropriation of Japanese Colonial Heritage in Present-Day Taiwan," *Journal of Current Chinese Affairs* 40, no. 1 (2011): 19–62.
28. Stephen J. Hartnett, Patrick Shaou-whea Dodge, and Lisa B. Keränen, "Postcolonial Remembering in Taiwan: 228 and Transitional Justice as 'The End of Fear,'" *Journal of*

International and Intercultural Communication 13, no. 3 (2020): 241.

29. Regarding the history of the Chinese Civil War exiles, see Dominic Meng-hsuan Yang, *The Great Exodus from China: Trauma, Memory, and Identity in Modern Taiwan* (Cambridge: Cambridge University Press, 2020).
30. Amae, "Pro-colonial," 26.
31. Ching, *Anti-Japan*, 89.
32. Hartnett, Dodge, and Keränen, "Postcolonial Remembering," 243–245.
33. Richard L. Walker, "Taiwan's Development as Free China," *The ANNALS of the American Academy of Political and Social Science* 321, no. 1 (1959): 122.
34. George H. Kerr, *Formosa Betrayed* (Upland, CA: Taiwan Publishing Co., 1992).
35. Fu-chang Wang, "National Imagination, Ethnic Consciousness, and History: Content and Context Analysis of the 'Getting to Know Taiwan' Textbook Disputes," *Taiwan Historical Research* 8, no. 2 (2001): 170–171.
36. See Mao-kuei Chang et al., *族群關係與國家認同* [Ethnic relations and national identity] (Xinbei: Yeqian, 1993); Leo L. S. Ching, *Becoming "Japanese": Colonial Taiwan and the Politics of Identity Formation* (Oakland: University of California Press, 2001); Wan-yao Chou, *海行兮的年代* [The age of Umi Yukaba] (Taipei: Yunchen, 2003); Horng-luen Wang, *戰爭與社會: 理論, 歷史, 主體經驗* [War and society: Theories, histories, and subjective experiences] (Taipei: Lienjing, 2014).
37. Wang, "National Imagination," 155.
38. Xiao-fen Liu, "我國中學歷史教科書中台灣史教材的分析" [An analysis of the portion of Taiwan history in high school national history textbooks] (master's thesis, National Chengchi University, 1991).
39. *The Journalist* was established in 1987, the same year that Taiwan lifted martial law. It featured a critical stance toward the authorities. In 2017, the magazine was bought by The Storm Media Group, Taiwan, which closely collaborates with the PRC.
40. See Hsin-yen Yang, "Re-interpreting Japanomania: Transnational Media, National Identity and the Restyling of Politics in Taiwan" (PhD dissertation, University of Iowa, 2010).
41. Leo T. S. Ching, "'Give Me Japan and Nothing Else!': Postcoloniality, Identity, and the Traces of Colonialism," *The South Atlantic Quarterly* 99, no. 4 (2000), 763–788; Yu-fen Ko, "Consuming Differences: 'Hello Kitty' and the Identity Crisis in Taiwan," *Postcolonial Studies* 6, no. 2 (2003): 175–189.
42. Ji-qing Wang, "History Teacher Concerned about the Popularity of Japan-Mania" [哈日風盛行 歷史老師憂心], *United Daily*, December 29, 2000.
43. Wang, "National Imagination," 189.

44. Hsin-I Cheng, *Cultivating Membership in Taiwan and Beyond: Relational Citizenship* (Lanham: Lexington Books, 2021).
45. "Observation on ARO/MMX," *InsightXplorer Biweekly Report* 70, (2016): 9. https://www.ixresearch.com/wp-content/uploads/report/InsightXplorer%20Biweekly%20Report_20160830.pdf.
46. Ono and Sloop, "The Critique of Vernacular Discourse," 25.
47. Ibid., 20.
48. Hsin-i Sydney Yueh, "Theorizing Vernacular Discourse in Sinophone Transnational Space: On Namewee's YouTube Music Videos," *Critical Studies in Media Communication* 37, no. 2 (2020): 174.
49. For example, see Darrel Enck-Wanzer, "Race, Coloniality, and Geo-Body Politics: The Garden as Latin@ Vernacular Discourse," *Environmental Communication* 5, no. 3 (2011): 363–371; Michelle A. Holling and Bernadette M. Calafell, eds., *Latina/o Discourse in Vernacular Spaces: Somos de una voz?* (Lanham, MD: Lexington Books, 2011); Lori K. Lopez and Vincent N. Pham, eds., *The Routledge Companion to Asian American Media* (New York: Routledge, 2017).
50. Yueh, "Theorizing Vernacular Discourse," 174, 184.
51. Hanchard, *Party/Politics*, 14.
52. Xavier Guillaume and Jef Huysmans, "The Concept of 'the Everyday': Ephemeral Politics and the Abundance of Life," *Cooperation and Conflict* 54, no. 2 (2019): 287.
53. The original post was deleted by the administrator, but based on other members' responses, I can trace the original text, which was published on May 26, 2020.
54. These three examples were posted on April 30, 2019; March 25, 2019; and June 12, 2020, respectively. The first expression is very colloquial and informal. The expression "p4" is an informal transliteration that is equivalent to the English expression "what the hell . . ."? Austin Ramzy, "Singer's Apology for Waving Taiwan Flag Stirs Backlash of Its Own," *New York Times*, January 16, 2016.
55. Emphasis added. All the paragraphs quoted from Bahamut are translated by the author.
56. J. Michael Cole, "Attack of the KMT Dinosaurs," *The Diplomat*, November 21, 2014.
57. Ching, *Anti-Japan*, 93.
58. Chris Buckley and Austin Ramzy, "Singer's Apology for Waving Taiwan Flag Stirs Backlash of Its Own," *New York Times*, January 16, 2016.
59. Some examples can be found in the following news reports: Brenda Goh and Yimou Lee, "Taiwan Bakery Chain Disappears from Major Chinese Food Apps amid Tsai Visit Row," Reuters, August 16, 2018; J. Michael Cole, "Taiwanese Celebrities Who Bow to China: A Tempest in a Teapot," *Taiwan Sentinel*, September 30, 2020; Samson Ellis and

Argin Chang, "Tycoon Targeted by China Speaks Out Against Taiwan Independence," *Bloomberg*, November 29, 2021.

60. "Taiwan Election: How a Penitent Pop Star May Have Helped Tsai Win," *BBC News*, January 18, 2016.
61. An entry posted on May 26, 2020.
62. Sunny Lie and Benjamin Bailey, "The Power of Names in a Chinese Indonesian Family's Negotiations of Politics, Culture, and Identities," *Journal of International and Intercultural Communication* 10, no. 1 (2017): 82.
63. Ono and Sloop, "The Critique of Vernacular Discourse," 22.
64. An entry posted on February 2, 2020.
65. A response posted on February 3, 2020.
66. Selected comments from February 2 to February 4, 2020.
67. See the page "Celebrities on Baha," Bahapedia, https://bahapedia.fandom.com/zh/wiki/Category:%E5%B7%B4%E5%93%88%E5%90%8D%E4%BA%BA.
68. Ching, "Give Me Japan," 763–788.
69. Wang, "National Imagination," 188–194.
70. An entry posted on March 9, 2019.
71. An entry posted on December 17, 2018.
72. Joshua Keating, "China is Trying to Wipe Taiwan off the Map," *Slate*, August 1, 2018.
73. Shelley Rigger, "Kuomintang Agonistes: Party Politics in the Wake of Taiwan's 2016 and 2020 Elections," in *Taiwan in the Era of Tsai Ing-wen*, edited by June Teufel Dreyer and Jacques deLisle (London: Routledge, 2021), 39–63.
74. See Dafydd Fell, *Party Politics in Taiwan: Party Change and the Democratic Evolution of Taiwan, 1991–2004* (London: Routledge, 2005); Shelley Rigger, *Politics in Taiwan: Voting for Reform* (London: Routledge, 1999).
75. Jude Blanchette, Scott Livingston, Bonnie S. Glaser, and Kennedy Scott, *Protecting Democracy in an Age of Disinformation: Lessons from Taiwan* (Washington, DC: CSIS, January 2021).
76. See David Brunnstrom, "Trump Signs US–Taiwan Travel Bill, Angering China," Reuters, March 16, 2018; Jennifer Hansler and Rayn Browne, "Trump Administration Notifies Congress of $1.8B in Proposed Weapons Sales to Taiwan," *CNN*, October 22, 2020.
77. Wayne Soon, "Why Taiwan Is Beating COVID-19, Again," *The Diplomat*, July 29, 2021.

PART 2

Resistance in Hong Kong

Not Yet the Endgame

A Reflection on the Tactic of *Laam Caau* in the Anti-Extradition Movement in Hong Kong

Iam-chong Ip

The anti-Extradition Law Amendment Bill (ELAB) movement in 2019, a watershed event in Hong Kong political history, serves as a special case symptomatic of the organic crises of our era. It is characteristic of an alienation of the masses from their political representatives, apocalyptic fear, and emotionally charged agitations. The term *laam caau* (攬炒 *lanchao* in pinyin) literally refers to "holding someone firmly" and "(car) crash"; the neologism conveys a sense of mutual destruction. Yet, with its multiple connotations, the term also came to define and shape the tone, repertoires of contention, driving force, and affective intensity of the movement. This tactical rhetoric, rather than simply a response to the authoritarian state and the crises, articulated the people's political disappointments, frustrations, and anger. Its meaning evolved on the internet, especially on social media platforms such as Telegram, the LIHKG online forum (a local and popular news forum), and Facebook, which facilitated diverse forms of protests, fostering a sense of community. With semantic ambiguity and replicability, this *laam caau* meme constituted mechanisms of empowerment at different levels of the movement through the scenario of "endgame." Yet, failing to bridge the temporal gap between the coerced present and the fantasy future, it is not adequate for addressing our shared crises, for indulging in the fantasy of "endgame," an imaginative and adventurous space, forecloses the possibilities of interim political engagement.

Research on social movements has attended to the new temporal sense created by media technology, such as mobile phones and social media platforms, and its implications for political engagements. For example, Zizi Papacharissi maintains that the instantaneity afforded by such media platforms, which not only provide 24/7 news but also facilitate netizens to immediately share and repeat the information, encourage them to comment and endorse emotionally charged remarks (e.g., "like" and hashtags), which then intensify and convey urgency.[1] All these online actions and interactions happen in the moment that individuals are watching and touching their mobile phone screens. Wondering if these impulsive and effortless actions would evolve into meaningful activism, some scholars are worried about the shifting of rational deliberation to indulgence in protest spectacle, the reinforcement of politically correct stance without self-reflexivity, and the failure to address inequalities and making changes.[2] Some scholars even argue that this type of "instant activism" allows activists to spread fake news, sway less-informed people's opinions, and manipulate their behavior.[3]

The concern of instantaneity largely emerged out of scholarly attention to advances in information technologies, yet I argue we should not overlook other forms of temporality. For example, while some critics have expressed concern about shrinking youth participation in electoral democracy due to their emergence in social media, youth's political engagement has been increasingly characterized by their impatience with conventional politics, leading to new forms of activism exercised through emotionally charged moments of political mobilization, such as referenda, occupations, and confrontation with police.[4] This shift partially points to a preference for the moments of political agitation over the gradual and prolonged movement of time coordinated by representative democracy, legislation, and political deliberations. Therefore, these transformations in how youth engage with the political process indicate governance crises, rather than the direct outcome of new media technologies. Put simply, the embrace of digitally mediated mobilization must be explained as a phenomenon entangled with politico-social changes and their ensuing temporal structures. Put differently, youth are not dropping out because of their immersion in social media; rather, they are evolving new forms—and new senses of time—in how they undertake political action.

According to critics such as Anthony Giddens and Pierre Bourdieu time is a critical dimension constituting social formations, as demonstrated, for example, by the link between the making of industrial capitalism and the modern state and the synchronization of clock time with work discipline.[5] Since the late 1980s, experiences of velocity and acceleration have permeated the contemporary discussion on capitalism, culture, and human conditions. But temporal experience is not only about speed, or the rate at which one changes, moves, operates or innovates, as suggested by the popularity of such temporally inflected terms as "time compression," "fast capitalism," and acceleration.[6] Time is usually perceived as either a naturalized flow of cycles that "pass" without our notice, or as routines and schedules, a sort of silent but ever-present structure we are obliged to follow. However, time is also portrayed as a narrative figure. As Paul Ricoeur notes, time is organized in the manner of narratives, whereby any sense of the strict objectivity of time gives way to deeply personal responses to temporal experiences.[7] In this light, the instantaneous moment, triggered and supported by media technologies and their uses, is freighted with contested meanings. The sense of urgency is not simply technically facilitated, a sort of clock/now-time, but also made possible by varied discourses and narratives of time.

The goal of this chapter is to understand not the temporal features of new media technologies, such as instantaneity and acceleration, but the affordances of the human–environment–technology interaction,[8] in which people perceive, experience, make, and imagine their political time. I draw examples from Hong Kong's anti-ELAB movement in 2019 and demonstrate that some activists, in the midst of political setbacks and fear, devised a discursive tactic under the banner of *laam caau*, which came to articulate political disappointments, frustrations, fear, and anger while also encapsulating a new will to power—a phrase that implied disaster but generated hope and engagement. It functioned as a meme on the internet, especially on social media platforms such as Telegram, the LIHKG online forum, and Facebook. While social media might have facilitated prompt actions, the commitment to *laam caau* on the ground was what really mattered, for it was on the streets, in moments of political engagement, that the curious mixture of endgame and hope was experienced, felt, and repurposed for specific contexts. While the meme helped to motivate Hong Kong's young activists, the phrase could not adequately address the draconian measures taken by the Beijing government against civil society, such as the direct introduction of a new national security law into the city, wiping out pro-democracy politicians, and weeding out "non-patriots."[9] In short, the meme was potent and effective for generating emotions, feelings of solidarity, and a shared sense of time, but was not equipped to sustain a movement in the long run.

These political setbacks drove a diaspora of dissident refugees across the world; once they departed from the scene of action, their political significance to Hong Kong and China became negligible. For example, Nathan Law, once the youngest lawmaker and a student leader, gained public support in Hong Kong. After leaving the city and becoming a political exile, he could only engage in lobbying in Western countries to urge the international community to support the Hong Kong protesters. The grief, anger, and pessimism conveyed by the rhetoric of *laam caau*, as I will demonstrate later, uniting people during agitations rather than building up resilience among the populace, ironically ended up driving more activists to retreat from politics and even to flee Hong Kong after the peak time of mobilization was over.

Articulation, Hegemony, and Conjuncture

My analysis of *laam caau* is informed by post-Marxist cultural theories of articulation, which denote communicative practices connecting two or more elements to establish a meaningful unity. Articulation serves as a suture or closure happening in a particular moment.[10] The ideological elements involved are not related to one another by nature but are brought together for the moment.[11] In this light, unity is produced through the interactions among different parties working in alliance. In other words, any temporary conjunctures built by activists may shift according to changing historical contexts. Articulation theories thus help us to comprehend how activists respond to specific contingencies by defining and redefining identities and antagonisms in action. In Ernesto Laclau's words, this organic and iterative notion of articulation is crucial to understanding the political character of social identities, especially as they form, recalibrate, and reform in the midst of intense struggles over hegemony.[12]

Hegemony refers to both the politico-moral leadership of existing elites and the processes by which they try to inculcate a stable political order by building forms of consent. Ideally, this stability-building consent is not imposed from above; instead, it relies on enduring articulations. It contrasts, yet is also complementary, with rule through coercion, which is deployed whenever consent wavers. Domination runs smoothly when the power bloc maintains its hegemony and keeps its means of organized violence to a minimum, making public consent appear natural, not constructed for the purposes of domination. However, when counter-hegemony is successfully rearticulated through struggles on various fronts, an organic crisis of hegemony occurs—this is what some critics call a "legitimation crisis."[13] As the symbolic system of the status quo is shattered and radically recast,[14] authorities' representativeness becomes disputed and elites seek to rebuild their legitimacy by either engaging in consent-building concessions or resorting to repression or, as in the case in Beijing's response to the Hong Kong protests, implementing new levels of violence. In this sense, articulation theory invites us to see all political life as a constant process of communicative persuasion, with varying parties seeking to represent themselves as legitimate voices of authority.

Theories of articulation and hegemony could shed some light on the growing body of literature on Hong Kong politics, which is prone to explaining all political phenomena through identity. In view of the rise of political nativism (本土主義 *buntou zyuji*) in Hong Kong, a couple of social scientists began to explore the notion of "Hong Kong nationalism" and use it to characterize Hong Kong's post-war/late-colonial history or the post-handover era as the making of Hong Kong nationalism, explaining its emergence as a peripheral nationalism in response to the threat of the geopolitical center.[15] Despite their rich accounts of the historical backgrounds, these scholars—knowingly or not—assume a coherent concept of nation/nationalism for understanding Hong Kong's political changes rather than explain how the discrete elements were momentarily articulated. The simple attribution of the political conflicts to "Hong Kong" versus "China" inadequately addresses the hegemonic changes happening to Hong Kong's politics. In other words, Hong Kong's political identity neither preceded political agitations, nor was a "natural" and spontaneous response to authoritarian threat. Instead, it was articulated in conjuncture. In other words, the politico-ideological drives behind the constitution of "the social" remain to be explained. A rigorous examination of the political contingency, a complexity in which institutional pressures, collective experience, and reflexive practices are involved, is needed.

Another issue concerns conjuncture—that is, the plurality of temporalities.[16] Using the case of the anti-ELAB movement, this article elucidates the complexity of temporal experience, which should not be simplified as "historical background." That said, time, rather than simply a flow passing at the present or something that happened in the past, is experienced and imagined. Whatever identity Hong

Kongers embrace and imagine "now" is always a temporal experience of the present mediated by narratives of the past (e.g., memory, stories, historical writing, etc.) and the future (e.g., prediction, expectation, hope, vision, etc.). In Martin Heidegger's terms, human existence is a stretching back to the past (toward birth) and the future (toward death).[17] In view of temporal complexity, rather than explaining the movement as the outcome of technological advancement, I conduct a conjunctural analysis of how the instantaneity of new media plays out in instant activism.

"Social Movement" in Hong Kong

To understand the significance of *laam caau*, one must foreground Hong Kong's political trajectory, in particular, how the paradigm of social movement in Hong Kong emerged, grew, and declined before the anti-ELAB movement. What happened in 2019 is neither a social movement nor a type of contentious politics often seen in the past three decades in Hong Kong. The "messiness" and decentralization of the anti-ELAB movement illustrate the inadequacy of the traditional concept of social movement in understanding the new forms of mass politics. Instead of focusing on the organizers' strategic production and circulation of information, one must attend to the multiple types of participants, their reception of information, the communication environment, and connective emotions.[18]

The term "social movement" is a Western concept, as it originated in Europe and the United States. Therefore, when I refer to the previous paradigm of "social movement" in Hong Kong, I borrow the definition from the historical sociologist Charles Tilly, who, in his late writings, argues that social movements as a distinctive form of mass politics have developed in Western Europe and North America since the mid-eighteenth century. Tilly explained that since then new elements gradually became dominant and coalesced into a vehicle for expressing public demands (i.e., the prototype of collective action).[19] The particular mode of action, organization, and rhetoric then eventually spread to other places of the world. In a nutshell, social movements contain three elements: (1) collective demands; (2) a series of conventional performances of demands, including rallies, demonstrations, public statements; and (3) public expressions that demonstrate the value, size, and commitment.

At the beginning, social movements as a form of mass politics looked similar to unorganized riots, lootings, and carnival-like disturbances. In other words, the distinction between a revolution and a social movement remained blurred, as the specter of revolution still haunted Europe in the early nineteenth century. Nevertheless, modern social movements, as Tilly explains, began to emerge. The rise of the new form of collective action coincided with its relatively peaceful and constructive engagement with the government, creating a legal and civic space in which people could gain political status by advocating, protesting, and expressing their values and commitments. In this sense, social movements, unlike revolution as an attempt to topple authority, are underpinned by institutional arrangements and practices. They address issues of human rights, nation-states, representative systems, and formal political affirmative action. From the populace's perspective, social movements represent an extra form of popular demand, and from the state's perspective, the response to a social movement is comparatively benign, rather than outright repression. Both sides' moderate stances facilitate a kind of space indispensable to building civil society and conducting socio-political reform. The development of modern Western social movements is consistent with Charles Taylor's idea of a modern social imaginary or moral order, which stresses the gradual expansion of the rights and obligations in the legitimacy of political authority over the last three centuries.[20]

This seemingly simple process of shaping modern social movements has taken Western Europe and North America since the mid-1700s. Around World War II, the ideas and practices of social movements gradually became mature and standardized. In the case of Hong Kong, it was not until the 1970s that the local term "social movement" and its related practices became popular. Before then, people in Hong Kong associated the idea of mass politics with the Chinese Revolutions in the first half of the twentieth century and accompanied wars. More specifically, during the Cold War, people in Hong Kong viewed social movements as confrontations between the Communist Party and the Kuomintang (KMT). For example, pro-KMT groups organized the "Double Ten Riot" in 1956.[21] They attacked and even killed pro-communist groups. The pro-communist riots in 1967 were triggered by labor disputes, but soon became an extension of the Cultural Revolution in China.

After the riots in 1967, the British colonial government launched its social reforms, allowed freedom of speech, and fostered civil rights. Influenced by movements in Europe and the United States in the 1960s, as well as by the overseas Chinese Diaoyutai movement,[22] a significant number of young people in Hong Kong started to organize demonstrations and protests in the 1970s. These became the prototype of the social movement in Hong Kong, which consisted of pressure groups and local political organizations, making them different from the pro-communist and pro-KMT groups. After the riots, the colonial government drastically adjusted its means of governance, which made more social reforms possible. A mutually constructive interaction between the government and the people began to form.

Then, in the 1980s, the issue of Hong Kong's political future dominated the public agenda. In 1984, China and Britain signed the Joint Declaration, which confirmed that China would take back Hong Kong after 1997. In addition to becoming a special administrative region under "one country, two systems," Hong Kong would move toward democratic autonomy. The power elites managed to maintain their hegemony by articulating the rules for civic engagement with Hong Kong's political prospects in the remaining decade of colonial rule. Against this background, Hong Kong's identity emerged out of "tacit popular acceptance of the existing regime of power."[23] However, this Hong Kong identity was not a strong claim of self-determination, but a sense of belonging to the city and its way of life.

At the time, limited political and legal reforms were carried out to provide more opportunities for social movements, such as enacting human rights laws and encouraging party politics. During the transition period and the early post-handover years, although many political disputes and conflicts took place, Hong Kong civil society generally followed a strategy: conforming to the rules of the game, protecting them, and making moderate changes. For example, all pan-democrats and social activists were fighting for reform according to the following themes: maintaining the status quo, defending the rule of law, protecting freedom, maintaining autonomy from China's political interferences, and promoting democratization. Democratic political parties and civic groups, despite their nuanced differences, played a leading role, representing civil society and engaging in political and social reform. During this period, despite the Chinese Communist rule, Hong Kong's political oppositions were allowed to practice their Western political values in such a moderate way that local mass politics were regarded as an orderly, peaceful, and rational street protest movement. In other words, Hong Kong's social movements in the 1980s developed according to Tilly's definition and represented a form of political gradualism.

The Sino–British Joint Declaration was not the sole influence on the development of modern social movements in Hong Kong. The rise of China and its attempt to change geopolitical relations also impacted the direction of Hong Kong's social movements. In the early 1980s, Deng Xiaoping launched economic reform and an open-door policy in order to seek collaboration with capitalist countries. Some Western elites saw Hong Kong as a springboard for global capital to enter the

Chinese market. Such an outlook was evident in Margaret Thatcher's conciliatory attitude in her negotiations with Beijing over Hong Kong's sovereignty in order to regain the "financial confidence" of the foreign capital in Hong Kong.[24] In this political moment, China was no longer a threat to the West; it might be still be "backward," but it was not considered "dangerous" anymore. Within this context, China's resumption of its sovereignty over Hong Kong was not regarded as a political disaster, either. Broadly speaking, since the 1980s, most Western governments had been using an "engagement policy" to deal with the Chinese Communist Party (CCP), so that only temporary sanctions were imposed after the June 4 crackdown on the Beijing Student Movement in 1989. Many Western governments and observers imagined Hong Kong and China that they would be the successors or remnants of the "third wave of democratization."[25] Western governments believed that China would evolve peacefully if they engage with it in more trades and societal interactions and let it enter the Western-dominated world.

However, China's political evolution was not moving in the direction Western governments expected. The economic reforms under the CCP were capitalist, led by state-owned enterprises, fostering state-regulated markets of all kinds, and actively integrating into the global capitalist system. This kind of economic progress was acceptable to—and perhaps welcomed by—Western political and economic elites. The CCP leaders even became the most important advocates of free trade and the most loyal supporters of the World Trade Organization. As early as 2007, the term "Chinameria" appeared in the media, and the seemingly opposing viewpoints, "Washington Consensus" and "Beijing Consensus," were in fact structurally complementary.[26] At the same time, China's short-lived political reform agenda in the 1980s, including the separation or division of party and government, checks and balances of power, and the monitoring of public opinion, has been completely suppressed since the 1990s. Since around 2011, the CPP's top leaders have repeatedly stressed the need to guard against Western values and their corresponding political reform initiatives.[27] After coming to power, Xi Jinping emphasized a self-defined "path" for the CCP, advocating a form of Chinese political exceptionalism.

In recent years, the Chinese party-state regime has become increasingly eager to rein in its surrounding regions to build up a China-centered geopolitical order. To counter the CCP's efforts, Western countries, led by the United States, have adjusted their "engagement policy." Since Donald Trump took office in 2017, the U.S. government rolled out a series of strategic sanctions targeting key industries in China and Hong Kong. For example, the Hong Kong politician Ho Chi-ping was imprisoned for bribing African officials in the United States, and the Chinese business executive Meng Wanzhou was detained in Canada in response to a U.S. extradition request.[28] Amid progressively hostile conflict between the United States and China, as an offshore Chinese civil society, Hong Kong is the first to bear the brunt.

Gradualism, as the temporal structure of local politics, lost its favor and footing in geopolitical politics and the city as well. Since 2011, the "Hong Kong is dying" or "The city is dying" narrative has been interspersed with livelihood problems and social conflicts. Due to the enactment of the Individual Visit Scheme,[29] a huge number of mainland visitors had swamped Hong Kong on a daily basis until the outbreak of Covid-19 pandemic. Hong Kong's public healthcare system had also encountered a crisis because many mainland Chinese citizens travelled to Hong Kong to give birth to gain right of abode for their children before 2012. Moreover, parallel traders who take advantage of the multiple entry visa policy had introduced traffic congestion and disruption to the daily lives of ordinary people.[30] In addition, the Beijing government repeatedly delayed Hong Kong's universal suffrage, from the original starting point in 2007/2008 to 2012. Then, in 2014, the Standing Committee of the National People's Congress (NPC) established harsh methods for nominating the Chief Executive, triggering the Umbrella Movement. At the same time, the CCP officially announced that it will "fully govern" Hong Kong.

The decline of political gradualism had two major effects politically. The first one is a growing distrust of the governmental system; public support for Leung Chun-ying's and Carrie Lam's governments has been declining. Second, the public support of the pan-democratic camp has also fallen, as its proposals for gradual social change and non-violent social movements seem to be ineffective amid the worsening political situation. Against this background, some activists, identifying themselves as nativist, advocated their "valiant" (*yungmou* 勇武) struggles to differentiate themselves from the pan-democrats. Fashioning themselves as more grassroots, youthful, brave, and spontaneous, the nativists were prone to confrontation and violent tactics.[31] In this light, they attributed the failure of the Umbrella Movement to its peaceful strategies and the incompetence of its leadership. The leaders of the movement, including the Hong Kong Federation of Students and Scholarism, as well as the Trios of Occupy, Tai Yiu-ting, Chu Yiu-ming, and Chan Kin-man, gradually lost their ability to lead the masses in the movement and in street politics. In the subsequent riots in Mong Kok in early 2016, and in the immediate aftermath of the Legislative Council by-election and election, nativist candidates who proposed self-determination and who were inclined to or openly supported Hong Kong's independence stepped onto the political stage. In response, the Beijing government used legal and administrative measures to disqualify many young candidates from standing for election, and to imprison the protesters of the Umbrella Movement and the Mongkok riots. Beijing's suppression eventually created a deeper sense of political fear, further suspicion of the system, and political resistance to China.

While an increasing number of people became disillusioned with political gradualism, Hong Kong youth especially felt it meaningless to follow the rules of game by participating in moderate social movements. The anti-ELAB movement in 2019 was a turning point in Hong Kong's social movement. Before the anti-ELAB movement, Hong Kong did not experience significant mobilization. Even though the pan-democrats lost two by-elections and the broad opposition masses felt pessimistic and depressed, society was relatively quiet and peaceful. However, when Carrie Lam's government took advantage of the murder case of Hong Kong resident Poon Hiu Wing in Taiwan to propose an amendment to the Fugitive Offenders Ordinance, it triggered a fierce controversy and a great sense of crisis in the community.

Lam attempted to establish a new legal mechanism to cover areas without extradition agreements and mutual legal assistance in the past, including Taiwan and mainland China. But many Hong Kongers were worried that China and the SAR government were conspiring to repatriate political dissidents from Hong Kong to the mainland. In other words, many ordinary citizens and media saw this amendment bill as a move to tear down the judicial firewall between mainland China and Hong Kong, which is crucial to the local identity. Amid the panic, the opposition camp launched several marches beginning in March 2019 and culminating on June 12, when a large group of young people wearing masks surrounded the Legislative Council on their own initiative, making it impossible to convene the meeting. While the government refused to back down, confrontations between protesters and police escalated. Since then, social movement in Hong Kong has generated different meanings.

The political crisis in June 2019 triggered many nativists and their followers to reemerge from sectarian isolation and win mass support for their causes, thereby sidelining the leadership of the pan-democrats. Some activists' confrontational tactics, break-in action and siege of the Legislative Council building and police stations, resulted in more use of brutal force from the police. Both sides became involved in a vicious cycle of violence. Beginning in late June, the protesting crowd started to chant the nativist slogans "Revolution of Times" and "Reclaim Hong Kong." Against this background, the slogan and tactic of *laam caau* also emerged.

Laam Caau

The term *caau* originated in a Hong Kong poker game in which a player who holds more than a certain number of cards at the end of a round will be penalized double or triple (*caau*). *Laam caau* refers to the attempt by the underdog to make other players get penalized together. Politically, it dates back to the so-called scorched earth policy, a doomsday scenario promoted by nativists in the 2017–2018 by-elections. This gaming term, widely used by the protesters in 2019, constitutes a special tactic or strategy. For example, protesters on the street would characterize their confrontation with full-gear riot police with their goggles, metal rods, Molotov cocktails, and roadblocks as *laam caau*. Risking injury, arrest, and imprisonment, they believed causing chaos would make the police restless, expose the regime's brutality to the public, and undermine its rule. Those who launched online signature campaigns calling to boycott Hong Kong and mainland Chinese officials regarded their own actions as *laam caau*, too. It is difficult to pin down its references given the wide variety of actions under this banner. What unites these variations, however, is a roughly defined gesture and reasoning peculiar to the activists in 2019. Protesters believed *laam caau* was the most effective way to put pressure on the government. It registered the political ethos when protesters engaged in contentious political processes, conjuring the image of a "dueling moment." The popularity of *laam caau* signaled a loss of patience with the conventional social movement and a refutation of the efficacy of opposition party politics and civic maneuvers. In other words, it opened up a new horizon for temporal experience.

This political background elucidates the significance of online platforms to the movement. In June 2019, a young man with the alias "I want *laam caau*" (later nicknamed "*laam caau* Brother"), made use of LIHKG and Telegram to form diverse task groups to engage in the anti-ELAB movement. Their aims included raising money for international publicity, networking overseas Hong Kongers, and lobbying foreign governments to support the protesters. In a short article published in *Financial Times* in June 2019, the members of the task force of "I want *laam caau*" identified their engagements as a "leaderless movement." They made use of various kinds of information technologies to form a decentralized and transparent network.[32] Regarding the current political institutions and deliberations as ineffective, they exploited new sites online to engage in an intense type of political participation that involved both the ephemeral digital time of agitations and the apocalyptic moment of Hong Kong's struggle. This was a temporal solution to their disappointment about malfunctional political institutions and deliberations.

On August 16, "*laam caau* Brother" made a statement with a prerecording at an assembly at the Chater Garden, Central Hong Kong. He explained that his original plan of "I want *laam caau*" was to target government officials and pro-Beijing officials. He attempted to lobby foreign governments to revoke these politicians' foreign passports for their "betrayal" of Hong Kong. Denying the gains of democratic struggles over the past few decades as "making concessions" and useless, he endorsed all tactics of the movement in 2019. He also highlighted three remarks made by protesters, indicative of three moments of the movement, into a will to act. The first remark was made by a young protester on June 10: "There is no future anyway, why not shoot me to death!" The second moment was when Leung Kai-ping stormed the LegCo building on July 1, and said: "If we lose this time, we will lose in the next ten years." The final one was the slogan "Reclaim Hong Kong, Revolution of Times," chanted by a frontliner after the police shot through his handmade shield with a rubber bullet on July 28. While the first two conveyed the tragic mood of the final struggle, the last referred to fundamental changes to the whole system, if not the sense of revolutionary immortality.[33] The urge of radical changes is evident in the slogan of "Five Demands, Not One Less," demanding the withdrawal of the extradition bill, inquiries into police brutality, and the relaunching of universal suffrage reforms.

Apart from seeking international support and calling for solidarity, "*laam caau* Brother" did not propose any broad strategy. His campaign for international connectivity with Hong Kong and revoking pro-Beijing politicians' foreign passports, which was a quite moderate move, was not consistent with the militant acts seen in Hong Kong's streets. Examined more closely, one may find the strategy of "*laam caau* Brother," to a certain extent, incoherent and unconvincing. Although the street violence might have deterred foreign governments from giving full support to the protesters, his notion of *laam caau* reconfirmed a strong message shared by many locals—"This is the final struggle for Hong Kong! Act now!" This message is less descriptive than performative in demanding an instant change of personal gesture or environmental condition. His call for change, although vague and subject to multiple interpretations and adaptations, showed uncompromising determination and helped sustain people's active engagement in spite of their fragmented social media circles.

In October 2020, "*Laam caau* Brother" revealed his real identity as Finn Lau, a young Hong Kong man working as a surveyor in London. Subsequently, the Hong Kong authorities sought him under the promulgation of Hong Kong National Security Law. However, Lau was by no means the leader of the movement. The leading role he played was largely confined to the campaign for international support and solidarity. But his rhetoric was captivating enough to be echoed by many neophyte activists who followed and joined the movement through social media, encrypted group communication (e.g., Telegram), and the local 24/7 online live news updates of street confrontations. The radical acts on the streets were largely organized on the internet. Along with seditious speeches against the authorities, a lot of protesters shared dangerous information and views on social media, such as sharing information about making Molotov cocktails, vigilantism, and planning to attack the police, which are not in the repertoire of your average social movement. But the term *laam caau* served to fast track many participants to get involved in the movement quickly and intensely as its doomsday scenario helped them skip careful calculations of the cost that they and society as a whole would have to bear.

To say all protesters or the frontliners are ready to sacrifice their lives is hyperbole. But many of them did risk arrest and imprisonment. Disrupting street safety and public transportation, and violent counter attacks on police sounded acceptable to people who engaged in *laam caau*. These challenges to authority and public order were largely seen as unidirectional. For example, some protesters believed that more pressure on police could likely place more stress on the government; then it would be possible to force the government to back down.[34] But would it trigger the government's revenge on the Hong Kong people in the future? Would the violent tactics justify more draconian measures against civil liberties? Putting aside all of these questions, the protesters seemed to believe there was only one option: to further escalate the violence. In the end, "What's next?" was not a question in their consideration. During the anti-ELAB movement, politics was compressed into an instant and an imagined moment of *laam caau*, which gave protesters a strong justification for turning a deaf ear to any moderate veterans. Their logic was, "If the whole game of Hong Kong is coming to the end and I am ready to burn myself with my enemies, why should I care about the price or consequences?" This reasoning was evident in the incident referred to as the "Storming of the Legislative Council Complex" on July 1, 2019. When the black-clad protesters attempted to break through the glass walls and metal doors of the building, a couple of pan-democratic legislators tried to persuade them to stop. But the protesters, not bothering to argue with them, simply removed the legislators from the scene by force.

While the upside of *laam caau* is that the movement's participants have been able to create their own political imagination, experience, and rich tactics, the downside is that the ethical norms of civil society have become blurred—sometimes even completely disregarded. One of the most famous examples of *laam caau* is the gaming tactics. Since July, an ACG-like campaign approach called Hoengseng (Hong Kong) Online was launched to mobilize and recruit participants. The danger of street protests was divided into game-like levels, and roles were assigned using ACG (animation-comics-game) terms, such as "fire magician" for those who threw petrol bombs and "boundary master" for those who set up roadblocks, and so on. The street clashes became a dangerous game. Young people could simply follow the online guidelines to join and upgrade their level of action at any time, and connect with fellow protesters online and in the streets. In November, after the limited success of launching mass strikes, protesters tried to block roads and create "three suspensions" to stop classes, work, and the market. A few radicals even tried to organize terrorist-like actions, such as making bombs and planning to assassinate police officers.

The intensity felt by the protesters and their supporters emerged spontaneously out of a series of emotionally charged incidents and the police's aggressive responses. The fear and pessimism that preceded the movement underwent a sea change after a couple of suicides in the name of "anti-extradition" in June. In August, a young girl named Chan Yin-lam died mysteriously. In November, Chow Tsz-lok, a university student died from falling from a building. Apart from grief and anger, there was a sense of comradery, expressed by the word *sau zuk*, literally meaning "hands and feet." This solidarity connected the participants and forged the sense of a common destiny, or even a collective political will to overcome adversity and build a collective future. A significant number of people "share the pain and desperation as a result of the common experience of oppression," in the words of well-known protester Leung Kai-ping.[35]

In retrospect, this sense of community and political will have gradually replaced the mild expectations for reform in the past, and the struggle has infused local politics with the sense of an existential struggle. However, the voices of *laam caau* could not have spread and taken root so quickly without the police's (and government's) excessive measures. For example, on July 14, the police broke into a shopping center in Shatin. On August 31, they chased protesters down into the Prince Edwards metro station. Then, in November, they conducted the siege of two university campuses. All of these reports of police brutality on the streets and other supposedly peaceful places not only terrified the Hong Kong people, but also aroused rage and sympathy with young protesters. Moreover, clips of young protesters' suffering on social media mobilized more people. In other words, in these surreal scenes, the police, unwittingly or not, revealed the bankruptcy of Hong Kong's status quo and the principle of "one country, two systems." Police behavior did not bring the city back to normalcy; instead, it fueled the people's imagination of life and death moments. In sum, both sides of the confrontations were locked in "terminal reciprocity."[36]

Conclusion: Agency and Time

My analysis of the anti-ELAB movement might give an impression reminiscent of the theories of collective behavior developed by early sociologists; for example, it features spontaneity, ad hoc organizations, an emotional charge, and short-livedness. The agents seem to regress into irrational outbursts after their faith in the institutional norms and values, the social supports of "rational action," breaks down. According to the structural functionalist perspective, collective behavior based on "magical belief" serves as "short-circuiting" a structural problem by diverting attention from its political and institutional complexity.[37] In addition, the leaderless character of the anti-ELAB movement almost rendered useless or irrelevant all analyses of collective action based on "rational choice," "political opportunities," or "resources mobilization."[38] It barely left room for any positive self-correction within the system. Instead, the authorities took advantage of some *laam caau* moves and their rhetoric to justify severe crackdowns and more repressive policing over the years after the anti-ELAB movement.

My intention, however, is not to explain the movement as an outcome of structural strains caused by the collapse of the dominant norms and values. My primary goal is to draw attention to the changing character of social mobilization, specifically to its peculiar temporality. Despite the unruliness of the anti-ELAB movement, the protesters' actions and agency by no means fit the model of collective behavior. It would be a mistake to deem their engagement as a primitive psychological reaction to the breakdown of the system. This movement emerged as a critical episode of the hegemonic struggles not simply for challenging the authorities but also for winning the leadership of mass politics. The idea of a leaderless movement was first advocated by the nativists to dismantle the long-standing leadership of pan-democrats and other civic groups during the Umbrella Movement in 2014. However, they did not end up with the establishment of another leadership. Instead, by accident, a local and decentralized form of instant activism surfaced during the anti-ELAB movement. Under the banner of *laam caau*, the protesters created a mode of agency alternative to that coordinated by pan-democrat-led social movement groups. This renewed intervention features instrumental calculations and a restrained manner of affective expression, if not preclusive of all. The prospect of gradual and long-term democratization, along with the people's expectation for progressive reform and the leadership of the opposition camp, lasting for more than three decades, was eventually shattered. Therefore, the charm of *laam caau* lay in its compressed temporal experience, which conveyed a sense of urgency through grief and anger. It was an intensity mediated by an apocalyptic narrative about Hong Kong's political future, strongly felt through the new media's instantaneity. Even though all *laam caau* moves may not do much to improve or resolve the situation in Hong Kong, they are as understandable and "persuasive" as we mean by "rational," however problematic.[39]

This phenomenon is not unique to Hong Kong. Ashish Rajadhyaksha insightfully juxtaposes Hong Kong's political crisis to the military lockdown of Kashmir in 2019. In his discussion on the *jihad* and *laam caau*, he correctly points out "an anthropocenic incapacity to imagine a future for any of us,"[40] a space of psychosocial dynamics leading to the decomposition of subjectivization and social integration. The similar symptom, symptomatic of the legitimacy crisis of the nation-state and the collapse of the public sphere, is characterized differently by others as fragmented futures of "erratic and anarchic sovereignties," "forms of paranoid apocalypsis," and evacuation of near futures.[41] All these depictions remind us that by not rebuilding the space for a rigorous reexamination of the past (rather than an outright rejection of or nostalgic adherence to it) and envisioning an interim future, reclaiming reflexivity from instant activism and online communicative practices cannot succeed. If our game is not confined to instant activism, it is still too early to call it over.

NOTES

This research is supported by the Direct Grant (DG) sponsored by the Lingnan University in Hong Kong (DR20A7 [101123]).

1. Zizi Papacharissi, *Affective Publics: Sentiment, Technology, and Politics* (Oxford: Oxford University Press, 2015), 45.
2. Jodi Dean, *Publicity's Secret: How Technoculture Capitalizes on Democracy* (Ithaca: Cornell University Press, 2002), 172–173; Thomas Poell and José van Dijck, "Social Media and Activist Communication," in *The Routledge Companion to Alternative and Community Media*, edited by Chris Atton, 527–537 (London: Routledge, 2015); Heidi Herzogenrath-Amelung, "The New Instantaneity: How Social Media Are Helping Us Privilege the (Politically) Correct over the True," *Media Culture & Society* 38, no. 7 (2016): 1080–1089.
3. Keonyoung Park and Hyejoon Rim, "'Click First!': The Effects of Instant Activism via a Hoax on Social Media," *Social Media + Society* 6, no. 2 (2020): 1–13.
4. Ipsos MORI, "How Britain Voted in the 2015 General Election," Ispos, https://www.ipsos.com/en-uk/how-britain-voted-2015; Richard H. Kimberlee, "Why Don't British Young People Vote at General Elections?," *Journal of Youth Studies* 5, no. 1 (2002): 85–98; Andrew Russell, Edward Fieldhouse, Kingsley Purdam, and Virinder Kalra, *Voter Engagement and Young People* (London: The Electoral Commission, 2002); Pippa Norris, *Young People and Political Activism: From the Politics of Loyalties to the Politics of Choice? Report for the Council of Europe Symposium, Young People and Democratic Institutions: From Disillusionment to Participation* (Strasbourg, 2003); Jorge Benedicto, "The Political Cultures of Young People: An Uncertain and Unstable Combinatorial Logic," *Journal of Youth Studies* 16, no. 6 (2013): 712–729; James Sloam and Matt Henn, "The Silent Revolution in Youth Political Engagement," in *Youthquake 2017: The Rise of Young Cosmopolitans in Britain* (Cham: Springer International Publishing, 2019), 43–69.
5. Anthony Giddens, *New Rules of Sociological Method: A Positive Critique of Interpretative Sociologies* (London: John Wiley & Sons, 2007), 127; Johannes Fabian, *Time and the Other: How Anthropology Makes Its Object* (New York: Columbia University Press, 2014), 24; Pierre Bourdieu, *Pascalian Meditations* (Stanford: Stanford University Press, 2000), 206.

Edward P. Thompson, "Time, Work-Discipline and Industrial Capitalism," *Past & Present* 38, no. 1 (1967): 56–97.

6. David Harvey, *The Condition of Postmodernity* (London: Polity, 1989); Ben Agger, *Fast Capitalism: A Critical Theory of Significance* (London: Routledge, 1989); Hartmut Rosa, *Social Acceleration: A New Theory of Modernity* (New York: Columbia University Press, 2013).
7. Paul Ricoeur, *Time and Narrative*, vol. 1 (Chicago: University of Chicago Press, 1984), 3.
8. Peter Nagy and Gina Neff, "Imagined Affordance: Reconstructing a Keyword for Communication Theory," *Social Media + Society*, 1, no. 2 (2015): 1–9.
9. Since the implementation of the National Security Law in Hong Kong in July 2020, a number of pro-democracy parties, unions, media, and other independent organizations have closed down. Hundreds of opposition politicians and activists were arrested and placed into custody. The Beijing government also overhauled Hong Kong's electoral system to guarantee that only the candidates deemed "patriotic" by authorities could run for election. For details, read: Michael Smith, "China Says 'Non-patriots' to Be Banned from HK Government Roles," *Financial Review*, February 23, 2021, https://www.afr.com/world/asia/china-says-non-patriots-to-be-banned-from-hk-s-government-roles-20210223-p5751f; Zen Soo and Huizhong Wu, "How Democracy Was Dismantled in Hong Kong in 2021," Associated Press News, December 30, 2021, https://apnews.com/article/china-hong-kong-beijing-democracy-national-security-9e3c405923c24b6889c1bcf171f6def4.
10. Stuart Hall, *The Hard Road to Renewal: Thatcherism and the Crisis of the Left* (London: Verso, 1990), 10.
11. Stuart Hall, "Signification, Representation, Ideology: Althusser and the Post-Structuralist Debates," *Critical Studies in Mass Communication* 2, no. 2 (1985): 91–114.
12. Ernesto Laclau, *New Reflections on the Revolution of Our Time* (London: Verso, 1990), 160.
13. Jürgen Habermas, *The Legitimation Crisis* (London: Heinemann, 1976).
14. Bob Jessop, "The Organic Crisis of the British State: Putting Brexit in its Place," *Globalizations* 14, no. 1 (2017): 133–141.
15. Brian Fong Chi-hang, "Stateless Nation within a Nationless State: The Political Past, Present, and Future of Hongkongers, 1949–2019," *Nations and Nationalism* 26, no. 4 (2019): 1069–1086; Alvin So Yiu Cheong, "The Making of Hong Kong Nationalism," *Asian Nationalism Reconsidered* (London: Routledge, 2016), 135–146; Rwei-ren Wu, "The Lilliputian Dreams: Preliminary Observations of Nationalism in Okinawa, Taiwan and Hong Kong," *Nation and Nationalism* 22, no. 4 (2016): 686–705.
16. Vittorio Morfino, "The Layers of History and the Politics in Gramsci," in *A Companion to*

Antonio Gramsci: Essays on History and Theories of History, Politics and Historiography, edited by Davide Cadeddu, 47–56 (Leiden: Brill, 2020).

17. Martin Heidegger, *Being and Time* (Oxford: Blackwell, 1980), 426; Craig A. Clancy, "The Politics of Temporality: Autonomy, Temporal Spaces and Resoluteness," *Time & Society* 23, no. 1 (2014): 28–48.
18. Jordana J. George, and Dorothy E. Leidner, "From Clicktivism to Hacktivism: Understanding Digital Activism," *Information and Organization*, 29, no. 3 (2019): 1–45; Jennifer Earla and R. Kelly Garrett, "The New Information Frontier: Toward a More Nuanced View of Social Movement Communication," *Social Movement Studies* 16, no. 4 (2017): 479–493; Lawrence R. Frey and Kevin M. Carragee, eds., *Communication Activism* (Cresskill, NJ: Hampton Press, 2007).
19. Charles Tilly, *Social Movement, 1768–2004* (Boulder: Paradigm Publishers, 2004).
20. Charles Taylor, *Modern Social Imaginaries* (Durham: Duke University Press, 2004), 5.
21. In the post-war era, both the pro-KMT camp and the local communists developed their grassroots organizations in squatter areas and resettlement housing areas. On October 10, 1956, in Lei Cheng Uk Estate, a resettlement housing area in Kowloon, the pro-KMT people hang the national flag of the Republic of China (ROC) and the large "Double Ten" (the national day of ROC) emblem on the wall of the housing blocks. The resettlement office staff removed them, which resulted in violent attacks by protesters. The confrontations escalated into strikes, arson, and attacks on police and pro-communist people in the following days. The rightist trade unionists and the Triad were involved in them. Finally, the colonial government sent riot police and British forces to disperse the rioters. The riots led to fifty-nine deaths and hundreds of injuries. Thousands were arrested, and some of them were deported.
22. The government of the ROC has asserted its sovereignty over the Diaoyu Islands, a group of uninhabited islands in the East China Sea. However, they were under the U.S. army's occupation of Okinawa in the postwar years until 1972. In 1970, the announcement of the U.S. government's decision to return Okinawa and the Diaoyu Islands to Japan triggered overseas Chinese students' protests. In 1971, in the name of "defending Diaoyu Islands," Hong Kong students staged protests against the U.S. and Japanese governments.
23. Stephen Chan Ching Kiu, "Future Un-imagined," *Hong Kong Cultural Studies Bulletin* 4 (1995): 24.
24. Margaret Thatcher, *The Downing Street Years* (New York: HarperCollins, 1993), 260.
25. Stephan Haggard and Robert R. Kaufman, "Democratization During the Third Wave," *Annual Review of Political Science* 19, no. 1 (2016): 125–144; Samuel P. Huntington, "Democracy's Third Wave," *Journal of Democracy* 2, no. 2 (1991): 12–34; Mathew Y. H.

Wong, "Democratization," in *Comparative Hong Kong Politics: A Guidebook for Students and Researchers*, 105–135 (Singapore: Springer Singapore, 2017).

26. Handel Jones, *Chinamerica* (New York: McGraw-Hill Professional Publishing, 2010); Niall Ferguson, "Team Chimerica," *Washington Post*, November 17, 2008.
27. Guoguang Wu, "'Repressive Capitalism' as the Institutional Crystallization of China's Transition," in *China's Transition from Communism: New Perspectives*, edited by Guoguang Wu and Helen Lansdowne, 188–210 (London: Routledge, 2016).
28. Jufei Wan, and Bryan R. Reckard, "Huawei and the 2019 Cybersecurity Crisis: Sino–US Conflict in the Age of Convergence," in *Communication Convergence in Contemporary China: International Perspectives on Politics, Platforms, and Participation*, edited by Patrick Shaou-Whea Dodge, 97–126 (East Lansing: Michigan State University Press, 2021); Oriana Skylar Mastro, "Cooperation and Competition with China: The Need for New Approaches" (Statement before the Senate Committee on Foreign Relations Subcommittee on East Asia, the Pacific, and International Cybersecurity Policy On the China Challenge, Part 2: Security and Military Developments, September 5, 2018).
29. In 2003, the Beijing government launched the Individual Visit Scheme to allow mainland travelers to visit Hong Kong and Macau on an individual basis rather than in tour groups.
30. These trading activities caused shortages of household goods in Hong Kong and traffic congestion. For details, see Iam-chong Ip, "Politics of Belonging: A Study of the Campaign against Mainland Visitors in Hong Kong," *Inter-Asia Cultural Studies* 16, no. 3 (2015): 410–421.
31. Iam-chong Ip, *Hong Kong's New Identity Politics: Longing for the Local in the Shadow of China* (New York: Routledge, 2020).
32. Linden Chai and Ko-ng Lui, "Leaderless Hong Kong Movement Thrives on Open Use of Technology," *Financial Times*, June 20, 2019.
33. "The Laam Caau Declaration at the Rally 'UK–US–Hong Kong Alliance, Power to the People,'" YouTube video, 5:47, posted by "HongKonger," August 16, 2020, https://www.youtube.com/watch?v=djPjML29NPw.
34. Aaron Mc Nicholas, "Hong Kong's 'Frontliners' Say They're Ready to Die for the Movement," *Bloomberg*, September 28, 2019, https://www.bloomberg.com/news/articles/2019-09-27/hong-kong-s-frontliners-say-they-re-ready-to-die-for-movement.
35. Brian Leung Kai-ping, "I am Leung Kai-ping," video-recorded public speech, "Stand with Hong Kong, Power to the People Rally," Chater Garden, Central, August 16, 2019.
36. Stephen Chan Ching-kiu, "Some Thoughts on the Endgame of Resistance: Ngo-Yiu Laam-Chaau as Terminal Reciprocity," *Inter-Asia Cultural Studies* 21, no. 1 (2020): 99–110.
37. Neil Smelser, *Theory of Collective Behavior* (New York: The Free Press, 1962), 8, 73.

38. Mancur Olson, *The Logic of Collective Action* (Cambridge, MA: Harvard University Press, 1965); John McCarthy and Mayer Zald, "Resource Mobilization and Social Movements," *American Journal of Sociology* 82, no. 6 (1977), 1212–1241; Sidney Tarrow, *Struggling to Reform: Social Movements and Policy Change during Cycles of Protest* (Ithaca: Cornell University, 1983).
39. Nick Crossley, *Making Sense of Social Movements* (Buckingham: Open University Press, 2002), 49.
40. Ashish Rajadhyaksha, "The Great Transition: Our Battles over History," *Inter-Asia Cultural Studies* 21, no. 1 (2020): 57–89.
41. Charles Piot, *Nostalgia for the Future: West Africa after the Cold War* (Chicago: University of Chicago Press, 2010); Kathleen Stewart and Susan Harding, "Bad Endings: American Apocalypsis," *Annual Review of Anthropology* 28, no. 1 (1999): 285–310; Jane I. Guyer, "Prophecy and the Near Future: Thoughts on Macroeconomic, Evangelical, and Punctuated Time," *American Ethnologist* 34, no. 3 (2007): 409–421.

Public Transportation as a Vehicle of Resistance against the Mainlandization of Hong Kong

Andrew Gilmore

Since 1997, when Hong Kong was handed back to the People's Republic of China (PRC) from Great Britain, the challenge of mainlandization—the Communist Party of China's (the Party) ever-increasing influence over the city—has been a source of great tension. Although regular protests regarding Hong Kong's future have taken place across the city in the years following the handover, Hong Kong's democratic plight has been etched into the global consciousness through several prolonged, colorful, and sometimes violent protests—namely, the Umbrella Revolution of 2014 and the Hard Hat Revolution of 2019. Intrigued by some of the protest tools and strategies used throughout the Umbrella Revolution, in late 2017, I wrote and later published an essay about the use of double-decker buses as *in-situ* tools of protest that communicated an air of "creative disrespect" and functioned as artistic billboards promoting resistance to mainlandization.[1]

In June 2019, Hong Kongers once again took to the streets of their city in response to an extradition bill proposed by the Hong Kong government that, if passed, would have allowed suspected criminals in Hong Kong to be transferred to mainland China to face trial. This time, however, the protest—now rebranded by some as the Hard Hat Revolution—quickly escalated. While the Umbrella

Revolution was described as "civil," "humorous," "charming," "polite," and "artistic," the Hard Hat Revolution was described as "a war," an "escalating humanitarian crisis," and "a de facto war about the future of democracy" not just in Hong Kong and China but across the globe.[2] What began as peaceful opposition to a proposed government policy grew into "something much more fundamental" as Hong Kong "unraveled" and "descended into chaos."[3]

Using the Umbrella and Hard Hat Revolutions as case studies, in this chapter, I highlight the contrasting ways in which pro-democracy-supporting Hong Kongers used public transportation as a vehicle to express their resistance to mainlandization. I point to the contrasting protest tactics of the two revolutions, revealing how resistance to mainlandization was communicated through the performance of two different (post)colonial Hong Kong identities. I extend my earlier bus-themed essay by adding analysis of another form of public transportation and its infrastructure that was harnessed by protesters in 2019: Hong Kong's Mass Transit Railway system (MTR).

To advance my analysis, I use Jean Paul Ricœur's strategy for appropriating historicity or the "historical condition." For Ricœur, historicity provides "creative possibilities for framing an alternative reality" by weaving together "perspectives of the expectation of the future, the reception of the past, and the experience of the present."[4] Using Ricœur's framework, my analysis uncovers three transformations of public transportation for each protest that converted mobility from the mundane to the political and, in doing so, became narratives that expressed Hong Kong's resistance to mainlandization. The three transformative narratives of the Umbrella Revolution are: an allegory of history (a British past), a monument of living death (a Chinese present), and dreams of democracy (a Hong Kong future). The three transformative narratives of the Hard Hat Revolution are fueling recolonization (Hong Kong's past), an illusion of death (Hong Kong's present), and facing a nondemocratic nightmare (Hong Kong's future).

Analyses of political discourse to frame resistance—such as those offered by Hsin-I Cheng and Ming Xie and Chin-Chung Chao earlier in this volume—are vital to enriching our understanding of political engagement. However, in a bid to look beyond the discursive nature of political analysis, scholars have sought to explore how materiality might help to analyze both political power and political action in a bid to unpack the relations among society, the public, the economy, and the state.[5] A city's infrastructure—its roads, tracks, bridges, tunnels, cables, and sewers is often figured as unremarkable, remaining largely invisible and taken for granted by those who use it and benefit from it.[6] However, infrastructure "undergirds modern society" and represents the backbone of a city, thus its communicative capacity as a potential form of resistance should not be overlooked.[7] Indeed, when disrupted, infrastructure can transform from tedious to remarkable. Anthropologist Hannah Knox refers to this disruption as "infrastructural rupture." For Knox, ruptured infrastructure offers an "imaginative resource" for political participation, wherein citizens can harness political possibilities to articulate their claims and desires.[8]

When considering the political possibilities of infrastructure, transportation infrastructure is often a "go-to" vehicle for resistance. Although Rosa Parks's refusal to give up her seat on a bus to a white man in Montgomery, Alabama, in 1955 is perhaps the most well-known example of public transit acting as "a space of dissent," for multiple reasons, public transit systems have continued to serve as platforms for resistance.[9] Public transit is a part of "the commons" and thus is a shared space in which individuals from varying demographics, neighborhoods, and levels of social privilege interact and coexist.[10] However, despite offering "a lifeline for citizens," public transportation systems are also viewed by many as an "apparatus of governmentality."[11] For example, in Hong Kong, the Government of the Hong Kong Special Administrative Region of the PRC (GovHK) owns 76 percent of the city's MTR system and, as a result, became "a ripe setting" for acts of civil disobedience in 2019.[12] Although the "tsunami of protests that swept across six continents" in 2019 were not all directly linked to public transportation services, it is no coincidence that public transit and its infrastructure act as a site of agitation that connects the dots among specific, localized incidents such as resistance to fare hikes (Santiago), increased policing (New York City), and more widespread dissatisfaction with policies and policymakers (Hong Kong).[13]

The repetitive nature and mundaneness associated with the everyday use of public transportation means that, when used as a tool of resistance, parallels can be drawn to Michel de Certeau's notion of the recomposition of spaces and the use of everyday rituals and familiar practices that he describes as "poetic ways of making do" or "bricolage" that can "offer a voice to the silent majority."[14] For de Certeau, everyday life is a "sphere of resistance," and acts that appear to be mundane and routine can, in fact, be used as a form of rhetorical invention that transforms them into the extraordinary through "artisan-like inventiveness."[15] This inventiveness can serve as a "lightning rod" that transforms the often banal into symbolic communicative modes that harness meaning and communicate contested fears, emotions, concerns, and hopes.[16] Hong Kong protesters' use of public transportation enacted this transformative process.

The Mainlandization of Hong Kong

The anger and consternation of many Hong Kongers had been bubbling since Hong Kong was returned to the PRC in 1997 following 150 years of British colonial rule. Since the city's return to China, many Hong Kongers report having increasingly experienced the effects of the "mainlandization" of their city.[17] *Mainlandization* is defined by David Gruber as "the encroaching influence" of mainland China in Hong Kong.[18] Ching Cheong, meanwhile, is more specific, positing that mainlandization represents the "the erosion of freedom, plurality, tolerance, respect for human rights and the rule of law" in Hong Kong.[19]

I argue that mainlandization is shorthand for Chinese nationalism through which President Xi seeks to achieve his "Chinese Dream." Xi's goal is to rejuvenate the Chinese nation through the "peaceful reunification" of Chinese territories. However, the "Chinese Dream" also seeks to extend China's reach and challenge the global might of foreign powers, including the Unites States.[20] Thus, although this chapter focuses on Hong Kong, to think more about the wider context of this volume, my analysis of the Umbrella and Hard Hat Revolutions has relevance much further afield. Indeed, Hong Kong's desire for independence and political and social reform is not unlike events occurring across the globe. A study of Hong Kong's protests is salient because it contributes to the study of social movements that focus on identity in an era of nationalism. Donald Trump's U.S. presidential election victory in 2016, the United Kingdom's (UK) decision to leave the European Union, and the mainlandization of Hong Kong are examples of events that are "largely products of rising nationalism" and highlight global issues of localist and nationalist divides.[21] Consequently, similarities can be identified between the events that have taken place and the protest strategies in Hong Kong and those that have occurred across the globe, including in Chile, India, Mexico, Germany, Iraq, Kazakhstan, Myanmar, and, of course, the United States.[22]

Returning to Hong Kong, as the Party has sought to exert greater political, economic, social, and cultural control and influence over the city, many people in the city believe they are being forced to converge with China in a way that amounts to a form of colonization that Stephen J. Hartnett refers to as "postcolonial colonialism."[23] As a result of this forced convergence and China's ever-growing influence over Hong Kong, many Hong Kongers claim that the uniqueness of their city and its culture are slowly ebbing.[24] However, as I point to in the conclusion to this chapter in the face of Party provocation, as many Hong Kongers have worked to differentiate themselves from the mainland and resist the Party's attempts to homogenize and recolonize Hong Kong under one Chinese national identity, Hong Kongers have unintentionally created their own sense of close-minded nationalism.

Although the foundations of the Umbrella and Hard Hat Revolutions were built on calls for a democratic Hong Kong, many of the tensions that underpin the protests are identity conflicts between Hong Kong and the mainland and, as I will highlight, the changing identities of Hong Kongers. Like Hong Kong's social and political context, the notion of identity in the city is also unique, complex, and far from homogeneous. Since Hong Kong's return to China, the city has become a "powder keg" of "narrower and more combative" ideologies and identities that have resulted in a toxic and often violent mentality of us (democracy-supporting Hong Kongers) versus them (mainlanders), but even among Hong Kongers, the notion of identity is not black and white.[25] A "battlefield of ideologies" means Hong Kong citizens share diverse perspectives.[26] For example, while "yellow" supporters (mainly comprised of young Hong Kong activists) hold grievances against GovHK and the city's police force, "blue" supporters (mainly comprised of older Hong Kongers) support the same institutions their children and grandchildren are battling against.[27]

These divisions stem largely from the fact that older Hong Kongers have firsthand experience of the extreme efforts the Party will deploy to support its totalitarian rule. Having risked their lives by migrating from the mainland in the 1950s to escape "the chaos of the Chinese civil war and Maoist repression," these experiences have led some members of Hong Kong's older generation to value stability over radical political change, a mindset that appeases the Party.[28] Instead of stability, many young Hong Kongers—a cohort that Ben Bland refers to as "Generation HK"—want real change; a life that is not dictated by the Party. They have a "stronger sense of belonging" to the city than older generations, in part because they have only experienced Hong Kong as a fairly free society that is separate from the mainland.[29] Prior to the Umbrella and Hard Hat Revolutions, unlike their parents and grandparents, young Hong Kongers had not witnessed Party brutality and its heavy forms of governance firsthand.

The Umbrella Revolution: Double-Decker Buses as Artistic Canvases of Democracy

When activists spontaneously flooded the streets of Hong Kong in 2014, vehicles including taxis; a police van; and, most notably, seven buses were abandoned in the Nathan Road area of the city's Mong Kok district.[30] Positioned on the Kowloon side of Hong Kong, the area of Mong Kok is one of the most densely populated places on the planet. A major transportation hub, Mong Kok is served by multiple subway lines, train tracks, and countless bus and mini-bus routes. The recently opened Express Rail Link enables travel between Hong Kong and multiple mainland cities in less than an hour. If Hong Kong is, as it is so often labeled, *China's gateway to the West*, Kowloon is Hong Kong's gateway to the mainland.

As the first road built in Kowloon in 1861, Nathan Road has historical connections to Hong Kong's former colonizer, the United Kingdom. Referred to as the *Golden Mile* in the years preceding World War II, Nathan Road today is Kowloon's main thoroughfare, passing through the heart of Mong Kok. Lined with shops, museums, high-end hotels, and restaurants, Nathan Road is a mecca for tourists as well as locals going about their daily routines. On the night of September 28, 2014, however, the bustling Nathan Road came to a grinding halt.

As an uncontrollable swell of pro-democracy-supporting Hong Kongers filled Nathan Road, a number of double-decker bus drivers abandoned their vehicles and fled the scene, perceiving that no safe driving routes were available to them, the stricken buses took on a new life form. As the sun rose on Hong Kong after a night of unrest that resulted in police's deployment of teargas and pepper spray, photographs began to circulate that showed the abandoned double-decker buses that protesters had transformed from large, mobile machines into static, artistic canvases calling for democracy. I now move to present the three transformations of double-decker buses that encapsulated the tensions among UK, Chinese, and Hong Kong cultures by communicating narratives of Hong Kong's past (colonization), present (mainlandization), and future (democracy).

Buses as an Allegory of History: A Portrayal of the (British) Past

From department stores to restaurants to numerous streets named after British figures and places, British architecture remains imprinted onto Hong Kong's postcolonial landscape, and British influence is still deeply woven into everyday life in Hong Kong. One of the strongest and most distinctively British symbols can be found driving on the left-hand side of the city's roads—double-decker buses. A century after the first double-decker Omnibus was manufactured in the UK, the Kowloon Motor Bus Company (KMB) introduced the first double-decker bus onto the streets of Hong Kong in 1949.

Hong Kong protesters used double-decker buses to communicate their sense of Britishness via a nod to Hong Kong's period of British colonization. Hong Kong protesters' use of double-decker buses to portray the past aligns with communication scholars' Gerard Hauser and Erin McClellan's assertion that the "polyvocal" aspects of everyday discourse can be hidden under the surface of its denotative meanings and often do not appear in full view of official discourse. Because polyvocal discourse is "situated in the present as symbols of the past," it is able to communicate interpretations and reinterpretations of messages that are "not necessarily recognized as contrary or resistant by those in power."[31] Similarly, de Certeau writes of the use of "clandestine" tactics or "tactical ruses" and the "clever tricks of the 'weak' within the order of the 'strong'" that can reconfigure dominant spaces" to communicate something unanticipated, and thus "challenge systems of order."[32] And so, the humble double-decker bus and its ties to British colonialism became a canvas to communicate democratic desires.

One of the functions of history, suggests Ricœur, is to "lead us back to those moments of the past where the future was not yet decided, where the past was itself a space of experience open to a horizon of expectation." For Hong Kongers, the overtly British symbol of the double-decker bus represented a reenactment of the past in the present. Ricœur asks if the past is "intelligible any other way than as a persisting present,"[33] and for many Hong Kongers, the persistent present was an ever-increasing sense of mainlandization. As a result, Umbrella Revolution protesters used double-decker buses and the past they represented to showcase their fears about mainlandization and Chief Executive CY Leung.

A Monument of Living Death: A Representation of the (Chinese) Present

To many, CY Leung—Hong Kong's chief executive from 2012 to 2017—perfectly encapsulated the tenets of Hong Kong's mainlandization.[34] Leung's position as the "synecdochical embodiment of the [Chinese] nation" and his acceptance of and compliance with the will of the Party made him a divisive and unpopular figure among many Hong Kongers.[35] During the Umbrella Revolution, protesters applied "artisan-like inventiveness" to two buses to send a message to Leung.[36]

The front center panel of any bus, displaying the route number and final destination, is highly visible. Several buses abandoned on the streets of Hong Kong had their route numbers changed to #689 or #N689 (the night bus equivalent) and their destinations changed to "HELL." A highly symbolic number in Hong Kong, 689 represents the small number of votes that Leung needed to be elected to preside over a city of more than seven million-people. Umbrella Revolution protesters' transformation of one bus, however, went beyond a simple renumbering and displayed "an attitude of creative disrespect, a radical opposition to the illegitimately powerful."[37] The bus, which I refer to as *Bus 689*, was transformed into a monument commemorating the death of a living person—CY Leung. In addition to decorating Bus 689 akin to a Chinese-style shrine to a deceased person, complete with flowers, candles, and an image of the "deceased," Hong Kongers redesigned the route for the bus. Created to replicate authentic Hong Kong bus-stop signage, the new route included fictitious stops to mock Leung and the Party. These stops included renaming the Hong Kong and Shanghai Bank Corporation as *Hell Shade Banking Corporation*, Earth Temple as *Death's Door*, and Gloucester Road as *High Protest Road*.

Although the selection of a cemetery plot and the installation of a gravestone by individuals who wish to plan their self-commemoration before death is a rather unusual act, a larger public gesture of commemorating the death of a living individual is undeniably eerie, especially for the individual who is still living and breathing.[38] Jack Santino posits that temporary memorials at sites of trauma are often seen as "a portal to the otherworld, a place where two-way communication can occur" between the living and the dead.[39] While the number of Hong Kong protesters occupying the city's streets continued to grow, and demands for Leung's resignation reached a fever pitch, Leung persisted in refusing to communicate with protesters. Acting out Leung's living death was perhaps the only way Hong Kong protesters could directly communicate with their unelected leader. Moreover, the portrayal of Leung's death via a bus transported Hong Kongers to an "otherworld," in which Leung ceased to exist and democracy had been achieved.

A hope for protesting Hong Kongers—and, perhaps, a fear for Leung and the Party—may have been that designing Leung's coffin and commemorating his death would lead to a loss of face for Hong Kong's perceived oppressors. An important sign of respect in Chinese culture, to save face is to maintain one's reputation and to keep dignity and honor intact at any cost; to lose face is embarrassing and shameful.[40] A loss of face functions as possibly the only realistic victory for Hong Kong protesters. Thus, the use of death—a taboo subject in Chinese culture that many citizens are afraid of speaking about for fear it will come true[41]—and marking the passing of a living individual also can be viewed as an immense loss of face for Leung.

By bringing Leung's death into the present, Hong Kongers manipulated time by preempting his demise and bringing the future into the present. To this end, by commemorating the demise of Leung and the system of mainlandization he represented, the Hong Kong protesters combined representations of their British past and Chinese present in a bid to communicate an aspirational vision of the city's future in which possibilities for a democratic Hong Kong could be realized.

Buses as a Democratic Dream: A (Hong Kong) Future

Umbrella Revolution protesters used the exteriors of the abandoned double-decker buses to explicitly communicate their visions for Hong Kong's future. Although a majority of the handwritten signs placed on the buses were in Cantonese, a number of messages were in English. Most of these messages were situated around the area where the buses' license plate would normally be visible. In addition to covering the license plate with "HK 1997"—a clear gesture to the city's 1997 handover from the UK—one sign simply stated "Peace please," accompanied by the globally recognized peace symbol. The back of one bus carried an image of one of the most famous nonviolent activists of all time, Martin Luther King, Jr. A man who used the "power of words and acts of nonviolent resistance . . . to achieve seemingly-impossible goals,"[42] King fit the bill as a father figure to oversee the protesters of the Umbrella Revolution. He also was no stranger to the protest function of buses—in 1955, King served as spokesperson throughout the thirteen-month bus boycott in Montgomery that was sparked by the arrest of Rosa Parks.

Because protesters had covered the buses' wheels, the vehicles no longer looked like buses. The buses took on a new skin—a new life through the materiality of paper—through which paper and cardboard carried Hong Kongers' democratic pleas. The wheel-less buses not only communicated the powering down of everyday transportation but also the shutdown of the city and the closure of a global financial hub. However, although road closures led to the abrupt halt of the city's "unfettered capitalism"—an element of the city's existence that distinguishes it from the mainland—both local and international organizations and brands were unwittingly embroiled in Hong Kongers' resistance to mainlandization.[43]

One bus (which I have named the Lukfook Bus) was forced to stop under the sign outside of a Lukfook Jewellery store.[44] As one of the most prestigious jewelry chains in Hong Kong, the organization claims to be the "Brand of Hong Kong, Sparkling the World."[45] Despite being forced to close its doors, however, the ephemeral paper skin added by protesters to the Lukfook Bus connoted the organization's corporate mission "to contribute to the community through enforcing communications with the public."[46] In one advertisement on the wall of the Lukfook store's exterior, a young woman who usually would be casting a watchful eye over the store is now looking down at the store's latest piece of merchandise: the Lukfook Bus. The serendipity of the bus's resting place meant that Umbrella Revolution protesters had unknowingly harnessed the branding of one of the city's billion-dollar businesses that, incidentally, has a huge footprint in mainland China. The artwork of the Umbrella Revolution superseded the branding of Lukfook and became a brand associated with Hong Kong's democratic desires and resistance to mainlandization.

Other brands also became inadvertently tangled in Hong Kongers' fight for democracy. While most of the reachable surfaces on the buses were covered with messages, the logos of two companies were still visible and recognizable. The first was a brand with which Hong Kongers were familiar: *Advanced Toiletries*. A local company specializing in toiletries and health and hygiene products, the decision not to fully cover over the Advanced Toiletries logo could be seen as connoting Hong Kong's pro-democracy supporters' desires to clean up and sanitize the political and plutocratic mess that had befallen Hong Kong. While the Advanced Toiletries logo was still largely visible, on another bus, part of a logo in the top left-hand corner of the bus was covered with a handwritten protest sign. While only the letters *S* and *O* were visible, the globally recognized brand that was partly obscured was unmistakable—the oval shape, white background, blue edging, and red lettering were clearly parts of the *Esso* logo. Having its branding on the side of a static bus appeared to go against what Esso is known for: producing the fuel that helps vehicles and machinery to operate. The bus may have been static and not using Esso-produced fuel, but by being unwittingly featured on a static billboard, Esso—an organization founded and based in the United States—was communicating resistance to mainlandization and fueling the Umbrella Revolution.

Serving as the city's bus provider since 1993, KMB's slogan is "moving forward every day."[47] For seventy-nine days, however, the promise of its slogan was not fulfilled as traffic came to a standstill in Hong Kong, and immobile buses were transformed into static walls showcasing protesters' attempts to move Hong Kong forward to a time of genuine universal suffrage. The handwritten and visual calls for democracy on a static bus transformed the vehicles into fixed billboards. By doing so, Umbrella Revolution protesters successfully used elements of their present and past to communicate their desired vision for a democratic future.

Throughout the Umbrella Revolution, pro-democracy-supporting Hong Kongers predominantly protested in ways that aligned with the ideological beliefs for which they have been historically renowned. The Umbrella Revolution protesters' actions were disciplined and orderly; the protest was "rooted in community"; and the participants were "unique," "sweet," "polite," and "not in the least threatening."[48] For many Umbrella Revolution protesters, the on-street occupation was simply an extension of their everyday life, albeit in a very public setting, as they continued to do the same things they did in their homes on any given day. They slept, cooked, ate, and studied on the streets and continued to use public transport, albeit not to travel. Instead, double-decker buses became signboards and monuments to telegraph their democratic desires, their resistance to mainlandization, and their commitment and determination to remain steadfast in embracing their identity as nonviolent and artistic protesters. The Umbrella Revolution, then, "retained that uniquely Hong Kong character."[49] Four-and-a-half years later, however, Hong Kong was in the midst of a very different kind of protest, and the city's protesters were forced to reconsider the foundations of their Hong Kong identity.

The Hard Hat Revolution: The Subway as a Relic of Democracy

As they had done during the Umbrella Revolution, many Hong Kongers treated the city's public transportation in respectful and thoughtful ways during the early stages of the Hard Hat Revolution. For example, after police used teargas to disperse protesters at Kwai Fong MTR station, a number of Hong Kongers arrived with washcloths to wipe down soiled surfaces.[50] A similar scene unfolded as Hong Kongers armed with face masks, gloves, and wet wipes cleaned up teargas residue at Sham Shui Po MTR station.[51] The artistic side of Hong Kong protesters was also on display in the early stages of the Hard Hat Revolution. Safety and information stickers from MTR trains were redesigned in a move that paralleled Hong Kongers' redesign of bus routes in 2014. Mimicking the colors and other graphic design elements of existing MTR signage, the redesigned safety stickers offered "guidelines" to help MTR "get [on] the right track." The rules, shared by Joshua Wong on Twitter, included: "no more closing stations," "do not allow police to use stations as satellite police stations," and "don't cancel trains."[52] Like the 2014 redesign of route for Bus 689, in 2019, the 777 bus service (representing the number of votes that Carrie Lam required to become the city's chief executive) was rerouted to "Hell." These moments of creative protest were fleeting, however, and, as the Hard Hat Revolution progressed, chaotic scenes of fire and smashed glass became common as the city's MTR stations became sites of violent conflict.

In late July 2019, clashes broke out when masked assailants, purported to be members of Hong Kong's organized crime syndicates, attacked other citizens in Yuen Long MTR station.[53] Video footage shows masked individuals indiscriminately attacking people on platforms, concourses, and trains with sticks and steel rods. As Hong Kongers scrambled for cover, at least forty-five individuals, including journalists, a Hong Kong Democratic Party lawmaker, pro-democracy protesters, and non-protesting citizens, including a pregnant woman, were reported to have been injured.[54] The most violent episode that linked the Hard Hat Revolution to Hong Kong's MTR network occurred on the night of August 31, 2019 (hereafter 831), when dozens of MTR stations were vandalized. As police began to disperse the crowds and clear streets after another day of heavy protests, protesters vandalized ticket machines and customer-service booths at Mong Kok MTR station, broke turnstiles at Tung Chung MTR station, spray painted ticket machines at Kwun Tong MTR station, smashed glass platform screen barriers at Prince Edward MTR Station, and threw objects onto tracks that connect Hong Kong Island to the city's airport. The *South China Morning Post* reported that, by the end of the weekend, a third of MTR stations had been severely damaged.[55]

Hong Kong's Recent Past: Fueling Recolonization

First operating in 1979, today, Hong Kong's MTR system is the most popular mode of transport in the city, covering over 140 miles of the city and transporting over six million passengers a day.[56] Celebrated for its affordability, first-class safety record, and world-class efficiency, the MTR is regarded as a jewel in Hong Kong's crown.[57] Although tenuous links are evident between Hong Kong's British colonial past and the architecture of the MTR system—it was commissioned by the UK government—unlike the use of double-decker buses throughout the Umbrella Revolution, the ways in which public transportation infrastructure was used during the Hard Hat Revolution was built upon a past that was not linked to Britain's occupation of Hong Kong. Instead, the violent use of public transportation during the Hard Hat Revolution communicated an exigency that was linked to and fueled by a past comprised of the years between the end of the Umbrella Revolution and the beginning of the Hard Hat Revolution.

In the years following the Umbrella Revolution, Hong Kong, China, and, indeed, much of the world underwent seismic change. In Hong Kong, as the Party's influence and control over Hong Kong increased, further calls for democratic reform in the city were repeatedly ignored. In 2015, Hong Kongers' anxieties about increasing mainlandization were heightened when five employees of a Hong Kong book shop were reported missing. The employees of Causeway Bay Books—a shop that stocked controversial texts banned in mainland China—were widely believed to have been taken to the mainland for interrogation.[58] In the midst of these events, the Party announced plans for its Greater Bay Area project, an economic plan that would see nine southern mainland cities, Macau, and Hong Kong linked through the joint development of technology, infrastructure, and finance.[59] These developments, along with the opening of the world's longest sea-crossing bridge that links Hong Kong to the mainland Chinese city of Zhuhai, meant that, for many Hong Kongers, the mainland and the reach of the Party felt closer than ever before.[60] This uneasy feeling was exacerbated when, in 2018, the Party approved the removal of the two-term limit for its leader.[61] Effectively, President Xi Jinping can lead the Party until his death.[62]

Returning to Hong Kong politics, in 2016, Scholarism—the student-led activist group that played a major role in the Umbrella Revolution—disbanded. Realizing that "street activism is not enough if we want to fight for a better future," Scholarism leader Joshua Wong stated that in order to make real change in Hong Kong, a new political party—called Demosistō—was needed to "enter the system" and "shape the political agenda" of the city.[63] As members of "Generation HK" were putting forth plans to forge a new political future for the city, Leung surprised everybody by announcing he would not be running for his expected second term as the city's chief executive.[64]

In March 2017, Carrie Lam became the Party's "preferred candidate" to become Hong Kong's next—and first female—chief executive.[65] Lam professed to be "honest and straightforward" and her promise to embark on a new style of governance and "heal the city's social and political divide" gave Hong Kongers hope for a better future.[66] This hope, however, was short lived and, in hindsight, previous calls for "anyone but CY" were shortsighted.[67] Within weeks of Lam being sworn in as the chief executive, six pro-democracy politicians—including Demosistō's Nathan Law—were disqualified from Hong Kong's legislative council after refusing to take the oath pledging allegiance to the Party. For Law, the oath was a "political tool being used by the regime to suppress Hong Kong's people."[68] Later, Law along with fellow pro-democracy activists Joshua Wong and Alex Chow were sentenced to serve jail time for their parts in the Umbrella Revolution that had ended almost three years earlier.[69]

The past events and experiences that Hard Hat Revolution protesters used as fuel for their treatment of public transportation may not have covered as long a historical period as that of British rule used by Umbrella Revolution protesters in 2014. However, returning to the work of Ricœur, the trauma, fallout, and experiences of the four-and-a-half years that separated the Umbrella and Hard Hat Revolutions led to a "horizon of expectation" that stoked fears among many Hong Kongers about the future of their city.[70] The events in the years that divided the Umbrella and Hard Hat Revolutions meant that, by August 2019, Hong Kong was a vastly different place from the one that showcased fun and artistic appeals for democracy in 2014. The impending passing of the extradition bill meant that a sense of immediacy had gripped the city, which, in turn, led to an increase in and intensity of violent events. In 2014, protesters did not go home because they decided to erect tents and sleep in the streets. In 2019, however, protesters were concerned that they might not make it home, wondering if they would have to die for their cause. Some young Hong Kongers even admitted that they had written letters to their families in case they died while attempting to achieve their goal of a democratic future.[71]

Hong Kong's Present: Commemorating an Illusion of Death

By August 2019, the two-month-old Hard Hat Revolution had taken "a darker turn" and entered "a dangerous new phase." Images broadcast in the United States and across the globe showed "marauding mobs" and masked individuals attacking police, and civilians and setting fire to the city.[72] Hong Kong resistance could no longer be characterized as predominantly nonviolent. Instead, a city renowned for being orderly and civil had turned into a chaotic, almost dystopian society. Protesters wearing military-grade gas masks and protective equipment damaged property and infrastructure with hammers, iron rods, and Molotov cocktails; police, also in military fatigues, responded with teargas, pepper spray, and rubber bullets. Almost every image of Hong Kong from this period is filled with clouds of smoke from either police or protesters. Indeed, as thick plumes of acrid teargas hung over all corners of the city on a daily basis, reports suggest that 88 percent of Hong Kongers were exposed to its effects.[73] Hong Kong had morphed into a violent and, at times, lawless city.

As Special Tactical Squad officers of the Hong Kong Police Force made their way inside Prince Edward Station firing pepper balls and teargas on the night of 831, chaos ensued. For many observers and commentators, police officers who entered train carriages and began beating passengers with batons acted no differently from the masked gang members who had beaten passengers in Yuen Long station a little over a month earlier.[74] For de Certeau, by their very nature, railway trains constitute a "closed system." Trains may be moving, but those onboard are immobile. Passengers can see things flashing by the window, but they cannot get to them because they are only permitted to alight at designated and predetermined stops. Those on board a train, then, are "incarcerated" and forced to follow rules and procedures.[75] Although trains at Yuen Long station were stationary, those inside the cars were essentially imprisoned and unable to flee as police approached.

In terrifying scenes captured by *Stand News*, police officers were seen storming a subway car and using batons to beat cowering passengers who were trying to defend themselves with umbrellas. In the same video and accompanying images, officers were seen firing pepper spray directly into the faces of a family huddled on the floor of the same subway car. One man tried to cover his face as a jet of pepper spray ricocheted off the side of his face and bounced off the door of the subway car behind him. To his left, a man whose face mask slipped below his mouth and whose hair was visibly wet after having faced a deluge of teargas could be seen raising his hands as though surrendering. As the video ends, the man is screaming as his female companion cowers while she grabs his leg for protection.[76] According to Senior Police Superintendent Yu Kaijun, officers used "professional experience" and "appropriate force" when dealing with the situation.[77]

Reports suggest that, in the immediate aftermath of the police's storming of Prince Edward Station on 831, journalists and medics were denied entry to the station. These reports led to fears that something sinister was taking place beneath the streets.[78] As rumors continued to circulate in Hong Kong that three—or as many as six people—were killed in Prince Edward Station on 831, discrepancies fueled reports among Hong Kongers of three "missing" people presumed to have been beaten to death by police officers. Despite a lack of evidence that anyone had died or was even missing, in the days and weeks that followed, the B1 entrance/exit of Prince Edward Station was transported into an ephemeral monument to the "deceased." Each night, Hong Kongers gathered at the B1 entrance/exit of Prince Edward Station to lay white flowers—representing death in Chinese culture—in memory of those reported to be missing and presumed dead. They lit candles, burned incense, and surrounded the station with handwritten signs that lamented the failing of "one country, two systems"; accused the city's police force of being "corrupt" and "lawless"; and called for the "truth" behind the beatings on 831 to be revealed. Images show the entrance to Prince Edward Station completely covered in flowers and cardboard signs calling for justice. The retractable gate was no longer visible as a wall of flowers had grown to the ceiling of the entrance, and the MTR logo had been spray painted over, leaving only the words *Prince Edward Station*.[79] The removal of the MTR branding meant that Prince Edward Station no longer belonged to the majority-government-owned MTR: it now belonged to mourning Hong Kongers.

In 2014, Umbrella Revolution protesters used double-decker buses and their "experience of the present" to appropriate historicity and frame an "alternative reality" in which CY Leung was dead and Hong Kong had achieved genuine universal suffrage. In reality, however, everybody knew that Leung was still alive. In 2019, the Hard Hat Revolution used the B1 entrance/exit of Prince Edward Station to communicate another illusion of death, but a different, less positive future for Hong Kong. Hong Kongers turned Prince Edward MTR Station into an ephemeral monument that mourned the "loss" of fellow citizens and, in doing so, communicated Hong Kong's present during which citizens were missing and presumed dead and their calls for justice were ignored by the government.

As was the case with Bus 689, of course, there were no bodies; nobody had died. Unlike the use of CY's image on Bus 689, however, pictures of the "dead" could not be displayed at Prince Edward Station; there were no names or other identifying links to any individuals. The only thing that was dead was Hong Kong's way of life. As one interviewee told me, "Hong Kong is over, there's no way back for us. Hong Kong is dead."[80] As the specter of common threats—mainlandization and the Party—increases, perhaps the frequent cycle of violent protests, clouds of teargas, and police-government collusion is simply "a new normal" for Hong Kong as Hong Kongers face a future in which they are "condemned to live in a permanent political crisis."[81]

Hong Kong's Future: Facing a Nondemocratic Nightmare

Despite multiple appeals from protesting Hong Kongers and the general public, MTR refused to release CCTV footage of the events that took place inside Prince Edward Station on the night of 831. Under pressure, MTR did eventually release still images through a press release stating that comprehensive footage was not available because three of the CCTV cameras had been "damaged or defaced" by protesters.[82] Although Civic Party lawmaker Jeremy Tam Man claimed that the "selective screenshots" left more questions than answers, Party newspaper *China Daily* reported that the CCTV "reconstruction . . . squashed" rumors of any deaths occurring on 831.[83] Home to eight of the top-ten most surveilled cities in the world, China has "reached a nadir" as a modern surveillance state. As the Party "exploits and weaponizes" data to control its citizens, China is "a harbinger of what society looks like when surveillance proliferates unchecked."[84] Consequently, despite possessing comprehensive CCTV footage, the refusal to release it further highlights the mainlandization of Hong Kong, showcasing the Party's desire to control all aspects of daily life to meet its own ends.[85]

MTR's decision to close Prince Edward Station for three days after 831 did little to quell conspiracy theories claiming that MTR was in cahoots with the Hong Kong police by allowing them to remove and destroy evidence of any wrongdoing.[86] These persistent accusations were fueled by a number of events that took place throughout the Hard Hat Revolution. On multiple occasions throughout the protest movement, MTR stations near protest sites were closed by officials. By halting services, reducing trains, and ending scheduled services early, MTR appeared to be intentionally keeping Hong Kongers from attending street occupations by enacting a "de facto curfew."[87] MTR responded to these accusations by claiming that the reduced services were a result of needing to repair the extensive damage that had been caused by protesters.

Since the events of 831, many Hong Kongers avoid using the service because they believe the subway system had been "weaponized" by the city's government.[88] By doing so, the MRT—now rechristened by protesters as the Communist Party's Railway or, as one interviewee told me, Commie-MTR—had morphed from being regarded as "the lifeblood" of the city to being "another tool of government suppression."[89] Graffiti on one customer-service booth at Mong Kok Station labeled the MTR "dogs," while a ticket machine at Sha Tin station was tagged with the Cantonese character for "Party."[90] For many Hard Hat Revolution protesters, the MTR was no longer a "public thing" or part of "the commons"; it was now simply a tool through which the Party and the Hong Kong police could control Hong Kong and its citizens. Protesters, many of whom pride themselves on the politeness, punctuality, and law-abiding tendencies that typify Hong Kong culture, turned against the method of transportation that makes their city run like clockwork. At multiple points throughout the Hard Hat Revolution, MTR was forced to temporarily close almost half of its stations to ensure passenger safety.[91] Hong Kong's ever-reliable and much-lauded subway system designed to transport life across the city had stopped and become a relic of any form of democracy that the city once had or could hope to have—an act that provided a glimpse into the future of Hong Kong.

Although basic infrastructure such as transportation systems may seem less alluring than flags, songs, and other patriotic symbols, it still has the power to bind communities together. Indeed, as a "public thing," transportation is one of "democracy's necessary conditions" and, without it, "democratic life is not just impoverished but unsustainable."[92] For some, the disruption of the MTR had nothing to do with calls for democracy. For non-protesters, the act of blocking travel was "not merely an inconvenience"; it was tantamount to taking away from Hong Kongers "a piece of freedom to go about their own business."[93] Although commenting on the MTR, the Hong Konger quoted here could easily have been sharing her fears about mainlandization and Hong Kong's future. In 2014, Umbrella Revolution protesters made temporary adjustments to a handful of double-decker buses, and those not participating in the protest could avoid the disruption by choosing other routes or modes of transportation. In 2019, however, Hard Hat Revolution protesters forced the closure of multiple subways lines and thus severely disrupted the daily lives of nonparticipants in the movement. Everybody was made aware of and forced to face Hong Kong's present and potential future.

Even double-decker buses—the vehicles that Hong Kongers transformed with creative disrespect in 2014—were treated differently in 2019. Abandoned buses, once again stranded in the road, had their tires slashed and their windshields smashed. The words "Join Us" were spray-paint on the front windows of one bus.[94] Although the damage could eventually be repaired, in 2019, Hong Kongers were prepared to deface their city and create more lasting damage. Unlike the use of nonpermanent and easily removable sticky notes and paper that gave double-decker buses ephemeral skins in 2014, the tactics in 2019 had a more enduring effect. A week after the events of 831, Hong Kongers' disdain toward MTR intensified. Burning MTR stations became a persistent theme as stations at Causeway Bay, Wanchai, Mong Kok, Cheung Sha Wan, and Central were all set on fire. Entrances to multiple stations were set on fire using cardboard, traffic cones, wood, and any other flammable material available.[95] Meanwhile, below ground, ticket machines, turnstiles, and customer-service and ticket booths were smashed and set on fire.[96] Fire and the act of burning is "a key form of resistance" that allows for powerful statements about rebirth, resurrection.[97] Quite simply, as a form of protest, the act of setting something alight removes or alters traces of what was there before and, moreover, demands attention and forces individuals to bear witness to the destruction that is taking place.

Businesses immediately outside MTR stations also suffered. In 2014, the Lukfook Bus was framed by a designer brand that originated in Hong Kong. In 2019, however, the situation in Hong Kong had escalated and, as fires set by Hard Hat Revolution protesters impacted businesses that surrounded MTR stations, high-end, luxury brands that are recognized globally became inadvertently involved in Hong Kong's resistance to mainlandization. The Italian luxury brand Bulgari is clearly visible in one picture on one side of Exit F of Central Station as flames engulf the front of the station.[98] Another luxury brand, Louis Vuitton, also unwittingly became embroiled in the protests. In an image that shows protesters running from police, the Louis Vuitton store next to Central Station is barely visible behind plumes of teargas. Wearing all black, the fleeing protesters could easily be mistaken for window-display mannequins showcasing the latest Hong Kong essential fashion accessories of gas masks, backpacks, and umbrellas.[99] Although there is no indication that protesters targeted Bulgari or Louis Vuitton, several globally recognized brands were intentionally targeted by pro-democracy protesters. Apple; video game company Activision

Blizzard; and Starbucks, were just some of the organizations that were damaged as a result of their perceived connections to Beijing or, even worse, their willingness to toe the party line in order to protect their revenue streams.[100]

The act of destroying businesses and other important infrastructure in a city that prides itself on its capitalism led to yet more deep divides among Hong Kongers. For some, vandalizing stores and disrupting transportation systems crossed a line and amounted to "an infringement on regular people's right to daily life." For others, however, although regrettable, damaged stores and transport infrastructure were "worthy sacrifices."[101] The enactment of violence was for "the greater good" and represented the only strategy through which these Hong Kongers perceived they could achieve their goal.[102] Thus, Hong Kong is perhaps more divided than ever before as a wedge is driven between the city's conflicted mindsets and approaches to resisting mainlandization.

Conclusion

In this chapter, I have analyzed the use of public transportation and its infrastructure as a vehicle to explore different approaches to resistance in Hong Kong in a bid to reveal the changing protest strategies and (post)colonial identities generated by mainlandization. My analysis revealed six transformations that politicized public transportation and its infrastructure during the Umbrella and Hard Hat Revolutions to express Hong Kong's resistance to mainlandization and, with it, two contrasting identities.

In 2014, participants in the Umbrella Revolution embraced artistic flair and innovative ideas that transcended the confines of regular social movements to ensure that their message reverberated around the globe. Umbrella Revolution participants harnessed and maintained everyday practices and ways of being that were familiar to them. Although unsuccessful in their plight, Hong Kongers were applauded for their polite and predominantly nonviolent forms of protest as an expression of resistance to mainlandization. These actions of polite protest—which extended to their transformation of double-decker buses—aligned with the values that were traditionally associated with Hong Kong and a majority of its citizens.

In the face of the increasing threat of mainlandization through the enactment of the extradition bill and with the failure of the Umbrella Revolution weighing heavily on their minds, in 2019, Hong Kong's pro-democracy protesters responded in a different way from how they had in 2014.[103] Hard Hat Revolution participants changed the nature of their strategies dramatically by abandoning most things that were familiar to them. The Hard Hat Revolution was violent and, at times, deadly. Instead of maintaining the city and its infrastructure, as had been the case throughout the Umbrella Revolution, Hard Hat Revolution protesters turned to destruction as the city's MTR was vandalized, fires were lit across the city, and physical violence became prevalent.

The scars of the Hard Hat Revolution were more permanent than the Umbrella Revolution not just by way of the graffiti and scorch marks on the city's infrastructure. By allowing violence, the very nature of what, for many, being a Hong Konger meant had been eroded. Acts of physical violence; showing a lack of respect to authority figures, such as the Hong Kong police, GovHK, and the Party; and destroying the city's infrastructure violated Hong Kong identity. In short, Hard Hat Revolution protesters fought fire with fire, thus adhering to the Chinese proverb, "use the barbaric way to fight against the barbarian" (以夷制夷). However, this approach violated the renowned and well-trodden approach to protest that Hong Kongers have traditionally taken.

Hong Kongers' attempts to resist mainlandization have seen them embrace a "glocal consumer identity." However, while uniting many pro-democracy-supporting Hong Kongers, this new-found identity has bought with it some troubling undercurrents, including hints of xenophobia, nativism, ethnocentrism, and anti-immigrant sentiment directed toward those from mainland China. Troublingly, as Lee notes, these sentiments harness the potential to legitimize the xenophobic, "superiority stance" rhetoric expressed by U.S. president Donald Trump and his supporters. Indeed, in 2019, Hong Kong—a city where, historically, "orderliness is sacrosanct" and diversity is embraced—became a battleground as Hong Kongers caught "a disease that has plagued the United States: partisan polarization" regarding nationalism.[104] Some Hong Kongers accused those from the mainland of stealing jobs, taking school places, and inflating house prices. Furthermore, mainlanders in Hong Kong were referred to as "yellow thugs," "savages," "locusts," and "Chinazis" who should "go back" to where they came.[105] Echoing Trump's slogan of "Make America great again," calls to "reclaim Hong Kong" were increasingly heard across the city throughout the Hard Hat Revolution as large groups of democracy-supporting Hong Kongers became "closed and inward-looking."[106]

Trump was on the minds of many Hard Hat Revolution protesters, and the divisive U.S. president was an ever-present topic of conversation with many of the protesters whom I interviewed. When I was in Hong Kong during the early stages of the Hard Hat Revolution, I asked protesters what message I should take back with me to the United States. "Tell Trump to help us" and "Tell the president we need him" were frequent responses.[107] Despite repeated calls for assistance from—and despite embracing some of his rhetoric—Trump and the U.S. government were not allies of Hong Kong's city's pro-democracy supporters. Trump's decision—after much deliberation—to sign the Hong Kong Democracy Legislation to impose possible sanctions on Party interference in Hong Kong affairs was a fleeting victory as Trump's tone and stance toward Hong Kong changed.[108] The city lost its "special status" as, among other things, a trade partner to the United States as a result of a newly enacted National Security Law. As far as Trump was concerned, Hong Kong was "no longer sufficiently autonomous from mainland China."[109] In response, U.S. Customs and Border Protection announced that any product entering the United States from Hong Kong was now to be labeled "Made in China."[110] The U.S. government's rhetoric made many shudder, but it only clarified what was already known: Hong Kong's future is clear; mainlandization has fully taken hold.

With a new U.S. administration came hope. Calling out the Party for undermining the "enjoyment of rights and freedoms" in Hong Kong, Biden offered fleeing Hong Kongers a "temporary safe haven" in the United States.[111] However, this approach only encourages Hong Kongers to completely abandon their home. Hong Kongers who choose to stay in the city are powerless. Neither of Hong Kong's (post)colonial identities and their approaches to resistance that I have highlighted in the chapter will be tolerated. Indeed, under the city's new National Security Law, sabotaging transport is deemed a "terrorist activity," and damaging government buildings is considered "an act of subversion," both punishable by life in prison. As the first anniversary of 831 approached, Hong Kongers were warned that they faced arrest if they laid flowers at Prince Edward MTR Station.[112] The introduction of the National Security Law means that, in Hong Kong, "the price of bravery has risen dramatically," requiring that Hong Kong's pro-democracy supporters reassess how to resist mainlandization and reimagine what it means to be a Hong Konger.[113]

NOTES

1. Andrew Gilmore, "Hong Kong's Vehicles of Democracy: The Vernacular Monumentality of Buses during the Umbrella Revolution," *Journal of International and Intercultural Communication* 13, no. 4 (2020): 329, https://doi.org/10.1080/17513057.2019.1646789.

2. Wendy Gan and C. Haut, "Puckish Protesting in the Umbrella Movement," *International Journal of Cultural Studies* 20, no. 2 (January 23, 2017): 162–176, https://doi.org/10.1177/1367877916683823; Samanthi Dissanayake, "Things That Could Only Happen in a Hong Kong Protest," *BBC News*, September 30, 2014; Verna Yu, "Hong Kong: 'Revolution Is War, and No War Is without Bloodshed,'" *Guardian*, August 31, 2019; Jimmy Choi, "HK On Verge of Humanitarian Crisis: Protesters," *Radio Television Hong Kong*, August 12, 2019, https://news.rthk.hk; "Anatomy of a Protest: Inside Hong Kong's Fight for Freedom," *Washington Post*, November 1, 2019, https://www.youtube.com/watch?v=I7pxzy4rwb8.
3. "Hong Kong: Violent Standoff between Police and Students," *News Night*, BBC, November 16, 2019, https://www.youtube.com/watch?v=1qfDzK3qYg4; Lillian Suwanrumpha, "Hong Kong Is on Fire," *ABS-CBN News*, September 1, 2019; Stuart Heaver, "Hong Kong's Quiet and Determined 'Hard Hat Revolution' Is Braced for a Lurch towards Civil War," *Independent*, July 26, 2019; "Hong Kong Streets Descend into Chaos on China's National Day," *Guardian*, October 1, 2019.
4. Gerard A. Hauser, *Vernacular Voices: The Rhetorics of Publics and Public Spheres* (Columbia: University of South Carolina Press, 1999), 160; Jean Paul Ricœur, *Time and Narrative*, vol. 3 (Chicago: University of Chicago Press, 1990), 206.
5. Jürgen Habermas, *The Structural Transformation of the Public Sphere: An Inquiry into a Category of Bourgeois Society*, trans. Thomas Berger and Frederick Lawrence (Cambridge: Polity, 1989); Hannah Knox, "Affective Infrastructures and the Political Imagination," *Public Culture* 29, no. 2 (2014): 363–384, https://doi.org/10.1215/08992363-3749105; Bruno Latour, "Where Are the Missing Masses? The Sociology of a Few Mundane Artifacts," in *Shaping Technology / Building Society: Studies in Sociotechnical Change*, edited by Wiebe Bijker and John Law (Cambridge, MA: MIT Press, 1992), 225–258.
6. Knox, "Affective Infrastructures"; Susan Leigh Star and Karen Ruhleder, "Steps toward an Ecology of Infrastructure: Design and Access for Large Information Spaces," *Information Systems Research* 7, no. 1 (1996): 111–134, https://doi.org.10.1287/isre.7.1.111.
7. Brian Larkin, "The Politics and Poetics of Infrastructure," *Annual Review of Anthropology* 42, no. 1 (2013): 328, https://doi.org.10.1146/annurev-anthro-092412 15552.
8. Knox, "Affective Infrastructures," 374.
9. Robin D. G. Kelley, "Congested Terrain: Resistance in Public Transportation," in *Race Rebels: Culture, Politics, and the Black Working Class*, edited by Robin D. G. Kelley, 55–75 (New York: Free Press).
10. Bonnie Honig, *Public Things: Democracy in Disrepair* (New York: Fordham University Press, 2017).

11. Michel Foucault, *The Birth of Biopolitics: Lectures at the Collège de France, 1978–1979* (New York: Picador, 2010); Terry Nguyen, "Why Protests Around the World Often Involve Public Transportation," *Vox*, November 7, 2010.
12. Lucas Clay, "Train Operator at 99.9% Efficiency," *Sydney Morning Herald*, June 26, 2009; Nguyen, "Why Protests."
13. Robin Wright, "The Story of 2019: Protests in Every Corner of the Globe," *New Yorker*, December 30, 2019; Nguyen, "Why Protests."
14. Michel de Certeau, *The Practice of Everyday Life* (Berkeley: University of California Press, 1988), xi, xv, xvii.
15. Ben Highmore, *Everyday Life and Cultural Theory: An Introduction* (New York: Routledge, 2002), 151. de Certeau, *Practice of Everyday Life*; Michael Middleton, Aaron Hess, and Danielle Endres, *Participatory Critical Rhetoric: Theoretical and Methodological Foundations for Studying Rhetoric In Situ* (Lanham, MD: Lexington Books, 2015).
16. Candice Rai, *Democracy's Lot: Rhetoric, Publics, and the Places of Invention* (Tuscaloosa: University of Alabama Press, 2016), 5.
17. Alex Lai, "Thousands Protest Hong Kong's China-Fication," *CNN*, July 2, 2012.
18. David R. Gruber, "The (Digital) Majesty of All Under Heaven: Affective Constitutive Rhetoric at the Hong Kong Museum of History's Multi-Media Exhibition of Terracotta Warriors," *Rhetoric Society Quarterly* 44, no. 2 (March 15, 2014): 149, https://doi.org/10.1080/02773945.2014.888462.
19. C. Cheong, "Hong Kong Fears Mainlandization," *China Post*, September 9, 2011.
20. Patrick Shaou-Whea Dodge, ed., *Communication Convergence in Contemporary China: International Perspectives on Politics, Platforms, and Participation* (East Lansing: Michigan State University Press, 2020); Didi Kristen Tatlow, "Nationalistic and Chasing the 'Chinese Dream,'" *New York Times*, January 12, 2011.
21. Taisu Zhang, "The Anti-Mainland Bigotry of Hong Kong's Democracy Movement," *Foreign Policy*, November 29, 2016.
22. Fareed Zakaria, "Why Are There so Many Protests across the Globe Right Now?," *Washington Post*, October 24, 2019; Sarah Zheng, "From Belarus to Thailand: Hong Kong's Protest Playbook Is Spreading Everywhere," *Inkstone*, August 19, 2020; Tim Hume and Tess Owen, "Traffic Cones, Leaf Blowers, and Other Brilliant Tactics U.S. Protesters Are Taking from Hong Kong's Playbook," *Vice News*, June 3, 2020.
23. Stephen John Hartnett, "Alternative Modernities, Postcolonial Colonialism, and the Storm of Progress in Tibet," in *Imagining China: Rhetorics of Nationalism in an Age of Globalization*, by Stephen J. Hartnett, Lisa B. Keränen, and Donovan S. Conley, 91–138 (East Lansing: Michigan State University Press, 2017).

24. Lai, "Thousands Protest."
25. Max Fisher, "'One Country, Two Nationalisms': The Identity Crisis Behind Hong Kong's Turmoil," *New York Times*, September 27, 2019.
26. Xiang Li, "Hong Kong: A Battlefield of Ideologies," *Georgetown Public Policy Review* (blog), December 12, 2014.
27. Ge Yunfei, "Blue vs. Yellow: Divide Is Ripping Families in Hong Kong," *China Global Television Network*, September 3, 2019.
28. Tim Sullivan and Sylvia Hui, "Protests Reveal Unease over Hong Kong's Identity," *Washington Examiner*, October 12, 2014.
29. Ben Bland, *Generation HK: Seeking Identity in China's Shadow* (Melbourne: Penguin Press, 2017), 5; Chermaine Lee, "Hong Kong Protests Pit the City's Young against the Old," *Deutsche Welle*, June 28, 2019.
30. Philip Wen, "Hong Kong Residents Unite in the Fight for Democracy," *Sydney Morning Herald*, October 3, 2014.
31. Gerard A. Hauser and Erin Daina McClellan, "Vernacular Rhetoric and Social Movements: Performances of Resistance in the Rhetoric of Everyday Life," in *Active Voices: Composing a Rhetoric for Social Movements*, edited by Sharon McKenzie Stevens and Patricia M. Malesh, 23–46 (Albany: SUNY, 2009).
32. De Certeau, *Practice of Everyday Life*, 40; Robert J. Topinka, "Resisting the Fixity of Suburban Space: The Walker as Rhetorician," *Rhetoric Society Quarterly* 42, no. 1 (January 2012): 66, 75, https://doi.org/10.1080/02773945.2011.622342.
33. Ricœur, *Time and Narrative*, 227, 144.
34. David R. Gruber, "A Beijing Wolf in Hong Kong: Lufsig and Imagining Communities of Political Resistance to Chinese Unification," in *Imagining China: Rhetorics of Nationalism in an Age of Globalization*, edited by Stephen John Hartnett, Lisa B. Keränen, and Donovan Conley, 371–394 (East Lansing: Michigan State University Press, 2017); Katie Hunt, "C.Y. Leung: Hong Kong's Unloved Leader," *CNN*, October 3, 2014, https://www.cnn.com.
35. Gruber, "Beijing Wolf," 372.
36. De Certeau, *Practice of Everyday Life*.
37. R. Stamm, quoted in Tracey Pyscher and Brian D. Lozenski, "Throwaway Youth: The Sociocultural Location of Resistance to Schooling," *Equity & Excellence in Education* 47, no. 4 (October 2, 2014): 531–545, https://doi.org/10.1080/10665684.2014.958964.
38. Thomas R. Dunn, *Queerly Remembered: Rhetorics for Representing the GLBTQ Past* (Columbia: University of South Carolina Press, 2016).
39. Jack Santino, "Between Commemoration and Social Activism: Spontaneous Shrines, Grassroots Memorials, and the Public Ritualesque," in *Grassroots Memorials: The Politics

of Memorializing Traumatic Death, edited by Peter Jan Margry and Cristina Sánchez-Carretero, 97–107 (New York: Berghahn, 2011).

40. Joo Yup Kim and Sang Hoon Nam, "The Concept and Dynamics of Face: Implications for Organizational Behavior in Asia," *Organization Science* 9, no. 4 (1998): 522–534; "Saving Face in China," *New York Times*, December 13, 2010.
41. Henry Fersko-Weiss, "The Chinese Approach to Death and Dying," *International End of Life Doula Association*, June 23, 2017.
42. "About Dr. King," The King Center, https://thekingcenter.org.
43. K. K. Tse, "Hong Kong's Protests Are Just the Tip of the Iceberg: Capitalism Is in Crisis across the Globe," *South China Morning Post*, September 13, 2019.
44. Gilmore, "Vehicles of Democracy," 338.
45. "Corporate Profile: Lukfook Jewellery," Lukfook Jewellery, https://www.lukfook.com.
46. "Corporate Statement: Lukfook Jewellery," Lukfook Jewellery, https://www.lukfook.com.
47. "Mission & Vision," *Kowloon Motor Bus Company*, 2016, http://www.kmb.hk.
48. Victoria Hui, "Hong Kong's Umbrella Movement: The Protest and Beyond," *Journal of Democracy* 26, no. 2 (2015): 111–121; Matt Sheehan, "The Weird World of Hong Kong's Umbrella Movement in 9 Photos," *HuffPost*, December 6, 2017; Peter Ford, "Hong Kong's Umbrella Revolution: The Politest Protests Ever?," *Christian Science Monitor*, October 1, 2014.
49. Dissanayake, "Things That Could."
50. "Hong Kong Protesters Vandalise MTR Station," *Citizen Daily*, September 26, 2019, https://www.citizendaily.news.
51. Adam Withnall, "Hong Kong Protesters Return to Clean up after Clashes at Sham Shui Po Metro Station," *Independent*, August 19, 2019.
52. Joshua Wong, Twitter post, October 12, 2019, 3:34 a.m., https://twitter.com/joshuawongcf/status/1182952625106350080.
53. Karen Leigh and Kari Soo Lindberg, "Triad Gangs Linked to Hong Kong Protester Attacks: Who Are They?," *Bloomberg*, July 24, 2019.
54. Jeffie Lam, Danny Mok, and Alvin Lum, "White-Clad Mob Brutally Attacks Hong Kong Protesters in MTR Station, Injuring 45," *South China Morning Post*, July 22, 2019; Kris Cheng, "Chaos and Bloodshed in Hong Kong District as Hundreds of Masked Men Assault Protesters, Journalists, Residents," July 22, 2019.
55. Kanis Leung, "Dozens of Railway Stations Vandalised by Protesters over Weekend, Says Hong Kong's MTR Corporation, Warning Some Services May Not Resume by Monday," *South China Morning Post*, September 2, 2019.
56. "MTR Corporation: Annual Report, 2018," MTR Corporation, https://www.mtr.com.hk/

archive/corporate/en/investor/annual2018/EMTRAR18.pdf.

57. "Protesters Vandalise"; Lucas Clay, "Train Operator at 99.9% Efficiency," *The Age*, June 26, 2009; Matthew Keegan, "How Public Transport Actually Turns a Profit in Hong Kong," *Guardian*, March 19, 2019.
58. Alex W. Palmer, "The Case of Hong Kong's Missing Booksellers," *New York Times*, April 3, 2018.
59. "Greater Bay Area: China's Ambitious but Vague Economic Plan," *BBC News*, February 26, 2019.
60. "World's Longest Sea Crossing: Hong Kong-Zhuhai Bridge Opens," *BBC News*, October 23, 2018.
61. "China's Xi Allowed to Remain 'President for Life' as Term Limits Removed," *BBC News*, March 11, 2018.
62. Liu Zhen, "Donald Trump Praises Xi Jinping over Move to End Term Limit . . . 'Maybe We'll Have to Give That a Shot Someday,'" *South China Morning Post*, March 4, 2018.
63. "Hong Kong Student Leader Joshua Wong Forms Political Party," *BBC News*, April 10, 2016.
64. Gary Cheung and Joyce Ng, "Hong Kong in Shock as Chief Executive CY Leung Decides Not to Seek Re-Election," *South China Morning Post*, December 10, 2016.
65. Benjamin Haas, "Hong Kong Elections: Carrie Lam Voted Leader amid Claims of China Meddling," *The Guardian*, March 26, 2017.
66. Carrie Gracie, "I Am No Puppet of Beijing, Says Lam," *BBC News*, June 21, 2017; Gracie, "No Puppet"; Elizabeth Cheung, "Carrie Lam Says She and CY Leung Are 'Totally Different People' in Attempt to Distance Herself from Outgoing Chief Executive," *South China Morning Post*, January 19, 2017.
67. Alex Lo, "'Anyone but CY': How the ABC Bandwagon Is Making for Strange Bedfellows," *South China Morning Post*, June 13, 2016.
68. Tom Phillips, "Rebel Hong Kong Politicians Defy China at Chaotic Swearing-in Ceremony," *Guardian*, October 12, 2016.
69. "Hong Kong Activist Joshua Wong Imprisoned," *Time Magazine*, August 17, 2017.
70. Ricœur, *Time and Narrative*, 227.
71. "Hong Kong: Violent Standoff."
72. Amy Gunia, "Violence in Hong Kong Protests Marks a Dangerous New Phase," *Time Magazine*, July 25, 2019.
73. "A Crying Shame-Banned in Warfare, Tear-Gas Is the Default Response to Controlling Protest," *Economist*, November 14, 2019; Yu, "Hong Kong: 'Revolution Is War.'"
74. "Witnessed 8.31 Citizens of Prince Edward Station Being Beaten as Middle-Aged Chef: The Police Are More Terrifying Than the 7.21 People in White," *Stand News*, September 2,

2019.

75. De Certeau, *Practice of Everyday Life*, 111.
76. Pakkin Leung, "The Police Rushed into the Train at Prince Edward Station. Many People Were Arrested after Spraying Pepper and Waving Batons," *Stand News*, August 31, 2019.
77. "Witnessed 8.31."
78. Kimmy Chung, "No Protesters Killed, Government Says, Slamming 'Malicious' Rumours," *South China Morning Post*, September 7, 2019.
79. Chung, "No Protesters Killed."
80. Interview with the author, July 2020. To protect them from possible reprisal, all interview subjects are quoted herein anonymously; all interviews used herein were conducted according to Colorado Multiple Institution Review Board Protocol 19-9116H.
81. Ambassador Kurt Tong in a conversation entitled "Hong Kong in Turmoil: Implications for the United States and China," University of Denver, November 4, 2019; Javier C. Hernández and Elaine Yu, "Hong Kong Protest, Largest in Weeks, Stretches Several Miles," *New York Times*, December 7, 2019.
82. "Occurrence at Prince Edward Station on 31 August (MTR Press Release)," MTR Corporation,, September 10, 2019, https://www.mtr.com.hk/archive/corporate/en/press_release/PR-19-053-E.pdf.
83. Cannix Yau and Kimmy Chung, "Hong Kong Rail Operator MTR Corp Finally Releases Images of Station Clashes in Yet Another Bid to End Rumours That 3 Protesters Died in Tussle with Police," *South China Morning Post*, September 10, 2019; "MTR: CCTV Reconstruction Squashes Death Rumor," *China Daily*, September 10, 2019, https://www.chinadailyhk.com.
84. Charlie Campbell, "What China's Surveillance Means for the Rest of the World," *Time Magazine*, November 21, 2019.
85. Vincent Wong, "The '831' Prince Edward MTR Incident Proves Hong Kong Urgently Needs Access to Information Reform," *Hong Kong Free Press*, September 22, 2019.
86. Holmes Chan, "Hong Kong Lawmaker and Protesters Demand CCTV Footage of Police Storming MTR Station," *Hong Kong Free Press*, September 6, 2019.
87. Jennifer Creery, "Explainer: 'The Communist Party's Railway'—How Hong Kong's Once-Respected MTR Fell Afoul of Protesters," *Hong Kong Free Press*, September 22, 2019; Cannix Yau, "Are the MTR's Early Closures Necessary for Repairs or a 'de Facto Curfew'?" *South China Morning Post*, October 19, 2019.
88. Interview with the author, July 2020; Rosalind Adams, "Hong Kong MTR: How Hong Kong Weaponized the City's Subway against Protesters," *BuzzFeed News*, October 11, 2019.
89. Creery, "Explainer"; interview with the author, July 2020; Adams, "Hong Kong MTR."

90. Leing, "Dozens of Railway Stations"; "Hong Kong Protesters Vandalize Subway Station, Deface Chinese Flag," *Voice of America*, September 22, 2019.
91. "Embattled Hong Kong Subway Operator Appeals for End to Vandalism," *Straits Times*, October 4, 2019.
92. Honig, *Public Things*, 90.
93. Jessie Yeung, "Hong Kong Protests: Fed up with Violence, Some Supporters Are Turning Away," *CNN*, October 27, 2019.
94. Ken Moritsugu, "Tear Gas and Fires: Hong Kong Protests from Morning to Night," AP News, November 12, 2019.
95. "Entire Rail Network Suspended as Violence Escalates in Hong Kong after Face Mask Ban," *China News Asia*, October 5, 2019; Yujing Liu, "MTR Services Resume after Hong Kong Protests Forced Closure of Major Stations," *South China Morning Post*, September 16, 2019; "MTR Station Exits Set on Fire," *Standard*, October 6, 2019; Hillary Leung, "Hong Kong's Subway System Was Once the City's Pride and Joy. Now It's a Target for Violent Protest," *Time Magazine*, October 25, 2019.
96. "Embattled"; Mengjie Wang, "Behind the Scars: 1-Year Anniversary of HK Protests," *China Global Television Network*, June 9, 2020.
97. George Holmes, "Protection, Politics and Protest: Understanding Resistance to Conservation," *Conservation and Society* 5, no. 2 (2007): 195.
98. Alice Su and Ryan Ho Kilpatrick, "'The Whole System Is Rotten. We Want to Tear It Down': Hong Kong Protests Blaze On," *Los Angeles Times*, September 8, 2019.
99. Travis Fedschun, "Hong Kong Protests, Violence Brings City to 'Brink of Total Breakdown,' Police Say," *Fox News*, November 12, 2019.
100. Edward Wong, "Hong Kong Protesters Are Targeting Starbucks. Apple Could Be Next," *New York Times*, October 15, 2019.
101. Jessie Yeung, "Hong Kong Protests: Fed up with Violence, Some Supporters Are Turning Away," *CNN*, October 27, 2019.
102. Cong Peiwu, "In Hong Kong, the Priority Is to End Violence and Restore Order," *Globe and Mail*, November 22, 2019.
103. Wright, "The Story."
104. Sullivan and Hui, "Protests Reveal Unease"; Fisher, "One Country, Two Nationalisms."
105. Audrey Jiajia Li, "Hong Kong's Hatred of Mainlanders Feeds the Xenophobic Undercurrents of Its Protests," *South China Morning Post*, October 11, 2019; Timothy McLaughlin and Casey Quackenbush, "Hong Kong Protesters Target Beijing-Friendly Businesses in Latest Demonstrations," *Washington Post*, September 22, 2019.
106. James W. Ellis, "Hong Kong's Elusive Identity: Searching in the Past, Present, and Future,"

Asian Culture and History 10, no. 2 (August 31, 2018): 90, https://doi.org/10.5539/ach.v10n2p90.

107. Interview with the author, June 2019.
108. Emily Cochrane, Edward Wong, and Keith Bradsher, "Trump Signs Hong Kong Democracy Legislation, Angering China," *New York Times*, November 27, 2019.
109. Amy Gunia, "How Hong Kong's Loss of 'Special Status' Could Hit Business," *Time Magazine*, May 29, 2020.
110. Ryan Ho Kilpatrick, "'Made in China' Label Ruling Hits a Raw Nerve in Hong Kong," *Washington Post*, August 14, 2020.
111. Dan Mangan, "Biden Blocks Removal of Most Hong Kong Residents from U.S. for 18 Months, Cites China Repression," *CNBC*, August 5, 2021, https://www.cnbc.com/2021/08/05/biden-blocks-removal-of-hong-kong-residents-cites-china-repression.html.
112. "Placing Flowers at MTR Station to Mark Aug. 31 Incident Will Lead to Arrest," *Apple Daily*, November 29, 2020.
113. Stephen J. Hartnett and Patrick Shaou-Whea Dodge, "Memory Activism and the Rhetorical Politics of Public Secrets, Forced Forgetting, and Dangerous Remembering," *Rhetoric and Public Affairs* 24, no. 4 (2021): 685–726, https://doi.org/10.2307/48657636; Javier C. Hernández, "Harsh Penalties, Vaguely Defined Crimes: Hong Kong's Security Law Explained," *New York Times*, June 30, 2020.

Glocal Consumer Identity as Political Resistance during the Hong Kong Extradition Bill Protests

Micky Lee

This chapter argues that protestors and their supporters articulated "glocal" consumer identities as the basis of political resistance during the Hong Kong extradition bill protests from March 2019 to November 2020. In the 1990s, globalization theorists used the term glocal—a combination of "glo" as in "global" and local—to describe phenomena whereby local populations use global brands to construct new meanings and fulfill their needs in daily lives.[1] For example, McDonald's is a fast-food chain in the United States but a mid-range, sit-down restaurant in other countries. Glocalization means that global brands do not impose meanings on locals; instead, locals use their lived experiences to make meanings of global brands. In the context of the Hong Kong protests, locals used global brands as a form of political resistance to an imposed Chinese national identity.

Even though Hong Kong was a British colony for 150 years, the local Chinese population did not identify itself as British. For the generations born after the 1960s, when the economy took off, they identify themselves as ethnically Chinese but not as Chinese nationals. Therefore, they turned to the market to seek the meanings of who they are.[2] Even after the territory was returned to China in 1997, Hong Kong people have not embraced a Chinese national identity. Instead, they resist this identity imposed by the Chinese Communist Party and mediated by the Hong Kong government by continually looking at the market to make sense of who they are.

This chapter illustrates how the extradition protests in 2019 illustrated this glocal consumer identity of protestors and supporters. A focus on this identity enriches current scholarship on post-1997 protests in Hong Kong by demonstrating how protestors' political identity is intertwined with this glocal consumer identity. Global brands and popular culture are resources from which protestors draw to enact political resistance. I assess that this glocal consumer identity was effective at attracting international attention and expanding the reach of the protestors. However, this identity does not advance democracy—defined here as political actors' agency to determine a political and economic future—for Hong Kong people. However, this glocal consumer identity does not address the root of some grievances, such as wealth disparity.[3] In fact, a market-based identity reinforces inequities because only those who have economic means to consume can voice their political stance. More dangerously, a market-based identity became a form of localism and nativism, conflating access to consumption sites with the right to enjoy public services. Citizens and residents in the Hong Kong cannot enact democracy when the working class and underclass cannot exercise their political and economic agency.

The organization of this chapter is as follows: First, I summarize the cause of the extradition bill protests. After that, I suggest how this chapter adds to the current literature on protests in post-1997 Hong Kong. Next, I explore protestors' glocal consumer identity in relation to a Hong Kong identity. Then I discuss how this identity resists a Chinese national identity during the protests. Lastly, I assess the effectiveness and shortcomings of this identity in enacting political resistance. If Hong Kong people seek democracy, they need to rethink whether a market-based identity advances or limits the political and economic agency of the collective.

What Are the Extradition Bill Protests?

In March 2019, the Hong Kong government proposed the Fugitive Offenders and Mutual Legal Assistance in Criminal Matters Legislation ("extradition bill," hereafter) after a Hong Kong citizen killed his girlfriend in Taiwan and fled to Hong Kong.[4] Because there was no agreement to extradite criminal suspects between the two places, the Hong Kong government proposed this bill to transfer fugitives between Hong Kong, Taiwan, Macau, and mainland China. The bill attracted wide public attention and was seen as a smokescreen for the Chinese government to silence political dissidents in Hong Kong.[5] In early summer 2019, up to a million people joined a street protest against the bill in Hong Kong. The protests then became weekly and took place in different districts. The government's refusal to withdraw the bill and its use of police violence against protestors led to a call for "five demands": bill withdrawal, an independent investigation into police misconduct, the release of all arrested protestors, the retraction of using the word "riots" to describe the protests, and the resignation of Hong Kong chief executive Carrie Lam.[6]

The government eventually withdrew the bill but did not respond to the other four demands. Therefore, protests continued in different forms, including airport sit-ins, college campus occupations, and arson of storefronts and public transportation. Protestors added more demands: some protests called for universal suffrage in Hong Kong, some wanted it to become an independent city-state, still others called for the involvement of the United Nations, the United Kingdom, and the United States.[7]

In addition to the two major actors—protestors and the Hong Kong government—big and small private businesses also became (reluctant) major actors. A number of Hong Kong–based conglomerates issued front-page newspaper advertisements to express their stance: most openly condemned violence, while some asked for dialogue. Interestingly, Li Ka-shing, the wealthiest man in Hong Kong, issued cryptic front-page messages that neither supported Hong Kong and Chinese governments nor condemned the protestors. Some "decoded" the hidden secret message as "allowing Hong Kong to self-govern."[8] Regardless of the intended meaning, social media posts that circulated these messages were deleted within hours on the mainland. This response shows that even a wealthy individual had to carefully maneuver between governments and protestors.

Street protests were largely subdued in early 2020 due to the COVID-19 pandemic. Small-scale protests later resumed when the pandemic was largely under control. However, on the eve of the twenty-third anniversary of Hong Kong's return to China, the Central Chinese government drafted and passed the National Security Law of Hong Kong behind closed doors. This law severely undermines the autonomy of Hong Kong and its political and judiciary independence, which were stipulated in the Sino-United Kingdom Joint Declaration signed in 1984.[9] The National Security

Law was drafted without consultation with the Hong Kong government, let alone the Hong Kong people. Its language is also vague enough that it sparked fear among not only residents but also foreign nationals and companies. For example, the *New York Times* relocated one-third of its staff to Seoul after this law was enacted.[10] One year after the enactment, the fear became reality: protestors, including high-profile ones, were sent to jail; the pro-democracy newspaper *Apple Daily* was forced to close.[11]

Literature Review on Post-1997 Hong Kong Protests

This chapter contributes to the current literature about post-1997 protests in Hong Kong by attending to protestors' glocal consumer identity through their references to popular culture. Because of this focus, the extant literature most relevant to this discussion concerns protestors' identity—political, local/national—and their use of symbols in public places. The majority of past studies focused on the Umbrella Movement of 2014, even though big and small mass protests had taken place in Hong Kong since 1997.

Protestors' Identity and Agency

Scholars have pondered the enduring question of Hong Kong identities.[12] The Umbrella Movement, given the lengthy duration of protestors occupying public places, provided evidence about how they articulated their identity. Scholars agree that protestors embrace a Hong Kong identity that is defined by neither ethnic nor national identity. In fact, the idea of belonging to a nation, whether it is China or the United States, baffled many young Hong Kong people. When they saw an American pledging to the Bill of Rights, they believed that person was tricked by propaganda.[13]

The use of signage and arts in the Umbrella Movement protest sites helped construct Hong Kong identities, which strive to negate the mainland Chinese one.[14] For example, the use of English on signage set protestors apart from mainland Chinese, while the use of Cantonese showed local affiliation.[15] Because participants need to actively engage in protest arts to make meaning, such dissident communication created common identities and a sense of belonging among Hong Kong protestors. For example, the umbrella was first used as a shield during the Umbrella Movement, but it became a symbol that protestors use as resistance. Many installation arts used this utilitarian object to forge a sense of common purpose among the protestors.[16]

The question of a local identity also garnered scholarly attention. For example, Kwong pointed out the slippery nature of the term "localism,"[17] a term some activists embraced to reject a market-oriented Hong Kong identity. They instead adopted an anti-capitalist and anti-colonialist local identity. Others used their local identity to distinguish themselves from mainlanders and to seek less intervention from Beijing. Some scholars agreed that this local Hong Kong identity is a civic one:[18] a Hong Kong person, as defined by the protestors, is one who engages in an imagined political community autonomous from the mainland Chinese political space. This belief contrasts that of the older generation that wished to democratize China by democratizing Hong Kong first. The younger generation sees Hong Kong as a separate political entity so it prioritizes local interests. It does not believe a more democratic Hong Kong will lead to a democratic China.[19]

Protestors' agency is a major theme in the literature about the Umbrella Movement. Veg argues that activists exercise their moral and political agency to understand notions of democracy, universal suffrage, and civil disobedience. On a political level, democracy is seen as asserting one's agency and individual autonomy. Expressing a local identity affirms this sense of agency through the civic community. Protestors believed that Hong Kong people need to exercise their human agency to demand democracy as a moral choice between good and evil.[20] In other words, while protestors expressed grievances toward a local government, the action of protests compelled them to reflect on their relation with other publics that suffer from global injustice. To protest in Hong Kong is to fight not only for what is right for local residents, but also for global publics.

The Use of Symbols and Street Arts in Protest Sites

Scholars have examined the wide range of discursive tactics and communicative acts that protestors employed during the Umbrella Movement. In a special edition of *Journal of Language and Politics*, Flowerdew and Jones argue that street protests are the most complex forms of political discourse because they involve multiple actors, modes of discourse, media, and historical trajectories.[21] In this special edition, Lou and Jaworski show how discourses moved from a physical space to an online space, and then back again.[22] By moving from one space to another, the meanings of the discourses changed from one context to another. For example, protestors initially used umbrellas to shield themselves from tear gas shot by the police, but then umbrella itself became a symbol of the movement. Flowerdew adds that the bodies of the protestors were also discursive; the yellow umbrella is more than an object and a symbol—it has become an extension of the body.[23] Therefore, when there is a sea of yellow umbrellas, there is a sea of protestors. In the same special issue, Lim suggests that symbols can effectively essentialize and simplify complex ideologies, which in turn swayed public opinion and helped avoid direct confrontation between protestors and the government.[24]

Some scholars believe that street arts connect protestors to the public, attract media attention, and provoke collective action because they are collaboratively produced, ephemeral, portable, and non-copyrighted. These arts were deemed successful at effecting social change.[25] Other tactics that attracted a global audience are multi-modal signage with English (poster, street arts, slogan) and cultural references to other East Asian (such as Japanese anime) and western cultures (such as superhero movies).[26]

Other scholars have focused on the use of secular symbols. For example, Bosco argues that protestors borrow religious symbols from both Western and Chinese religions (such as Jesus and Kuan Kung—the God of loyalty, righteousness, and trust) to show a sacred embodiment of the community. However, protestors and pro-establishment supporters understood this sacred body differently: while the protestors saw this body representing autonomy, civil rights, and Hong Kong's distinct culture, the officials saw the sacred body representing the Chinese nation and nationals. However, both parties can agree that this sacred body needs to be protected from foreign interference and division.[27]

Some scholars have looked at the symbolic value of spaces of protests. For example, Yuen argues that public places facilitate political participation because they are embedded with meanings that evoked protestors' affects.[28] Some scholars have maintained that occupying public places will counter a hegemonic, capitalist understanding of urban space. For example, Tremlett believes that occupying urban space suspended commercial transaction and transit, both essential to the working of capitalism.[29] He pays further attention to the assemblage of different materials (such as the tents, chairs, cooking equipment, and bodies of the protestors) in the protest sites by arguing that they form an alternative imaginary of Hong Kong as a place for emotions and affects. Such a place challenges the perception of Hong Kong as a politically indifferent, capitalistic utopia.

This chapter adds to the literature about post-1997 Hong Kong protests by elucidating how protestors articulate their identity during the extradition bill protests. I argue that it is difficult to divorce a market identity from a political identity, thus it is questionable whether protest sites were "cleansed" from capitalism. In fact, political resistance toward the Chinese Communist Party was enacted by demonstrating what a glocal consumer is in Hong Kong.

Glocal Consumer Identities in Hong Kong

In this section, I define what "glocal" means, argue why a glocal consumer identity is ingrained in Hong Kong identity, and illustrate this identity using McDonald's as an example. An understanding of this identity sheds light on the current literature, which is overwhelmingly focused on protestors' political, national/local identities.

The "glocal" concept arose in the globalization debates in the 1990s.Glocalization shows that global and local cultures are neither dichotomous nor exclusive. Global culture was believed to be a result of economic globalization. The World Trade Organization (WTO) established in 1995, and the signings of treaties such as the North American Free Trade Agreement (NAFTA) in 1994 facilitated trade between countries and integrated more national economies into the global one. For example, NAFTA allowed freer trade between Canada, the United States, and Mexico. One consequence was that a number of car factories shut down in the United States and moved to Mexico because of cheaper labor cost.[30] These international organizations believed that economic globalization would benefit the world population because freer trade would "sharpen competition, motivate innovation and breed success."[31] Economic globalization also increased trade between China and the United States. Former U.S. president Bill Clinton strongly supported admitting China into the WTO in 2001, believing that American consumers would benefit from cheaper goods imported from China.[32]

However, some international non-profit organizations and academics did not believe that free trade would economically benefit local populations because, they maintained, open competition would lead to "a race to a bottom," forcing countries to drive down local wages.[33] In one example, investors were once attracted by low wages in China but wages have since gone up. As a result, many factories have moved to other Asian countries with still lower wages.[34] In addition, globalization opponents are wary that global brands would drive small businesses out of business and bring cultural homogenization and consumerism to local cultures.[35] McDonalds and Starbucks, two U.S.-based corporations with visible presence in global cities, have come to symbolize globalization and were prime targets of attack during WTO protests.[36] (As will be shown later, during the Hong Kong protests, Starbucks stores were vandalized, but for a different reason.)

Some scholars disagree with these assumptions of globalization proponents and opponents, and argue that global and local cultures are neither dichotomous nor exclusive. They therefore use the term "glocal" to describe how local populations adopt global culture for their daily needs. Glocalists ask how local populations make sense of global brands based on their lived experience.[37] McDonald's, a symbol of American culture, once again, served as a glocalization case study. As analyzed in Watson,[38] McDonald's does not have the same menus in all countries. In addition, local practices influence how consumers make meaning of fast food and the restaurant. Later, I use Hong Kong McDonald's as an example of consumer perceptions of a fast-food eatery as a local establishment rather than as an American restaurant. Hong Kong McDonald's is a good case study for how glocal consumer identity is articulated in a global site in an intensely local place.

Glocal consumer identity is ingrained in Hong Kong identity. The glocal consumer identity is important to understand because it was articulated in online spaces and physical places during the extradition bill protests. In Hong Kong, a glocal consumer is well-versed in local and global goods, such as what, where, and when to buy in Hong Kong and abroad. A glocal consumer is also knowledgeable about local popular culture as well as Japanese popular culture, the Korean Wave, and Hollywood.

Until 1951, the border between Hong Kong and the mainland was relatively malleable, and Chinese residents moved back and forth between the city and the mainland. Up until the 1960s, many Chinese residents saw Hong Kong as a temporary shelter for their eventual emigration to the United States, the United Kingdom, Canada, or Australia. However, sweeping political economic changes in the 1960s led the generation born in Hong Kong to cultivate a sense of cultural belonging. Many began to see Hong Kong as a permanent home instead of a transitional place.[39]

Given that Hong Kong people can identify as neither British nor Chinese nationals, the market became a site in which the locals found meaning. Matthew,

Ma, and Liu argue that this market-based Hong Kong identity is reflected in many aspects of Hong Kong life, Hong Kong people's obsession with money, and the number of shopping malls.[40] I argue that this market-based identity was developed in the context of a laissez-faire economic model during the colonial period and the rise of consumerism since the 1960s. Both contexts set the population living in Hong Kong apart from mainland Chinese, who experienced the Cultural Revolution during that time.

First, the laissez-faire market in colonial Hong Kong strongly contrasted with the state-planned economy of Communist China. In addition, the Hong Kong economy experienced dramatic growth from the 1960s to 1980s, transitioning itself into a wealthy city, ridding of some local populations' famine and poverty, which mainland Chinese experienced during the Cultural Revolution. Second, since the economy took off, consumption has become a way of life in Hong Kong. The city of 7.5 million is called a land of malls and a mecca of restaurants.[41] Since residents tend to live in small apartments, few socialize at home. Going to a mall and eating out are therefore popular activities to do with family and friends. Malls and restaurants are thus sites in which to form a glocal consumer identity.

Local and imported popular culture are also important sites for this identity formation. Before the arrival of cable and satellite television, the Hong Kong television landscape was dominated by one commercial station, TVB. The portrayal of mainland Chinese on this dominant television station shaped Hong Kong people's perception: mainland men are seen as country bumpkins and violent robbers; and mainland women as prostitutes and trophy wives. Popular culture is so influential that the name of a television show character, 阿燦 (*Ar Chan*), became a term to call all mainland Chinese. This character is portrayed as a new immigrant who works in seedy and illegal professions. He also exhibits outrageous behavior such as wolfing down twenty hamburgers in one setting. Popular media also shaped female prototypes. In the 1990s, when Hong Kong business people set up factories across the border, their mistresses in the mainland were commonly called the "second woman." Some newspapers covered sensational stories about mistresses breaking up families in Hong Kong. These media stereotypes suggested that mainland Chinese are culturally backward, materialistic, and morally bankrupt.

Popular culture in Hong Kong is also influenced by those in Japan, South Korea, the United Kingdom, and the United States. Hong Kong people have pride in their media landscape being more international than that in the mainland. Therefore, global popular culture is also site where Hong Kong people construct a glocal consumer identity. For example, the Hong Kong audience has more choices of foreign films compared to the limited number officially distributed in theaters in mainland China.[42] In addition, the Chinese government censors foreign popular culture that is seen to portray the country in a negative light. A good example is *Shang-Chi and the Legend of the Ten Rings*. The film was not officially distributed in China; speculation was that Chinese censors rejected the racist tone of the comic book from which the film was adapted.[43] Lastly, Hong Kong residents can access international news sites such as CNN and BBC, which the Chinese government bans.

A good example of how Hong Kong identity is based on the consumption of goods as well as global popular culture is the opening of Hong Kong Disneyland in 2005.[44] The launch of the theme park was met with little local resistance, showing locals' readiness to accept global culture. In addition, many local visitors compared Hong Kong Disneyland to the one in Tokyo, illustrating that some were already familiar with the park. Even though the Hong Kong government had to heavily invest in it and have little control over the park design and management, the Chief Secretary of Hong Kong called Hong Kong Disneyland a collaboration between two global brand names, comparing Hong Kong to Disney as a lifestyle brand.

Hong Kong Disneyland is a pure consumption site, but it also affirms Hong Kong identity. When it first opened, local media widely reported on the uncivilized behavior of mainland Chinese tourists, such as jumping queue or taking too many pictures,[45] suggesting that Hong Kong people—who are familiar with how to behave in a global consumption site—would not demonstrate such behaviors. As I show, monitoring mainland Chinese behaviors in the city and pointing out their undesirable behaviors mark them as the different and assert the Hong Kong identity.

The Articulation of the Glocal Consumer Identity in Hong Kong McDonald's and Starbucks during the Protests

Protestors articulated this glocal consumer identity during the extradition protests, using it to resist a Chinese national identity imposed by the Chinese Communist Party.[46] McDonald's, a global chain that is localized in Hong Kong, serves as a glocal consumption site for meaning-making. In comparison, Starbucks, a less localized global chain, was vandalized during the protests. The differential treatment must be explained through local ownerships of both global brands and the brands' meanings to the Hong Kong people. McDonald's arrived in Hong Kong in 1975. The U.S.-based company owned the franchise until 2017, when it was acquired by a tripartite entity of a former Chinese state-owned investment company, a U.S.-based private equity firm, and McDonald's Corporation.[47] In contrast, Starbucks arrived in 2000, and the local franchise is fully owned by a Hong Kong–based restaurant conglomerate named Maxim's Caterers.

Given the ownership, McDonald's was a more likely target of protestors. However, during the protests, Maxim's founder's daughter spoke at the United Nations to defend the Hong Kong police and called out "a small group of radical protestors [carrying out] systematic and calculated violent acts" in Hong Kong.[48] This comment outraged protestors so they spray-painted the words "evil heart" and "betrayed Hong Kong" in Chinese on Starbucks storefronts. Although the conglomerate issued a press release stating that the daughter plays no managerial role, the protestors did not stop attacking Starbucks in Hong Kong. The different treatment may be explained by what both brands mean to the Hong Kong people.

In the United States, McDonald's is a place where patrons buy takeout or grab a quick bite. In contrast, some McDonald's brands in Hong Kong are like neighborhood centers, where an inexpensive meal will buy one a seat for quite some time. Unlike local eateries where servers clear dishes away from patrons before they finish eating, McDonald's employees rarely ask patrons to leave. This treatment makes the restaurant a safe hangout for young people, retirees, and foreign domestic helpers with limited means.[49] Some twenty-four-hour restaurants also provide shelter for the homeless. "McRefugees," people who stay at McDonald's for the night, have opined that the restaurants are cleaner and more comfortable than partitioned flats for the underclass.[50] Additionally, McDonald's branches are located in working-class and more rundown neighborhoods as well as on high street.

McDonald's familiarity with locals earned it the nickname "McKee" (麥記; *ma iji*). The word "kee" may be translated into "the shop of." Such shop names are usually found in working-class neighborhoods or rural areas where the owners—assumed to care little about branding and more about selling cheap goods—name their shops by using their last name plus the word "kee." These shops are not only businesses but also neighborhood hangouts and gossip centers.[51] Thus, calling McDonald's "McKee" implies that this U.S.-origin brand is part of daily life in local neighborhoods throughout Hong Kong.

McDonald's restaurants served some important functions during the 2014 Umbrella Movement; for example, protestors staged sit-ins in three downtown locations. McDonald's restaurants close to these sites became "refuel" centers where protestors charged their phones and used free Wi-Fi during sit-in breaks. Some branches gave out toothpaste as promotional items, which protestors saw as a gesture of support for the Umbrella Movement.[52]

In contrast, Starbucks branches in Hong Kong are mostly located in high streets, shopping malls, and affluent neighborhoods. Food and drink at Starbucks cost much more than McDonald's so it is frequented by office workers, the middle-class, and expatriates. Starbucks has not become a way of life in Hong Kong like McDonald's has, which may explain why vandalizing Starbucks is not an attack on Hong Kong people's glocal consumer identity. In contrast, attacking McDonald's would inconvenience the daily lives of low-income people such as students, retirees, and the homeless; therefore the restaurants were spared.

Protestors are savvy glocal consumers because they understand that boycotting a global brand may catch U.S. executives' attention. A protestor explained that since Starbucks in the United States supports liberal causes, vandalizing Starbucks would call out their headquarters to put pressure on the Hong Kong franchise.[53] In contrast, McDonald's is not known to have a progressive political agenda. The Starbucks CEO issued a non-committal response to protestor grievances, suggesting that the company deals with geopolitical issues all the time and that the priority is employee safety.[54] Protestors also made it clear that they were protesting the Hong Kong owner of Starbucks, not the Starbucks brand, as illustrated by the spray-painted words "evil heart," a reference to Maxim's Chinese name, "Beautiful Heart." Accusations of "betrayed Hong Kong people" also suggested that the Hong Kong-based conglomerate should stand with the people, not the police, during the protests.

Unlike globalization protestors who attacked both McDonald's and Starbucks as symbols of globalization, Hong Kong protestors mostly spared McDonald's because the restaurants are seen as a Hong Kong way of life. Therefore, although McDonald's restaurants are global sites, they are located in intensely local places such as older and more rundown neighborhoods. Starbucks, on the other hand, is not part of Hong Kong life. Protestors showed their knowledge about the Starbucks brand because they understood that vandalizing the storefronts would force a response from U.S. headquarters.

Effectiveness of a Glocal Consumer Identity in Advancing Democracy

But is the glocal consumer identity the Hong Kong protestors articulate effective for advancing democracy?[55] Even though protestors fought for democracy, the paths that lead to democracy remain unclear: is it through intervention from the international community or through self-destruction? We cannot assume that protestors and scholars who study post-1997 Hong Kong protests have the same understanding of democracy.

I agree with Andrew Gilmore that one root of the extradition bill protests is anti-mainlandization,[56] understood as the forced assimilation of Hong Kong political, economic, and cultural realms by mainland Chinese ones. In this sense, I define the fight for democracy as a fight for political and economic agency in the future of Hong Kong. Democracy in Hong Kong and elsewhere means populations will have legitimate means to collectively decide their political and economic destinies. Therefore, advancing democracy for Hong Kong people would require more than publicly resisting an imposed Chinese national identity. With this definition, I believe a glocal consumer identity is effective when it attracts attention from media outside China; however, when activism is a form of consumption, this identity excludes those of limited economic means.

Garnering International Attention

The glocal consumer identity articulated by Hong Kong protestors attracted international attention and sustained interest for three prominent reasons: First, consumption-oriented visuals resonate with publics outside Hong Kong; second, some key figures drew on global popular culture to spread their messages beyond a Chinese-speaking audience; and third, protestors strategically vandalized shops to show that their prime motive was not to loot goods or criticize capitalism but to call out the shops owned by Chinese state-supported enterprises.

Indeed, protestors were savvy at "packaging" themselves and tailoring their messages for a global audience. For example, organizers issued flyers to encourage protestors to wear black.[57] Those who marched for political parties wore matching clothing to show unity. Protestors also favored professionally designed and printed signs rather than the homemade banners and cardboard signs seen in protests in the United States. The carefully packaged "look" reinforces the perceived civility and orderliness of the protestors; the crafted "look" suggests that they are undertaking rational, intentional actions.

Some of the more well-known protestors drew on global popular culture references to make their cases. One protestor, Chun-man Ma, donned the Captain America costume at protests. Even when he wore a simple black t-shirt with the statement: "Hong Kong independence, the only way out," he carried the Captain America shield as if the superhero were his alter ego. Agnes Chow, a leader in both the Umbrella Movement and extradition protests, said that she taught herself Japanese by listening to Japanese popular music (J-Pop) and watching anime. She shared her activism on a Japanese Twitter account and made videos for the Japanese public. She was also interviewed in the Japanese media in Japanese. When Chow was arrested for violating the National Security Law, Japanese Twitter users showed their support with the hashtag #FreeAgnes, indicating her celebrity status in the country.[58]

Protestors also gained sympathy from media outside Hong Kong because they did not arbitrarily attack *any* shop and loot goods. Instead they strategically chose shops owned by Chinese state-owned companies or supporters of the Chinese Communist Party. They also explained their actions to the international media. As they stated, they chose Starbucks over McDonald's because they understood that the coffee chain had a progressive stance in the United States; thus, they believed that vandalizing Hong Kong storefronts might compel the U.S. headquarters to respond. In another case, after protestors vandalized shops that were believed to channel money to the Chinese Communist Party, they left notes *in English* to explain their reasons to an international audience rather than to the owners. The international media also reported on incidents in which protestors righted a wrong: after protestors realized that they spray-painted on Taiwanese owned shops, they voluntarily removed spray paint from these shops. Lastly, the international media took note that protestors did not attack sites that are popular targets of anti-globalization protests, such as Apple Computers and luxury brands. Additionally, protestors did not loot any goods from vandalized shops; they left disheveled goods on the floor, signaling that the prime motive was not to steal but to destroy Chinese capital.[59]

Presenting a packaged "look," drawing on global popular culture references and selecting brands to attack show that Hong Kong protestors understand how to use commercial images and consumption to express their grievances to the international media. These actions were effective at publicly resisting an imposed Chinese national identity because Hong Kong protestors showed that they resonate with global popular culture rather than with the Chinese national culture imposed by the party.

Limitations of a Glocal Consumer Identity in Advancing Democracy

In this section, I assess the limitations of a glocal consumer identity in advancing democracy, defined as a sense of agency to collectively determine political and economic destinies. I argue that this identity limits Hong Kong people's imagination of a future with political and economic agency because this identity falls back to the market-based identity that Hong Kong people developed during the colonial era, an identity constructed to oppose their perception of mainland Chinese.

The first limitation of this market-based identity is that even though the glocal consumer identity was powerful to publicly resist an imposed Chinese national one, it fails to solve one root of the protests, which is economic disparity. When consumption is seen as a form of activism, it excludes those who have the least economic means. Moreover, on the global stage, Chinese nationals have more consumption power to pressure brands to take a political stance so this strategy reduces citizens of different nations into global consumers. The second limitation is that some activists used nativism to govern access to city space and public services. The conflation of the right to enjoy public services and that of consumption means that citizenry is about consuming the right products in the right way. Both limitations foreclose any meaningful dialogue about political and economic agencies.

Consumption as Activism

Victoria Park has been a commemoration site for the annual June 4 Massacre as well as the gathering point of many protests. From there, protestors marched to the Hong Kong government building in Admiralty. Protestors walked along major shopping streets such as Hennessy Street as if they were window shopping—colloquially known as "strolling in the streets" (行街; *xíng jiē*). As mentioned, shopping has been a major pastime in Hong Kong since it became prosperous in the 1980s. The cityscape against which the protests took place also reflects consumption as a way of life in Hong Kong. Protestors were shown to favor certain brands, such as 7-Eleven umbrellas, the Japanese energy drink Pocari Sweat, iPhones, and Samsung phones. Noticeably absent from the protest sites were brands originated in mainland China. This may be unsurprising given that the protestors were against Chinese hegemony, which is partially constituted by state enterprises that own some consumer brands. In addition, Hong Kong youth do not have favorable impression of Chinese brands, they view them as unfashionable.[60] These brands do not have the soft power to be considered cool or modern.

Protest sites also illustrate the allure of consumption. For example, taking clues from the Baltic Way, where citizens formed a human chain of more than four hundred miles, Hong Kong protestors formed chains in a mountain and the harbor front at night. Protestors lit up their mobile phones to illuminate the chains. While the chains were attention-grabbing, they excluded low-income families that did not own smart phones or did not own the right brands. The human chains formed on the harbor front have the backdrop of neon signs of international banks (such as Bank of America and Bank of China) as well as global brands (such as Sony) on the top of crowded skyscrapers. The physical places where the human chains took place in Hong Kong sharply contrasted those of the Baltic Way, where citizens stood by the roadside or in fields in rural areas that are devoid of any brand names or logos.

Since the glocal consumption identity is ingrained in a Hong Kong one, patronizing shops that support protestors was a way to continue the movement. Protestors categorized businesses as "blue economy" and "yellow economy." The former tend to be conglomerates that side with the police, the Hong Kong government, and the Chinese government. For example, Maxim's Caterers, which owns the Hong Kong Starbucks franchise, was designated as part of the "blue economy." The yellow economy is constituted by mom-and-pop shops that side with the protestors. These shops gave food or financial support to protestors; some provided a wall (known as Lennon Wall) on which customers could write supportive notes for protestors.[61] Protestors advocated Hong Kong people to support yellow shops because doing so would strengthen the local economy and counter the blue economy.[62]

Activism by choosing where to consume is not effective at advancing democracy at all. On the global stage, Chinese nationalists employ the very same strategy to subject transnational corporations to economic pressure. These nationalists understand that due to its sheer size, the consumption power of the mainland Chinese population is much more significant to global brands than that of the Hong Kong population. Therefore, global brands would rather choose to not offend the

Chinese government.[63] The most high-profile case is that of the general manager of an American professional basketball team who voiced his support of Hong Kong protestors. He was subsequently criticized by mainland Chinese fans. As a result, both his team and the National Basketball Association had to distance themselves from him for the fear of missing out on the Chinese market.[64]

Conflating Private Consumption and Public Services

One of the most surprising sites of the Hong Kong extradition bill protests is the shopping mall. As previously suggested, shopping and going to malls are popular pastimes of Hong Kong people. But malls are essentially privatized spaces; they welcome consumers but discourage non-consumption public gathering. However, during the protests, malls became a safe space for protestors. To prevent confrontations between protestors and police, some mall management posted notes requesting that police not enter unless there is a crime.[65] However, the refusal to allow police entry does not mean that this private space has become a public space. Since protestors cannot be easily distinguished from regular shoppers—other than the former's tendency to wear black, malls cannot turn away all who *appear* like protestors. The management does not see police on duty as potential consumers. If their presence could lead to confrontation and damage property, not allowing them to enter preserves the space for regular shoppers to consume.

When shopping malls are seen as safe protest sites, there is danger of conflating the rights to consume with that of enjoying public services. Even though not all protestors advocated for localism and nativism, some of the localists' campaigns barred mainland Chinese from the right to space, whether it is a commercial street or a bed in public hospitals.

The slippery nature of the Hong Kong identity means some have embraced localism—a political ideology that advocates for preserving identity and autonomy.[66] Preserving this identity means mainland Chinese tourists and new immigrants in Hong Kong need to learn how to act and behave in public and consumption sites. For example, mainland Chinese in Hong Kong are supposed to observe personal conduct and civility in consumption sites, such as not buying in excess or consuming blindly.[67] Tourists websites give advice to Hong Kong people how to behave in tourist areas in the city and overseas. They often offer advice about how not to be perceived as mainland Chinese, such as not wearing t-shirts with luxury brand logos or speaking too loudly in public.[68] Some media outlets used foreign nationals' opinions to show the unworldliness of the mainland Chinese. Since Hong Kong people view the Japanese as expert consumers, the Japanese's opinions were used to validate those of Hong Kong people about mainland Chinese.[69] In online forums, some explained how Japanese distinguish tourists from Hong Kong, Taiwan, and mainland China. All of these tips show that there is a "right" way to consume; having the money to buy luxury goods does not mean one knows how to consume "correctly." Even when mainland Chinese have sufficient economic power to consume, they are unable to become glocal consumers because they do not know this "right" way.

Some localists opted for more confrontational tactics to deny mainland Chinese the right to the city. For example, some localists protested against mainland tourists who crowd luxury shopping malls. Others protested against parallel traders—mainland tourists who arrived in Hong Kong to buy highly in-demand goods (such as baby formula) and resell them across the border—and accused them of disrupting locals' daily lives.[70]

Localists' denying mainland Chinese's access to space is similar to nativists' complaint about mainland Chinese's abuse of Hong Kong public resources. Nativists use the slur "locust" to refer to mainland Chinese who take advantage of Hong Kong education and healthcare without giving back to society.[71] The "native-first" attitude was also adopted by the Hong Kong government who implemented policies that reinforce this localist stance by charging "non-eligible" persons a hefty fee to use public hospital facilities. Public hospitals explicitly named "non-eligible" persons as pregnant mainland Chinese who wish to give birth in Hong Kong. Even for those who are married to a Hong Kong citizen, public hospitals do not entitle them to use their services.[72]

The boundary between private consumption site and public space became blurred when protestors escaped to malls to avoid police harassment; when localists deny mainland Chinese tourists the right to consumption sites and mainland-born Hong Kong people the right to public services. Conflating private and public spaces, seeing consumption as activism both limit Hong Kong people's political and economic agencies, because the power to advocate for political change comes from the market. Even though the population in Hong Kong is much smaller than that in China, some protestors believe that Hong Kong people's economic power is robust enough to resist the Chinese Communist Party. Even if some mainland Chinese have economic power to consume, some Hong Kong people believe they do not know how to consume in the "right" way. When consumption is seen as a political tactic, it excludes many low-income residents because their meager economic means limits their choices. The strategy of consumption as activism reinforces unequal power relations, one of the grievances of the protestors. Protestors are aware of the collusion between political and economic elites. When consumption is a form of activism, the wealthy has the most political clout. Even for middle-class citizens who have some means to consume, they still have some power to take their stand. Unfortunately, the working-class can hardly voice their political opinions through consumption because there is not much means to choose what to buy.

Conclusion

This chapter contributes to the current literature of protests in post-1997 Hong Kong by focusing on the glocal consumer identity of protestors instead of the local/national identity as discussed in previous studies. The glocal consumer identity concept also shows that the symbols used to challenge the hegemony of the Hong Kong government and the Chinese government draw on global popular culture. I assert that this glocal consumer identity has been ingrained in Hong Kong identity since the city experienced dramatic economic growth in the 1960s. A laissez-faire market in colonial Hong Kong, coupled with local popular culture, gave meaning to the generations born in Hong Kong since the 1960s. This glocal consumer identity is a market-oriented one, and negates a mainland Chinese identity. The younger generation may identify itself as ethnic Chinese but cannot see itself as Chinese national.

The articulation of this glocal consumer identity was pronounced during the extradition bill protests in 2019–2020. Protestors' differential treatment of McDonald's and Starbucks shows that McDonald's has become a way of life in Hong Kong and was therefore mostly spared from attack. On the other hand, the local owner of the Starbucks franchise was seen as a traitor of Hong Kong people because the founder's daughter spoke out against the protestors. In addition, protestors knew that attacking this coffee chain would force the U.S. corporation to take notice.

This chapter assesses the effectiveness and shortcomings of protestors' glocal identity during the protests. This identity is effective at garnering international attention because of its use of global popular cultural references. However, it is limiting at advancing democracy for Hong Kong people when democracy is defined as collective actions to exercise political and economic agencies. When consumption is seen as a form of activism, it excludes the working-class population whose limited means offers fewer consumption choices. Therefore, it does not address one of the grievances during the protests, which is economic disparity in the city. In addition, the growth of localism and nativism leads to the belief that private consumption and public services are the same thing: protecting Hong Kong local identity means denying access to consumption sites to mainland Chinese tourists and the rights to enjoying public services for new immigrants from China.

NOTES

A note about my social positioning: I was born in Hong Kong at a time when the economy took off. I was educated in schools and universities where English was the preferred language even though many classes were conducted in Cantonese. I left for the United States for my PhD three years after the city was returned to China and have not lived in the Hong Kong Special Administrative Region since 2000. I was in the United States during the extradition bill protests. I recognize the privileged position from which I offer my critique. Although I expressed reservations about some choices made by the Hong Kong protestors, I support—with no reservation—their fight for freedom and democracy. I identify as a Hong Kong Chinese who works and lives in the United States. I am a British National (Overseas) passport holder who is no longer recognized by the Hong Kong government, a United States resident, and a Hong Kong citizen. I am married to a United States citizen and my son is also one. I have no plan to renounce my Hong Kong citizenship and become a United States citizen.

1. Roland Robertson, "Prologue," in *European Glocalization in Global Context*, edited by Robert Robertson (New York: Palgrave Macmillan, 2014), 2.
2. Gordon Matthew, Eric Kit-wai Ma, and Tai-lok Liu, *Hong Kong, China: Learning to Belong to a Nation* (London: Routledge, 2008), 18.
3. Po-keung Hui and Kin-chi Lam, "'Living in Truth' versus Realpolitik: Limitations and Potentials of the Umbrella Movements," *Inter-Asia Cultural Studies* 16, no. 3 (2015): 350.
4. "The Murder Behind the Hong Kong Protests: A Case Where No-One Wants the Killer," *BBC online*, October 23, 2019, https://www.bbc.com.
5. "Hong Kong-China Extradition Plans Explained," *BBC News*, December 13, 2019, https://www.bbc.com.
6. "Hong Kong Protests: What Are the 'Five Demands'? What Do Protesters Want?," *South*

China Morning Post, August 20, 2019, https://www.scmp.com.

7. "The Dream of Genuine Universal Suffrage in Hong Kong is Gone for Good, but Can the Democracy Movement Survive?," *Hong Kong Free Press*, March 13, 2021, https://hongkongfp.com.
8. Colin Dwyer, "Did a Hong Kong Tycoon Hide a Protest Message in His Innocuous Newspaper Ads?," NPR, August 22, 2019, https://www.npr.org.
9. Louisa Brooke-Holland, "Hong Kong: The Joint Declaration" (London: House of Commons Briefing Paper, 2019), 2. It was stated that Hong Kong "will enjoy a high degree of autonomy" with "executive, legislative and independent judicial power." It also stated that the existing rights, freedoms, and lifestyle enjoyed by Hong Kong people will remain unchanged up to 2047.
10. Michael Grynbaum, "*New York Times* Will Move Part of Hong Kong Office to Seoul," *New York Times*, July 14, 2020, https://www.nytimes.com.
11. Antony J. Blinken, "Marking One Year of Hong Kong's National Security Law," U.S. State Department, July 17, 2021, https://www.state.gov/marking-one-year-of-hong-kongs-national-security-law/.
12. Wing Sang Law, *Collaboration Colonial Power: The Making of Hong Kong Chinese* (Hong Kong: Hong Kong University Press, 2000).
13. Gordon Matthews, "The Hong Kong Protests in Anthropological Perspectives: National Identity and What it Means," *Critique of Anthropology* 40, no. 2 (2020b): 265.
14. Matthews, "Hong Kong Protests," 267.
15. John Flowerdew, "Understanding the Hong Kong Umbrella Movement: A Critical Discourse Historiographical Approach," *Discourse and Society* 28, no. 5 (2017): 466; Sebastian Veg, "Creating a Textual Public Space: Slogans and Text from Hong Kong's Umbrella Movement," *Journal of Asian Studies* 75, no. 3 (2016): 688. Cantonese is primarily a spoken language; when it is used as a written form, it is seen as informal and colloquial.
16. Georgios Patsiaouras, Anastasia Veneti, and William Green, "Marketing, Art and Voices of Dissent: Promotional Methods of Protest Art by the 2014 Hong Kong's Umbrella Movement," *Marketing Theory* 18, no. 1 (2017): 78.
17. Ying-ho Kwong, "The Growth of 'Localism' in Hong Kong: A New Path for the Democracy Movement?," *China Perspectives*, no. 3 (2016): 64–66.
18. Kwong, "Growth of 'Localism,'" 68; Veg, "Creating a Textual Public Space," 679, 699.
19. Kwong, "Growth of 'Localism,'" 66, 68.
20. Veg, "Creating a Textual Public Space," 682.
21. John Flowerdew and Rodney H. Jones, "Occupy Hong Kong: Historicizing Protest," *Journal*

of Language and Politics 15, no. 5 (2016): 519.

22. Jackie Jia Lou and Adam Jaworski, "Itineraries of Protest Signage: Semiotic Landscape and the Mythologizing of the Hong Kong Umbrella Movement," *Journal of Language and Politics* 15, no. 5 (2016): 634.
23. Flowerdew, "Understanding the Hong Kong Umbrella Movement," 454.
24. Lim, "Aesthetics," 85.
25. Patsiaouras, Veneti, and Green, "Marketing, Art and Voices of Dissent," 78.
26. Flowerdew, "Understanding the Hong Kong Umbrella Movement," 446; Lou and Jaworski, "Itineraries of Protest Signage," 634; Wai-man Lam, *Understanding the Political Culture of Hong Kong: The Paradox of Activism and Depoliticization* (London: Routledge, 2015), 84; Irmgard Wetzstein, "The Visual Discourse of Protest Movements on Twitter: The Case of Hong Kong 2014," *Media and Communication* 5, no. 4 (2017): 29.
27. Joseph Bosco, "The Sacred in Urban Political Protests in Hong Kong," *International Sociology* 31, no. 4 (2016): 376.
28. Samson Yuen, "Contesting Middle-class Civility: Place-Based Collective Identity in Hong Kong's Occupy Mongkok," *Social Movement Studies* 17, no. 4 (2018): 395.
29. Paul-François Tremlett, "Affective Dissent in the Heart of the Capitalist Utopia: Occupy Hong Kong and the Sacred," *Sociology* 50, no. 6 (2016): 1157.
30. "What Happened to Wages in Mexico Since NAFTA?," National Bureau of Economic Research, September 2003, https://www.nber.org/digest/sep03/what-happened-wages-mexico-nafta.
31. "The Case for Open Trade," World Trade Organization, https://www.wto.org/english/thewto_e/whatis_e/tif_e/fact3_e.htm.
32. Robert E. Scott, "Administration's Own Analysis Suggests Spiraling Deficits, Job Losses," *Economic Policy Institute*, February 1, 2000, https://www.epi.org/publication/issuebriefs_ib137/.
33. Jagdish N. Bhagwati, *Free Trade Today* (Princeton, NJ: Princeton University Press, 2002), 18; Edna Bonacich and Richard P. Applebaum, "Offshore Production," in *Sweatshop U.S.A.: The American Sweatshop in Historical and Global Perspective*, edited by Daniel Bender and Richard Greenwald (New York: Routledge, 2005), 141.
34. Prince Ghosh, "The Exodus of Chinese Manufacturing: Shutting Down 'The World's Factory," *Forbes*, September 18, 2020.
35. Fredric Jameson, "Notes on Globalization as a Philosophical Issue" in *The Cultures of Globalization*, edited by Fredric Jameson and Masao Miyoshi (Durham: Duke University Press, 1998), 62. See critique in David Held, Anthony G. McGrew, David Goldblatt, and Jonathan Perraton, *Global Transformations: Politics, Economics, and Culture* (Stanford, CA:

Stanford University Press, 1999), 328.

36. Fredric Jameson, "Notes on Globalization," 62. See critique in Held et al., *Global Transformations*, 328.
37. Jan Nederveen Pieterse, "Globalization as Hybridization," in *Global Modernities*, edited by Mike Featherstone, Scott Lash, and Roland Robertson, 54–77 (London: Sage, 1995).
38. James L. Watson, ed., *Golden Arches East: McDonald's in East Asia*, 2nd ed. (Stanford: Stanford University Press, 2006).
39. Matthews, Ma, and Lui, *Hong Kong, China*, 31.
40. Ibid.,15.
41. Christopher DeWolf, "How Hong Kong Became a 'City of Malls,'" *CNN*, January 27, 2020, https://www.cnn.com; "Dining," Hong Kong Tourism Board, https://www.discoverhongkong.com/us/explore/dining.html.
42. "Film Entertainment Industry in Hong Kong," Hong Kong Trade Development Council, December 6, 2021, https://research.hktdc.com/en/article/MzExMjc4NDIz.
43. "Marvel's 'Shang-Chi' Was Made with China in Mind. Here's Why Beijing Doesn't Like It," *NBC New York*, October 4, 2021, https://www.nbcnewyork.com.
44. Micky Lee, "Constructed Global Space, Constructed Citizenship," *Javnost—The Public* 16, no. 3 (2009): 21.
45. Ibid., 33.
46. Gordon, Ma, and Lui, *Hong Kong, China*, 57.
47. Xie Yu, "Citic, Carlyle to Buy McDonald's Franchise in Hong Kong, China in a Deal Worth U.S. $2.08 Billion," *South China Morning Post*, January 9, 2017, https://www.scmp.com.
48. "Why Starbucks? The Brands Being Attacked in Hong Kong," *BBC News*, October 11, 2019, https://www.bbc.com.
49. James L. Watson, "McDonald's in Hong Kong: Consumerism, Dietary Change, and the Rise of a Children's Culture," in *Golden Arches East: McDonald's in East Asia*, 2nd ed., edited by James L. Watson (Stanford: Stanford University Press, 2006), 105.
50. Zoe Low and Ho-him Chan, "Coronavirus: Hong Kong's Homeless 'McRefugees' Scramble for Places to Stay as McDonald's Axes Dine-in Services in Evening to Help Fight Pandemic," *South China Morning Post*, March 25, 2020, https://www.scmp.com.
51. When these places are busy, neighbors would often just stand so as not to drive paying customers away.
52. South China Morning Post @SCMPNews, Twitter post, October 4, 2014, https://twitter.com/SCMPNews/status/518600676742402048?s=20.
53. Lucy Craymer and Heather Haddon, "Hong Kong Protesters Find Fresh Targets: 'What I Taste from Starbucks Is . . . Shame,'" *Wall Street Journal*, October 4, 2019.

54. Amelia Lucas, "After Hong Kong Protestors Target Starbucks Stores, CEO Says Employee Safety Is His 'Focus' and 'Priority,'" *CNBC*, November 1, 2019.
55. Given that I was not physically in Hong Kong during the protests, information about them was drawn from local newspapers (*South China Morning Post*, *Ming Pao*, *Hong Kong Free Press*, and *Apple Daily*) as well as U.K. and U.S.-based media such as *BBC News*, *CNN*, and *The Economist*. Some information came from acquaintances' social media. They are university-educated professionals who were born and grew up in Hong Kong before 1997. Therefore, social media information on which I rely excludes lived experience and opinions of those who have less cultural capital and English competency; it also excludes younger people who were born after Hong Kong's return.
56. Andrew Gilmore, "Convergence and Fragmentation in the Umbrella Revolution: A Rhetorical Analysis of the Mainlandization of Hong Kong," in *Communication Convergence in Contemporary China: International Perspective in Politics Platforms, and Participation*, edited by Patrick Shaou-Whea Dodge (East Lansing: University of Michigan Press, 2021), 20.
57. Zoe Suen, "How Hong Kong's Protest Uniform Changed a Market," *Business of Fashion*, November 7, 2019, https://www.businessoffashion.com/articles/china/the-aftermath-of-hong-kongs-protest-uniform/.
58. Hiromi Makino, "Why Does Japan Media Call HK Activist Agnes Chow 'Goddess of Democracy'?," *Mainichi*, September 9, 2020.
59. Kirsty Needham, "Chinese Companies Targeted as Wave of Destruction Hits Hong Kong," *Sydney Morning Herald*, October 21, 2019, https://www.smh.com.au.
60. Matthews, Ma, and Lui, *Hong Kong, China*, 127.
61. Oiwan Lam, "In Hong Kong, Local Entrepreneurs Champion the Pro-Democracy Cause," *Hong Kong Free Press*, December 28, 2019.
62. Alexandra Chan, "'Buy Yellow, Eat Yellow': The Economic Arm of Hong Kong's Pro-Democracy Protests," *The Diplomat*, December 13, 2019. .
63. Angela Doland, "From McDonald's to Fendi: How a Few Brands Were Swept into the Hong Kong Protests," *AdAge*, October 9, 2014, https://adage.com; Terry Nguyen, "American Brands Are Trying to Play Both Sides of the Hong Kong-China Conflict," *Vox*, October 11, 2019, .
64. Derek Wallbank and Alfred Cang, "How a Quickly-Deleted Tweet about China Got Pretty Much Everyone Mad at the NBA," *Time Magazine*, October 7, 2019, https://time.com.
65. Antony Dapiran, "How Hong Kong's Shopping Malls Became a New Arena in the Fight for Democracy," *New Statesman*, September 6, 2019.
66. Kwong, "Growth of 'Localism,'" 64–66; Hayley Wu, "The Trouble of Localism in Hong

Kong," *Berkeley Political Review*, March 8, 2018, https://bpr.berkeley.edu/2018/03/08/the-trouble-of-localism-in-hong-kong/.

67. Iam-Chong Ip, "Politics of Belonging: A Study of the Campaign against Mainland Visitors in Hong Kong," *Inter-Asia Cultural Studies* 16, no. 3 (2015): 417; Micky Lee, "Localism Against Nationalism: Resisting Being Chinese in Hong Kong," *InMediaRes*, February 22, 2022.
68. There are many examples, one of them is Jer, "如何分辨中國人和香港人" ["How to distinguish between mainlander from Hong Kong people"], *YouTube*, May 8, 2020, https://www.youtube.com/watch?v=WPa4Wds4UGU.
69. Ernest, "【問問日本人】點樣分辨中國人VS香港人 中國旅客經常大聲說話？" ["Ask a Japanese: How to Tell the Difference between Chinese and Hongkongers? Chinese Tourists are Usually Loud?"], *Apple Daily*, October 10, 2019, https://hk.appledaily.com.
70. Ip, "Politics of Belonging," 413.
71. Kwong, "Growth of 'Localism,'" 65; Wu, "Trouble of Localism."
72. "Fees and Charges," Hong Kong Hospital Authority, https://www.ha.org.hk/visitor/fees_and_charges.asp?lang=ENG#b.

Discourses of National Identity in Hong Kong

Examining Media Coverage of Carrie Lam's Leadership

Ming Xie and Chin-Chung Chao

The street protests, the COVID-19 pandemic, and the U.S.–China trade war have all escalated political and social conflict in Hong Kong. As the trade dispute between the United States and China continues, the tension between these two countries has significantly impacted Hong Kong's privileged economic status, transforming the city's relationships with international trade partners and its sense of itself. But what the general public knows about these events and their causes mainly comes from media coverage. Benedict Anderson has shown that media is heavily involved in creating, promoting, and reflecting narratives about citizenship and the nation.[1] For this reason, media coverage of events such as the 2019–2020 Hong Kong protests, the COVID-19 pandemic, and the 2018–2020 U.S.–China trade war plays an essential role in shaping, organizing, and normalizing national identity in Hong Kong. This identity formation occurs at different levels, in pictures, texts, and language choices, which all reflect narrative structures and represents an identity-forming process within specific contexts, media users' embeddedness in both specific political contexts, and historically influenced notions about national identity. In short, different senses of national identity in Hong Kong have undergone a remarkably turbulent period, with local, regional, national, and international repercussions.

Compared to ethnic and cultural identity, national identity and nationalism are more related to political representation and discourse. For instance, nationalism has been viewed as a concept that "values membership in a nation greater than other groups" and emphasizes political representation by the nation.[2] Therefore, examining nationalism starts with questions such as whether a specific political choice or national identity is given priority. In the process of framing national identity, political leaders have been the core figures. During the process, political elites develop nationalist leadership strategies that emphasize national pride, patriotism, and international prestige to navigate power relations and elaborate nationalist discourse. The political elites' leadership, political stances, and interpretations of regional, national, and international relations are conveyed to the public largely through media coverage. Therefore, media can impact public opinion, mobilize social resources, and shape ethnic and group identification and national identity.

This chapter focuses on media coverage of Carrie Lam's leadership during the 2019–2020 Hong Kong protests, the COVID-19 pandemic, and the U.S.–China trade war. Carrie Lam has served as chief executive of Hong Kong since 2017. As the first female chief executive, Lam's leadership and her administration have faced some tough challenges. This research addresses two research questions: (1) What are Lam's nationalist leadership styles in dealing with these crises? (2) How has media coverage portrayed Lam's nationalist leadership? Examining Lam's nationalist leadership illustrates the dynamic relationship between democratic and authoritarian ideologies in Hong Kong. Since Hong Kong's handover to the mainland of China in 1997, its society has been divided between pro-establishment and pro-democracy advocates, with increasing tensions between democracy and authoritarianism.[3] Under Lam's administration, the tensions became more pronounced and further complicated with the turbulent relations between the United States, China, and the rest of the world. In addition, the literature on gender and nationalism has focused on the struggles in which women have had to participate in national political life.[4] As the first woman to assume the top leadership role in Hong Kong, Lam's discourse illuminates the relationship between gendered leadership styles and nationalism as well as Hong Kong's struggle against China's patriarchal authoritarianism. Studying Lam's discourse of nationalism thus points to issues of national identity, gender, and the ongoing tension between pro-democratic and pro-mainland forces in Hong Kong.

The central oddity in this case study is that Lam's nationalist leadership hinges on her representing herself as a pro-China force of resistance against Western support for democracy in Hong Kong. As such, the major media outlets in Hong Kong have not endorsed Lam, portraying her instead as a stooge of the Chinese central government. In addition, the media has depicted her as lacking in strategies to highlight charismatic leadership and civic nationalism. As a result, this research helps our understanding of how Lam's version of nationalism has evolved and changed in an increasingly polarized Hong Kong society. By comparing the pro-Chinese media's portrayal of Lam as a brave defender of threatened Chinese nationalism against the pro-democracy media's portrayals of Lam as a communist mouthpiece, we can observe as Hong Kong's evolving nationalism rotates from resistance against alleged Western encroachment to resistance against "mainlandization" from China. The chapter thus focuses on Lam's leadership to demonstrate the complexities and confusions of national identity formation in Hong Kong, in turn showing how Hong Kongers' competing versions of identity are influenced by China, the United States, and their different narratives about nationalism.

Media Coverage and Nationalist Leadership

According to Benedict Anderson, the nation is an imagined community "because the members of even the smallest nations will never know most of their fellow members, meet them, or even hear of them, yet in the minds of each lives the image of their communion."[5] Anderson's concept of the imagined community illustrates how mass media can create a social construction of nation and national identity. Media discourse has constantly engaged in the production of national identity, the protection of national interest, and the encouragement of ritual consumption.[6] Nationalist political leaders demonstrate their leadership by making crucial decisions, skillfully managing crises, and running complicated large-scale projects and initiatives.[7] As Hironori Sasada has discussed, nationalist leadership emphasizes national pride, patriotism, and international prestige.[8] Media coverage can be an effective tool for political elites to demonstrate their political standing, charismatic personality, and leadership skills, and therefore mobilize nationalism. In other words, the formation of national identity is related to leaders' abilities to build social relationships through symbols, discourses, and interactions. At the same time, citizens can engage in nationalist discourse and imagine themselves as a national community when they consume mass media. Mass media fortifies citizens' political knowledge, fosters their capability to contend with politics, promotes political participation, and makes governments accountable for political decisions. Also, mass media forms a national identity by exposing news coverage supporting national development or conveying a positive image of nationalist leadership, therefore reinforcing individuals' affection for the incumbent nation-state.[9]

Research on nationalism and national identity discusses two types of nationalism: civic nationalism and state nationalism. Civic nationalism is formed by culture, language, religion, geographical conditions, individuals' shared values, and social experiences.[10] Therefore, the concept of civic nationalism is based on the principle that the nation is formed through individuals' choices, bubbling up as an organic version of grassroots solidarity.[11] For example, civic nationalism has erupted in Hong Kong by rejecting a Beijing-centered nationalism and valuing democracy and freedom within a largely democratic international system.[12] The emphasis of a civic identity and sense of community among Hong Kong people is viewed as confronting cultural and economic "mainlandization."[13] The pro-democratic group of Hong Kong has expressed its resistance to mainlandization, in order to differentiate itself from the mainland, hence illustrating how this civic nationalism entails both a sense of solidarity with one's neighbors and opposition to encroachments by what are perceived as outside forces.

In contrast, state nationalism is a political concept related to the established nation-state and an imagined political community, as portrayed from the top down. If civic nationalism is grassroots and organic, so state nationalism tends to reflect the wishes of entrenched political elites. This top-down nationalism is based on the belief that "the world is (and should be) divided into identifiable nations, that each person should belong to a nation, that an individual's nationality has some influence on how they think and behave and leads to certain responsibilities and entitlements."[14] Overall, both civic and state nationalism distinguish and prioritize in-group members from others.

Ian Seckington has identified the deepened tension between state nationalism and civic nationalism in Hong Kong.[15] State nationalism has been a crucial pillar of the authoritarian regime in China.[16] Within the model of "one country, two systems" promoted by the Chinese central government, state nationalism emphasizes political solidarity and authoritarian political control. Moreover, the Hong Kong Special Administrative Region (HKSAR) government has attempted to foster a

Chinese national identity based on the political authority of the Chinese central government. For example, the Hong Kong Basic Law issued by the Chinese central government in 1997 "prohibit[s] any act of treason, secession, sedition, subversion against the Central People's Government."[17] State nationalism is most successful when it overlaps with civic nationalism, but as the Hong Kong situation indicates, when the two forces clash, state nationalism can sometimes feel like an imposition.

The challenge Lam has faced is a polarized and pluralistic society.[18] Civic nationalism focuses on Hong Kong people's self-determination and concepts such as the "rule of law, civil liberties, human rights, a free and vibrant press."[19] With the continuous economic, social, and political changes, Hong Kong people's feelings toward the Chinese central government have become complicated. On the one hand, the authoritarian central government has imposed absolute authority over the Hong Kong administrative government; on the other hand, Hong Kong people view their interests and values as the opposite of the Chinese central government.[20] Hence, pro-democracy groups advocate for democratic values and the initiation of social transformation to defend "their civic identity against real and perceived threats from the government."[21] They promote Hong Kong's separateness from the mainland of China and reject the "mainlandization" of Hong Kong.[22] One instance is the pro-democracy's advocacy for the universal suffrage of the chief executive in 2014 rather than the preapproved candidates selected by the Chinese central government. On the contrary, when the central government released the Hong Kong election law in March 2021, the pro-establishment groups tried to endorse the reform by collecting citizens' signatures and building trust between Hong Kong society and the mainland of China.[23] What makes the Hong Kong situation so complicated, then, is that the city's emerging sense of civic nationalism is rooted in increasingly strident opposition to China's state nationalism, rendering the very notion of national identity a source of pride, conflict, hope, and fear.

Complex international relations have also influenced Hong Kong's national identity. Historically, as a British colony, Hong Kong created a conqueror-colonial mentality in its political leadership.[24] That is, leadership was exercised in the interests of the sovereign state. Before the Hong Kong handover, national identity was formed by institutions, and the Hong Kong people value democracy, freedom, autonomy, and individual rights, which still profoundly influence the current national identity of Hong Kong. During the 2019–2020 protests, the

United Kingdom expressed concern regarding the Chinese central government's control over Hong Kong. As well, the United States has been deeply involved in Hong Kong's political and economic development. In 1992, the U.S.–Hong Kong Policy Act stated that the United States supported Hong Kong's autonomy by concluding and implementing bilateral agreements. During the 2019–2020 Hong Kong protests, protesters gathered in front of the U.S. Consulate in Hong Kong, asking for support from the U.S. administration to help confront the pro-China Lam Administration. In November 2019, U.S. president Donald Trump also signed the Hong Kong Human Rights and Democracy Act to support the Hong Kong protesters.[25] In July 2020, Trump signed the Hong Kong Autonomy Act, which imposes sanctions on officials and entities in Hong Kong and mainland China that are deemed as helping violate Hong Kong's autonomy.[26] The report on U.S. relations with Hong Kong released by the U.S. Department of State in August 2020 states, "Hong Kong is an independent customs territory and economic entity separate from the PRC and can separately enter into international agreements in commercial, economic, and certain legal matters, under the Basic Law."[27] In March 2021, U.S. Secretary of State Blinken stated that the United States would stand up for human rights and democratic values and take action against those responsible for violations of human rights in Hong Kong. The statement reinforced the pro-democracy groups' value of autonomy and freedom while escalating the tension among the different ideological groups.

As a result of these historical narratives and political discourses, Hong Kong has developed its unique national identity. Zhongdang Pan and three other scholars analyzed the media discourses of the Hong Kong handover. They identified how the Chinese Party-state constructed media discourses by reinforcing the official ideology of the Communist Party. Through the construction of historical narratives and political authority, mass media became state apparatuses on framing issues of identity and national interest. For example, regarding the Hong Kong handover in 1997, the mass media controlled by the Chinese central government used the metaphor of family and historical stories to highlight family fidelity and common ancestry, and to personalize political events.[28] Zhongshi Guo's coauthored research focused on specific events, such as China's entry into the World Trade Organization and the China–U.S. aircraft collision, and found that media coverage provided a consistent and routine contribution to the public imagination of nationalism.[29] These examples show how China's state-run mass media construct and reinforce national identity through event-related coverage.

Female Leadership in the Context of Hong Kong

Mass media is the lens through which citizens see politics in action. Carrie Lam's nationalistic leadership style is complicated by her female identity in Hong Kong's political arena. The public nature of politics makes women occupying traditionally male roles in the political domain highly visible.[30] The news media often situates female politicians as women first and politicians second by highlighting their marital status, sexuality, appearance, and domestic roles.[31] Political leadership has been a male-dominant arena in Chinese culture with masculine values and themes. As Chin-chung Chao and Yahui Zhang suggest, political issues are gendered. People trust women to handle issues such as education, health care, poverty, and the welfare of children and families. In contrast, men are trusted to handle issues such as defense and military affairs, foreign policy, crime, and economic management.[32] Gender-based assumptions have been one main obstacle for female political leaders. As leaders, they are required to be confident and assertive; as women, they are expected to be communal and feminine, which makes them perceived as weak and ineffectual.[33]

As the chief executive of Hong Kong, Lam has been navigating and balancing leadership between the local needs and interests in Hong Kong and the Chinese central government's authority and agenda. She has also been portrayed by mass media as "a defender of the regime as a tough iron lady or a utilitarian stooge of Beijing."[34] Based on Article 48(9) of Hong Kong Basic Law, the chief executive is responsible "to conduct, on behalf of the Government of Hong Kong Special Administrative Region, external affairs and other affairs as authorized by the Central Authorities." On October 11, 2017, Lam's first policy as the chief executive of HKSAR mandated a Chinese curriculum, requiring Hong Kong's young students to study China in junior secondary schools.[35] When the anti-extradition bill protests started in Hong Kong in June 2019, with the ongoing protests starting in 2019 and COVID-19, the media criticized the Lam administration as ineffectual, slow, uncoordinated, and lacking governance capacity.[36] Chun Man Rolian Lee analyzed Lam's responses toward these critiques and found that Lam tried to project a strong authoritarian voice while employing public engagement strategies to restore the public's confidence in her governance.[37] For instance, on February 4, 2020, Lam ordered Hong Kong officials not to wear masks to save stocks for medical workers. The newspaper *South China Morning Post* reported this information and criticized Lam for neglecting civil servants' safety.

The critiques were not only directed at Lam's authoritarian voice and her disconnection with Hong Kong society. Her leadership as a woman and the improper use of her role as a mother were also attacked. On June 12, 2019, she appeared on television and used her identity as a mother of two sons to justify her handling of the protest. Her response was viewed as condescending, which worsened the growing crisis of public confidence in the government.[38] Later, she was described as nervous and emotional while she appeared on mass media. The recent events of the 2019–2020 Hong Kong protests, the COVID-19 pandemic, and the U.S.–China trade war provide an apparent context to explore the constructions of a political woman leader influenced by the Chinese culture to understand the specific challenges they face as aspiring women in politics.

Overall, the current literature suggests that the interaction of media coverage and national consciousness closely relate to the legitimacy of leadership. Lam's controversial leadership styles have reflected the sociopolitical contexts of Hong Kong and the political dynamics between Hong Kong and the Chinese government within the complex international relationships. The Chinese central government has used the same governance and rhetorical strategies to build up top-down nationalism in the mainland of China and Hong Kong. The examination of Lam's leadership as Hong Kong's chief executive and media coverage of her leadership style offers a context-based understanding of Hong Kong's struggle over its national identity as well as the tensions between civic and state nationalism.

Methodology

This study adopted the discourse analysis method and gathered media coverage to analyze the reporting of Lam's nationalist leadership and woman leadership. Beyond texts and language, discourse is a broader term related to social context as well as to knowledge and power.[39] Examining grammatical and organizational aspects of discourse in relation to their social context helps expose or denaturalize implicit political agendas. Discourse analysis is appropriate for this research because of its capability to capture the qualitative nuances of media portrayals regarding Lam's leadership style, strategies, behaviors, and responses. The research method has been adopted by previous similar research on Australia's first female prime minister.[40]

Our research selected four newspapers from Hong Kong: *Ta Kung Pao*, *Apple Daily*, *Oriental Daily News*, and *Ming Pao*. *Ta Kung Pao* was chosen because of its reputation as a strong supporter of the Communist Party of China.[41] In addition to *Ta Kung Pao*, all three selected newspapers are the most popular newspapers in Hong Kong. *Apple Daily* was founded in the 1990s by a pro-democracy entrepreneur Jimmy Lai and has been one of the most popular newspapers in Hong Kong. It is viewed as mass-oriented, favorable of the pro-democracy camp, and critical of the Communist Party of China.[42] In August 2020, Jimmy Lai was arrested over allegations, including collusion with foreign forces under the national security law imposed in June 2020. However, following Lai's arrest, *Apple Daily* produced 550,000 copies—five times more than its average circulation, to urge people to buy the paper and show their support. In April 2021, Lai was sentenced to fourteen months in prison because he participated in unauthorized assemblies in August 2019. Following Lai's sentence, *Apple Daily* was shut down in June 2021. Lai's repeated arrests and *Apple Daily*'s shutdown have drawn criticism from Western governments and international human rights groups who raised concerns over waning freedoms in the global financial hub, including freedom of speech and assembly. Our data were collected before *Apply Daily* was shut down.

Oriental Daily is also a mass-oriented newspaper in Hong Kong but is more pro-government than *Apple Daily*.[43] *Ming Pao* used to be considered the most trusted and respected newspaper in Hong Kong.[44] Unfortunately, the Chinese central government decided to intervene in its operation. In 2016, the chief executive editor of *Ming Pao* was dismissed after a report revealing the offshore business dealings of influential citizens in Hong Kong and the mainland of China. His dismissal caused protests and critiques about the Chinese central government's censorship tactics over Hong Kong's press freedom.

We chose these newspapers with various backgrounds to offer a comparative perspective to identify, analyze, and interpret the recurrent themes.[45] This research analyzes the media coverage of Lam in dealing with the 2019–2020 Hong Kong protests, the COVID-19 pandemic, and the U.S.–China trade war between 2018 and 2020. We collected articles from the above four newspapers on Lam's statements regarding the three events published from May to August 2020. This period was significant because it covered the escalation of the U.S.–China trade war as well as the former U.S. president Trump's critiques of COVID-19 as the "Chinese virus." In August 2020, the U.S. Customs and Border Protection issued a notice requiring that goods produced in Hong Kong and exported to the United States be marked as originating in China. The notice implied that Hong Kong's exports to the United States might face the additional tariffs that the United States has imposed on Chinese products amid the trade war. In early August of 2020, the U.S. Department of Treasury accused Lam's "implementing Beijing's policies of suppression of freedom and democratic processes."[46] As a consequence, it has imposed sanctions on Lam and the other ten officials of Hong Kong and the mainland of China.

We conducted the search by using keywords "Carrie Lam," "protest," "COVID-19," and "the U.S.–China trade war" in the online databases of four newspapers: *Apple Daily, Oriental Daily, Ming Pao, and Ta Kung Pao*. As a result, one hundred articles including news reports and editorials were collected. Then, a qualitative content analysis of these articles was conducted. Data analysis began with reading the collected articles. The analysis integrated the social situation related to the media coverage, the function of the text, and how the functions have been fulfilled through specific discourse patterns. The examination of nationalism in media coverage of Lam's leadership focused on two main types: state nationalism and civic nationalism, especially the tension between these two types of nationalism. We read through the one hundred articles and listed 217 significant statements. The significant statements were selected based on classifications of civic and state nationalism. Based on the list, we sorted the relevant texts into three coherent categories as themes. A theme is a relevant issue, concept, opinion, understanding, knowledge, experience, or question. In the thematic analysis, we repeatedly read the significant statements and determined the themes of the research questions presented in the statements. To be specific, we identified three themes to address our research questions.

Discourse analysis helps develop suitable and effective strategies at the intersection of nationalist leadership and women's leadership. The discourses provide a feasible start to understand the various conceptions of civic and state nationalism in Hong Kong, explaining the current political and ideological conflict within the region, and exploring the significant roles exerted by China and the United States. In addition, our analysis provides an inductive examination of the fluctuations and salience of various media coverage of Lam's leadership under the 2019–2020 Hong Kong protests, the COVID-19 pandemic, and the U.S.–China trade war.

Research Findings

Our analysis identified three major themes: (1) polarized leadership: self-disclosure and media portrayal; (2) patriotism: alignment with the dominant political institutions and the national mission; and (3) negotiation of civic and state nationalism: the conflicting identities in Hong Kong. The themes, as well as summary statements and explanations of research findings, are addressed below.

Polarizing Portrayals of Lam as Caring Leader vs. Lam as Iron-Fisted Stooge

As a political leader, Lam has attempted to demonstrate her comprehensive leadership skills through self-disclosure in public. Being aware of Hong Kong people's distrust of politics, especially with regard to the relationship with the mainland of China, she has presented herself as a leader who does not know much about politics by saying "I am a managerial person."[47] Also, Lam has tried to highlight her contributions to Hong Kong society. She stated that she has served Hong Kong citizens for forty years "in good faith, without fear or favor," and would listen to the citizens' opinions and serve Hong Kong's future humbly.[48] In an interview conducted by *Ta Kung Pao* in May 2020, Lam said, "I encouraged my colleagues to confront the challenges and do not be afraid of others' critiques. The society will see what we have done correctly."[49] In response to the interview, *Ming Pao* commented that Lam is a brave, straightforward leader who dares to criticize and confront people with different opinions.

Lam also publicly showed herself as a responsible leader. According to *Oriental Daily*, Lam and some other Hong Kong government officials announced that they donated their one month's salary at the end of February 2020 to manage the COVID-19 pandemic. Also, on June 6, 2020, Lam told the public that all Hong Kong administrative officials would not receive a salary increase for one year "to deal with the current hardship in Hong Kong."[50]

Although Lam attempted to create a self-sacrificing image as Hong Kong's leader, media coverage has contrarily portrayed her as a selfish and greedy official. Her leadership was portrayed more negatively by a few of these newspapers. *Oriental Daily* reported that Lam received an HK$100,000 salary increase in 2020, which made her earn approximately HK$5.2 million (USD$672,000) in the year 2020. The report stated that Lam, as a government official, received the second highest salary worldwide. A report of *Apple Daily* on August 10, 2020, cited a public opinion poll, claiming that 47 percent of the respondents "despised" Lam and rated her overall leadership as zero out of 100. Similarly, on August 26, *Oriental Daily* reported that 70 percent of Hong Kong citizens did not want Lam to be the chief executive again. *Apple Daily* portrayed Lam as condescending, stubborn, shameless, and despicable. For example, a report on June 30, 2020, stated:

> She [Carrie Lam] is arrogant. She looks down on others, including doctors. The US–China relations were very tense, but all she did was add oil to the flames. Her extradition law bid split the community. She refused to visit young people who were beaten up [during protests]. Since the beginning, she has been a tough executor. The only difference is that she used to claim to serve Hongkongers, and now she serves the central government. She seems to have been taking orders from Beijing only and has ignored the feelings and opinions of most Hongkongers.[51]

These descriptions from various news outlets show that even though Lam attempted to present herself as a noble leader for the Hong Kong people, the mainstream media in Hong Kong viewed her leadership as undemocratic and self-serving.

Lam also faces challenges as a female leader. On the one hand, media coverage focused heavily on her family; on the other hand, her parenting style was criticized as ineffective leadership. For example, *Ming Pao* revealed Lam's concern over the impact of her political position on her family. A report on August 27 stated, "Lam's family is aware of the political pressures and is willing to compromise for Lam." In the report, Lam mentioned that she would not run for the chief executive position if her son disapproved, so that she would not have to go through all the stressful and painful processes. Additionally, she made statements to link her relationship with Hong Kong people to her relationship with her two sons. However, as previous research identified, emphasis on her family did not increase acceptance of her leadership during the government crisis. In fact, public critiques and distrust of her leadership reached a high.[52] Her communal and feminine features seemed to make her appear weak and ineffectual in dealing with the crisis. Also, media coverage positioned her as feeling superior to the Hong Kong people and as a pro-establishment representative of the patriarchal Chinese central government.

Patriotism Aligned with the Dominant Political Institutions and the National Mission

Patriotism has been one of the core values of state-centered nationalism in China.[53] It is also a recurrent and controversial issue in Hong Kong because of its complicated relationship with the Communist Party of China.[54] At the closing ceremony of the sixth plenum of the fourteenth Party Congress in 1996, the previous leader of China, Zemin Jiang, stated that the patriotism of the Communist Party is the highest principle of the Chinese nation. The official discourse on nationalism placed the Communist Party at the center of the country's development.

Historically, Hong Kong has not had a connection with the Communist Party. However, as the top political leader in Hong Kong, Lam is aware of and has explicitly expressed her political stand to fit the Party's expectations. All of her statements collected between May and August 2020 have aligned with the dominant political institutions, the Party-state power, and the Chinese authorities. Throughout her statements, bureaucratic power and a salient national consciousness have been core themes. For example, in a *Ming Pao* report on May 30, 2020, Lam cited Deng Xiaoping, the Chinese paramount leader who led the Hong Kong handover negotiation with the United Kingdom in the 1980s, to comment on the 2019–2020 protests of Hong Kong. She said, "In 1987, Deng Xiaoping claimed that it is unrealistic to allow Hong Kong people to manage Hong Kong fully. It will create chaos if the Chinese central government gives up all the governance authority in Hong Kong, and therefore Hong Kong's interest will be hurt."[55] Also, it is unacceptable, she remarked, that "some foreign countries are trying to use Hong Kong as a democratic base against the Chinese central government."[56] Among the foreign countries mentioned in the report, the United States has been one of the leading countries defending Hong Kong against the Chinese central government. In 2020, the relationship between the United States and China was increasingly conflicted. Soon after her comments in May, the Chinese central government released the *Hong Kong National Security Law* on June 30, 2020, which has been criticized by countries such as the United States and the United Kingdom as a violation of the freedom and autonomy of Hong Kong. In early August 2020, the United States imposed sanctions on Lam and ten other Hong Kong and Chinese officials due to the alleged curbing of Hong Kong's freedom and autonomy. Lam immediately reacted to express her loyalty toward the Communist Party of China and cut her connection with the United States by giving up her U.S. visa and credit cards. She explained, "The most important thing is that we feel honored to be trusted by the central government at such a historical moment to enforce this law to safeguard national security. The more people who oppose China attack us, the more effective the National Security Law in Hong Kong will be."[57] Her defiance against the Western sanctions was coupled with passionate pronouncements upon her loyalty toward the Chinese Communist Party. As a nationalistic leader, Lam spoke on half of Hongkongers to stand firmly with the Beijing government.

However, Lam's emphasis on patriotism has not been entirely successful because of the political gap between the mainland of China and Hong Kong. For example, on August 7, 2020, Lam announced that Beijing would send health officials to help Hong Kong cope with the third wave of the coronavirus pandemic. However, the support from Beijing was criticized by *Apple Daily* as lacking transparency and accountability, and thereby subjecting Hong Kong people to surveillance tactics. An article published on August 19, 2020 on *Apple Daily* stated:

> This began with Lam's announcement on August 7 that Hong Kong could not cope with the third wave of coronavirus pandemic and had asked the central government for help. In no time, Beijing sent unknown number of health officials to help the city increase its testing capacity of COVID-19 cases. Lam also announced that, with the support of Beijing, universal, free and voluntary COVID-19 testing would be provided to all Hong Kong people who want to be screened for the virus. The lack of transparency and accountability of the whole project of inviting Mainland experts to assist with fighting the pandemic and the involvement of mainland testing companies has raised alarm. Some people were concerned that universal testing could lead to harvesting of DNA samples by the mainland authorities and subjecting Hong Kong people to surveillance tactic such as digital contact tracing similar to what is being done in the mainland.

In this paragraph, we see that Lam's patriotism raised public concern about her leadership and distrust of her government. While Lam's actions and rhetoric demonstrated her alliances with the Chinese Communist Party's agenda in Hong Kong, there remained dissident voices from civic society. These contradictions illustrate the challenges over Lam's tendency to lead Hong Kong based on directions from the Chinese central government.

Negotiation of Civic and State Nationalism

As the second theme identifies, Lam has explicitly stated her political loyalty and compliance with the Chinese central government. Her patriotism is toward the Party-state. Mass media that favor state nationalism tried to describe Lam as a fighter and protector for Hong Kong from the Western domination. Additionally, Lam claimed that she would be the bridge between the central government and Hong Kong society to build a trustful relationship. She commented on the pro-democratic groups, explaining, "We should not compromise with [their] requests and blackmails toward the government. These requests are simply slogans and are not based on empirical evidence."[58] Hence, Lam's responses to pro-democracy groups' critiques and activities have clearly stated her stance. More so, she tried to demonstrate the common interest between Hong Kong and the mainland of China by criticizing pro-democracy groups. State nationalism has been the foundation for the legitimacy of Lam's leadership.

However, both Lam and the HKSAR government have suffered from low public trust and intense public scrutiny. The conflict between state nationalism and civic nationalism cannot be reduced easily. *Apple Daily*'s reports intensified the opposite stands between Lam and the Hong Kong people. Whether local events or international events, the media coverage on *Apple Daily* has compared Lam and Hong Kong people's actions and claimed that Hong Kong people would take the opposite action. An editorial on August 4, 2020, claimed that, "The [HKSAR] government is not seeking a way best to facilitate Hong Kong people's self-reliance and self-standing powers, instead is placing hope on China's help and following China's anti-epidemic arrangements." This media coverage demonstrated that Lam's efforts to establish state nationalism in Hong Kong was unsuccessful. Although Lam's leadership position receives a wide range of powers and authorities from the Chinese central government, she was not able to mitigate public discontent and build a unified national identity within Hong Kong society.

Indeed, identity constructions in Hong Kong were profoundly shaped not only by the political framing of a nation-state but also by the collective memory and shared history. As the above examples indicate, *Apple Daily* framed Lam's statements about cutting off her connections with the United States and the United Kingdom to make Hong Kong stronger as an indication that she does not care the Hong Kong people or Hong Kong society. Lam's immediate response to international criticism and pressure was interpreted as an intention to isolate Hong Kong. As a former colony of the British Empire, Lam's decision could be viewed as cutting ties with the previous master while aligning herself with another one. At the same time, these reports revealed the deepened values of democracy and freedom, which have been the main force in forming civic nationalism in Hong Kong, to counter the Communist Party's authoritarian governance. Regardless of Lam's hopes to be a leader who bridges differences, she continued to face the dilemma of building a positive relationship based on understanding the local needs rather than on a top-down, one-directional approach.

Discussion

The above research findings demonstrate the various portrayals of Lam's leadership, which has been used to reinforce state nationalism and patriotism in Hong Kong. A factional interplay between the Chinese central government's discourses and those of the Hong Kong society is evident. The authoritarian control of the Chinese government has profoundly influenced all of media's operations and reports, whether they are pro-establishment or pro-democracy. In this section, we address the two research questions based on the research findings.

Carrie Lam's Leadership Style

Regarding the first research question, concerned with Lam's leadership styles in dealing with the 2019–2020 Hong Kong protests, the COVID-19 pandemic, and the U.S.–China trade war, this research identifies that Lam has tried to depict a positive image for herself as a protector of the nation-state. In her statements, she reviewed her experience as a public servant of forty years as a means to establish her credibility. Through her many statements, she conveyed that the legitimate national membership of Hong Kong is the Chinese central government. Lam has tried to establish the image of a public servant who rationalizes and acts reasonably while engaging in politics. Therefore, she described the hardship and oppression she has experienced as a leader. She showed that she did not regret devoting herself and her family to Hong Kong and China through actions such as giving up the U.S. visa and her honorary title from the University of Cambridge. In particular, she was unafraid of the criticisms and sanctions of foreign countries in the name of protecting Hong Kong and China. Her tough and combative style in dealing with the criticism has been well-known.[59] Also, we have to note that from Lam's perspective, the interest and benefits of Hong Kong and China are the same. As the representative of the Beijing authority in Hong Kong, she expects that Hong Kong people will embrace the Chinese nationalistic patriotism, and that Hong Kong will be fully integrated with the mainland of China. Therefore, her leadership style has been patriotic to Beijing and resistive to the West. She tried to demonstrate her political skills, although somewhat limited, in navigating between the priorities of the Chinese central government and Hong Kong's local needs.

While attempting to convey a positive image of the nationalist leadership that reveals her commitment to the Chinese state nationalism, Lam has also tried to block out alternative and critical images of Beijing while legitimizing the Hong Kong administration under the control of the Chinese central government. According to her statements about international relations and domestic policies, we found that she adopted straightforward challenges and powerful attacks on the West as her resistant strategies. She has criticized the political interest groups and individuals against the Chinese central government, and emphasized the ideological correctness of controversial issues such as the Hong Kong National Security Law and the Hong Kong Basic Law. While there were challenges within Hong Kong as well as from foreign countries, she took an immediate action to confront them and clearly stated her political position. She critically and explicitly condemned the local protesters and called the behavior of foreign countries irresponsible and destructive. Additionally, her praise for the help from the mainland of China during the COVID pandemic, and her citing of Deng Xiaoping's rhetoric are strategies seek to garner support from and prove the legitimacy of her leadership to the People of Republic of China.

In addition, Lam faces the challenges of Hong Kong's unique identity, which is different from mainland China's national identity and the independent and free people promoted by the pro-democracy groups. An increasingly pressing question for the Hong Kong government, the Chinese central government, and the international society is whether the discourses and actions of Lam's nationalistic leadership can integrate Hong Kong people's desires and political and ideological confrontation from the Beijing government. In her acceptance speech, Lam said:

"Hong Kong, our home is suffering from quite a serious divisiveness and has accumulated a lot of frustrations. My priority will be to heal the divide."[60] At the beginning of the 2019–2020 Hong Kong protests, Lam announced that the Hong Kong government would foster dialogue and help Hong Kong society move forward.[61] However, Hong Kongers remain suspicious of and distrusting toward the Chinese central government, represented by Lam. Her leadership of state nationalism led to critiques of her igniting political crisis rather than healing the wounds. The authoritarian governance style of the Communist Party cannot fit with the current social structure and the deeply rooted democratic values in Hong Kong society. Lam's legitimacy granted by the central government makes her a representative of mainland China rather than of the Hong Kong people. The polemic, polarizing, and divisive media portrayals of Lam also reflect the multiple imageries of national identification in Hong Kong.

Media Image and Nationalist Leadership

Our second research question concerns the degree to which Lam's nationalist leadership has been portrayed by media coverage. Events such as the 2019–2020 protests, the COVID-19 pandemic, and the U.S.–China trade war further raised public discontent about political ideologies, values, as well as governance strategies. They increased the polarization of Hong Kong society, and produced crises and challenges to both the Hong Kong government and society. Our research findings show that most of the media coverage focused on Lam's political stance and her close relationship with the Chinese central government, which has alienated her from Hong Kong society. Because of the different political stances of these newspapers, they have portrayed Lam quite differently. For instance, in terms of Lam's style in dealing with crises, *Ming Pao* and *Ta Kung Pao* described Lam as brave and straightforward while *Apple Daily* and *Oriental Daily* criticized Lam as stubborn. Portrayals of Lam's political stance showed her lack of (desire to express) comprehension of Hong Kong society's social and political conflict. For example, the statement in which she cites Deng Xiaoping and the model of "one country, two systems" on Hong Kong's media increased rather than mitigated public discontent regarding the Communist Party's governance. Apparently, the emphasis of her stance with the Chinese central government does not serve Lam's effort to build a relationship with the Hong Kong public.

In examining these news reports, we found that most of the media coverage of Lam's leadership seems to be ineffective in building solidarity between the government and the public. Immediately following her election as the chief executive in 2017, Lam received mass popular support in Hong Kong. The media published photos of women taking selfies with Lam in public, becoming an inspiration for Hong Kong women. However, the media has portrayed her as "China's puppet" since 2020. Despite her decades of civil service in Hong Kong before her election, she became a "very mainland-Chinese bureaucrat" accountable to the Chinese central government rather than to Hong Kong people.[62] This research reveals that Lam's authoritative voice was strengthened through the media portrayal of her patriotism to Beijing.

Lam's leadership legitimacy mainly derives from the Chinese central government's endorsement. As the first woman who took office as the chief executive of Hong Kong, there is a pressing need for her to restore public confidence in her leadership. However, it appears that she might have missed the opportunity to adopt strategies to construct relationships and conversations with the civic Hong Kong community in achieving public consensus rather than enhancing legitimacy through authoritative means. The media coverage of her as a leader has demonstrated the divisions between pro-establishment and pro-democracy groups, reflecting an increasingly sophisticated and factional Hong Kong society.

Conclusion

Hong Kong's social and political context is unique and complex. Recent events have intensified the existing gap of political values between the Chinese central government conveyed through Hong Kong's first woman leader Carrie Lam, and the local Hong Kong society. We would like to highlight that this research is not intended to make a right or wrong judgment regarding the political debates and controversies. Instead, it aims to present the different perceptions and perspectives and explore the strategies of Lam's nationalist leadership.

Nationalism cannot be separated from politics and cultures.[63] This research focuses on Lam's political rhetoric and mass media's discourses about social upheaval. It examines how national identity is formed by and embedded in the dominant representations of the nation/region in political culture. The analysis of media coverage explores the symbolic interaction and framing of the nation/region's collective actions and struggles. As Michael Billig argues, "Nationalism, far from being an intermittent mood in established nations, is the endemic condition."[64] We hope this research provides some insight to inspire scholars to examine nationalism and national identity from a contextually specific perspective to understand Hong Kong society's uniqueness and political tensions and, therefore, to open dialogue among people with different opinions and values.

NOTES

1. Benedict Anderson, *Imagined Communities: Reflections on the Origin and Spread of Nationalism*, rev. ed. (New York: Verso, 2016). See also Anderson, *The Spectre of Comparisons: Nationalism, Southeast Asia, and the World* (London: Verso, 1998). He discusses the relationship between nationalism and identity in Southeast Asian countries such as Indonesia, East Timor, Thailand, and Philippines. Anderson's discussion is applicable in the current context of Hong Kong, especially the relationship between nationalism and cultural identity. His focus on newspapers further facilitates our analyses of print media.
2. Florian Bieber, "Is Nationalism on the Rise? Assessing Global Trends," *Ethnopolitics* 17, no. 5 (2018): 520.
3. Tai Wei Lim, "The 'Nanny,' the 'Fighter,' and the 'Puppet': A Brief Political Biographical History of Carrie Lam Cheng Yuet-Ngor Including the Earliest Days of Her Chief Executive Appointment," *East Asia* 35, no. 4 (2018): 379–394.
4. Joan Judge, "Talent, Virtue, and the Nation: Chinese Nationalisms and Female Subjectivities in the Early Twentieth Century," *The American Historical Review* 106, no. 3 (June 1, 2001): 765–803, https://doi.org/10.1086/ahr/106.3.765.
5. Anderson, *Imagined Communities*, 6.
6. Jan Herman Brinks, Stella Rock, and Edward Timms, *Nationalist Myths and Modern Media: Contested Identities in the Age of Globalization* (New York: Tauris Academic Studies, 2006).
7. John Breuilly, "Max Weber, Charisma and Nationalist Leadership," *Nations and Nationalism* 17, no. 3 (2011): 477–499.
8. Hironori Sasada, "The Electoral Origin of Japan's Nationalistic Leadership: Primaries in the LDP Presidential Election and the 'Pull Effect'—Document—Gale in Context: Opposing Viewpoints," *Journal of East Asian Studies* 10, no. 1 (2010): 1–30.
9. Chuanli Xia and Fei Shen, "Political Participation in Hong Kong: The Roles of News Media and Online Alternative Media," *International Journal of Communication* 12 (2018): 22.

10. Justin Kwan, "The Rise of Civic Nationalism: Shifting Identities in Hong Kong and Taiwan," *Contemporary Chinese Political Economy and Strategic Relations: An International Journal* 2 (2016): 941–973.
11. Sebastian Veg, "The Rise of 'Localism' and Civic Identity in Post-handover Hong Kong: Questioning the Chinese Nation-State," *China Quarterly* 230 (2017): 323–347.
12. Justin Kwan, "The Rise of Civic Nationalism: Shifting Identities in Hong Kong and Taiwan," *Contemporary Chinese Political Economy and Strategic Relations: An International Journal* 2, no. 2 (August 1, 2016): 941–973.
13. Jeff Hai-chi Loo, "The Myth of 'Hong Kong Nationalism,'" *Asian Education and Development Studies* 9, no. 4 (January 1, 2020): 535–545, https://doi.org/10.1108/AEDS-10-2018-0161.
14. Michael Skey, *National Belonging and Everyday Life: The Significance of Nationhood in an Uncertain World* (Basingstoke, UK: Palgrave Macmillan, 2011), 5.
15. Ian Seckington, "Nationalism, Ideology and China's 'Fourth Generation' Leadership," *Journal of Contemporary China* 14, no. 42 (2005): 23–33.
16. Jean-François Dupré, "Making Hong Kong Chinese: State Nationalism and Its Blowbacks in a Recalcitrant City," *Nationalism and Ethnic Politics* 26, no. 1 (2020): 8–26.
17. Hong Kong Basic Law 1997, Article 23.
18. Koon Wong and Chi Lee, "Learning to Live Together in Polarized and Pluralistic Societies: Hong Kong Teachers' Views of Democratic Values versus Patriotic Values," *Citizenship Teaching & Learning* 14 (2019): 307–330.
19. Malte Philipp Kaeding, "Identity Formation in Taiwan and Hong Kong—How Much Difference, How Many Similarities?," in *Taiwanese Identity in the 21st Century: Domestic, Regional, and Global Perspectives*, edited by Gunter Schubert and Jens Damm, 258–280 (London: Routledge, 2011), 271.
20. Agnes Shuk-mei Ku, "Constructing and Contesting the 'Order' Imagery in Media Discourse: Implications for Civil Society in Hong Kong," *Asian Journal of Communication* 17, no. 2 (2007): 186–200.
21. Kaeding, "Identity Formation," 271.
22. Martin Purbrick, "A Report of the 2019 Hong Kong Protests," *Asian Affairs* 50, no. 4 (2019): 465–487.
23. Tony Cheung, "Hong Kong's Pro-Establishment Heavyweights Push Elections Overhaul on Eve of Endorsement, Call it Key to Rebuilding Beijing's Trust," *South China Morning Post*, March 10, 2021, https://sg.news.yahoo.com/hong-kong-pro-establishment-heavyweights-115833983.html.
24. Jean Lau Chin, "Asian American and Hong Kong Chinese Women Leaders," in *Asian*

Women Leadership: A Cross-National and Cross-Sector Comparison, edited by Chin-chung Chao and Louisa Ha (Abingdon, UK: Routledge, 2020), 207–217.

25. Christopher H. Smith, "H.R.3289—116th Congress (2019–2020): Hong Kong Human Rights and Democracy Act of 2019," legislation, October 16, 2019, 2019/2020, https://www.congress.gov/bill/116th-congress/house-bill/3289.
26. Brad Sherman, "H.R.7440—116th Congress (2019–2020): Hong Kong Autonomy Act," legislation, July 14, 2020, 2019/2020, https://www.congress.gov/bill/116th-congress/house-bill/7440.
27. Bureau of East Asian and Pacific Affairs, "U.S. Relations with Hong Kong," U.S. Department of State, August 28, 2020, https://www.state.gov/u-s-relations-with-hong-kong/.
28. Zhongdang Pan et al., "Orchestrating the Family-Nation Chorus: Chinese Media and Nationalism in the Hong Kong Handover," *Mass Communication and Society* 4, no. 3 (2001): 331–347, 340.
29. Zhongshi Guo, Weng Hin Cheong, and Huailin Chen, "Nationalism as Public Imagination: The Media's Routine Contribution to Latent and Manifest Nationalism in China," *International Communication Gazette* 69, no. 5 (2007): 467–480.
30. Lauren J. Hall and Ngaire Donaghue, "'Nice Girls Don't Carry Knives': Constructions of Ambition in Media Coverage of Australia's First Female Prime Minister," *British Journal of Social Psychology* 52, no. 4 (2013): 631–647.
31. Linda Trimble, "Gender, Political Leadership and Media Visibility: Globe and Mail Coverage of Conservative Party of Canada Leadership Contests," *Canadian Journal of Political Science/Revue Canadienne de Science Politique* 40, no. 4 (2007): 969–993.
32. Chin-chung Chao and Yahui Zhang, "The 'First' First Lady of China and the 'First Black' First Lady of America in the Media's Portrayal," in *Asian Women Leadership: A Cross-National and Cross-Sector Comparison*, edited by Chin-chung Chao and Louisa Ha (Abingdon, UK: Routledge, 2020), 63–76.
33. Chin, "Asian American and Hong Kong Chinese Women Leaders."
34. Lim, "The 'Nanny,' the 'Fighter,' and the 'Puppet,'" 382.
35. Sonny Shiu-Hing Lo, "Ideologies and Factionalism in Beijing–Hong Kong Relations," *Asian Survey* 58, no. 3 (2018): 392–415.
36. Kris Hartley and Darryl S. L. Jarvis, "Policymaking in a Low-Trust State: Legitimacy, State Capacity, and Responses to COVID-19 in Hong Kong," *Policy and Society* 39, no. 3 (2020): 403–423.
37. Chun Man Rolian Lee, "Discursive Leadership of Anson Chan and Carrie Lam: How Do the Most 'Powerful' Hong Kong Women in Politics Take Their Stances?," (MA thesis, University of Hong Kong, 2019).

38. Purbrick, "Report of the 2019 Hong Kong Protests."
39. Fatih Bayram, "Ideology and Political Discourse: A Critical Discourse Analysis of Erdogan's Political Speech," *Arecls* 7 (2010): 23–40.
40. Hall and Donaghue, "Nice Girls Don't Carry Knives."
41. Bryce T. McIntyre, "Public Perceptions of Newspapers' Political Positions: A Perceptual Map of Hong Kong Newspapers," *Asian Journal of Communication* 5, no. 1 (1995): 126–135.
42. Qiaolei Jiang, "Celebrity Athletes, Soft Power and National Identity: Hong Kong Newspaper Coverage of the Olympic Champions of Beijing 2008 and London 2012," *Mass Communication and Society* 16, no. 6 (2013): 888–909.
43. Ku, "Constructing and Contesting the 'Order' Imagery."
44. Chen Wei, "The Image of China in Hong Kong Media: Content Analysis of the Coverage in Three Hong Kong Newspapers," *China Media Research* 8, no. 3 (2012): 65–71.
45. John W. Creswell, *Qualitative Inquiry and Research Design: Choosing among Five Approaches*, 3rd ed. (Thousand Oaks: Sage, 2013).
46. "Hong Kong: US Imposes Sanctions on Chief Executive Carrie Lam," *BBC News*, August 8, 2020, https://www.bbc.com/news/world-us-canada-53699084.
47. "Bei wen Meiguo zhi tsai she fo yo ying xiang jia ren, Lin Zheng Yue E: Jia ren ming bai yuan yee xi sheng" [Being asked about the impact of the U.S. sanction on family, Carrie Lam: My family understood and were willing to sacrifice], *Ming Pao*, August 27, 2020.
48. "Lin Zheng Yue E: Shi zheng bao gao bu zai yo hen duo dong yung gon gong tsai zheng xing tsuo shih" [Carrie Lam: Policy address no longer has many new measures to use public budget], *Ming Pao*, August 25, 2020.
49. "Te sho juang fang/yueh gang chu ru jing yang yueh ne fang kuan jian yi" [Interview with the Chief Executive: Entry and exit of Guangdong, Hong Kong, and Macau; Covid quarantine will be lifted in one month], *Ta Kung Pao*, May 11, 2020.
50. "Lin Zheng Yue E: Cheng chih wei jen kuan yuan chi hang hui fei kuan shou I yuan teng wei lai I nien tung xin" [Carrie Lam: Public officials will have salary freeze for one year], *Ming Pao*, June 9, 2020.
51. "Carrie Lam After Three Years in Power: The Verdict from All Sides," *Apple Daily*, June 30, 2020.
52. Purbrick, "Report of the 2019 Hong Kong Protests."
53. Seckington, "Nationalism, Ideology and China's 'Fourth Generation' Leadership."
54. Jiang, "Celebrity Athletes, Soft Power and National Identity."
55. "Lin Zheng Yue E ying shu Deng Hsiao Ping chiang hua cheng hung yang mo ke neng fang chi so yu kuan chih chuan" [Carrie Lam quoted Deng Xiaoping and claimed that the central government would not give up governance authority], *Ming Pao*, May 30, 2020.

56. “Carrie Lam Quoted Deng Xiaoping.”
57. “National Security Law to ‘Punish the Wicked’: Hong Kong Leader Carrie Lam,” *Apple Daily*, August 18, 2020.
58. “Interview with the Chief Executive.”
59. Lim, “The ‘Nanny,’ the ‘Fighter,’ and the ‘Puppet.’”
60. “Carrie Lam: The Controversial Leader of Hong Kong,” *BBC News*, September 28, 2020, https://www.bbc.com/news/world-asia-china-48646472.
61. The Press Release of HKSAR, September 4, 2019.
62. Timothy McLaughlin, “The Leader Who Killed Her City,” *Atlantic*, June 18, 2020, https://www.theatlantic.com/international/archive/2020/06/carrie-lam-hong-kong-china-protest/612955/.
63. Bart Bonikowski, “Nationalism in Settled Times,” *Annual Review of Sociology* 42, no. 1 (2016): 427–449.
64. Michael Billig, *Banal Nationalism* (Thousand Oaks, CA: Sage, 1995), 6.

A Conversation with Taiwan's Minister of Digital Affairs Audrey Tang on Communication, Technology, Identity, and Democracy

Hsin-I Cheng, Chiaoning Su, and Chiaochun Su

Audrey Tang, Taiwan's first Digital Minister, is well-known for contributing to Taiwan's democratization through free and open technology.[1] Tang is the youngest and first openly transgender minister in Taiwan. Prior to becoming Digital Minister, Tang was active in organizing efforts to move Taiwan toward a society with greater transparency.

On February 1, 2021, Minister Audrey Tang joined us for an hour-long conversation.[2] As Taiwan's Digital Minister, Tang articulated the role of technology—in both technical and social senses—in Taiwan's continuous evolution as a democratic and inclusive nation. Our conversation centered on three areas pertaining to the impact of communication technology: (1) fostering a democratic culture of bottom-up transparency; (2) addressing misinformation or policy designs; and (3) interacting with the growth of Taiwanese national identity. Minister Tang used significant sociopolitical events such as the Sunflower Movement in Taiwan, the Umbrella Movement in Hong Kong, and the COVID-19 pandemic to explain the roles communication technologies play in resisting China's unilateral policies and misinformation campaigns, which combine to threaten Taiwan's democratic ways of life.

This epilogue offers a poignant ending to this book, which aims to articulate various rising consciousnesses as resistant forces; whether about Hong Kong or

Taiwan, the work herein has focused on how publics are empowered to cocreate practices that support open communication networks and participatory democratic systems. We ended the conversation on Minister Tang's outlook on the ways the concept of "radical transparency" is engaged in societies such as Taiwan, where local identity formations and international connections are impacted by dynamic relations between the two most powerful countries in the world—the United States and China.

Building a Culture of Participatory Transparency from the Bottom Up

As early as 2018, English news outlets widely reported on Taiwan's gov (gov-zero) and vTaiwan (virtual Taiwan) as innovative applications of technology.[3] For example, *Wired UK* discussed how gov was started by civic hackers using open data to improve people's understanding of government policy making and spending.[4] In 2016, Tang became Taiwan's first "Digital Minister" and established PDIS (Public Digital Innovation Space), an open-source space for citizens to raise concerns and come to a consensus through deliberations on policies.[5] On our first topic related to technology and democracy, we focused on the significance of the inception, implementation, and impacts of gov in Taiwan. We also asked Minister Tang to explain their view of technology and democracy.

CHENG: Taiwan is one of the most technologically advanced nations in the world, yet it also faces many challenges as a post-authoritarian society. Minister, you were well-known for your talent and experience in innovative technology before you became Taiwan's Digital Minister. Could you please share with us about what your original thoughts were when you first became involved in activities like gov?

Tang: I joined the gov hackathons in early 2013. The gov Taiwan initiative started in late 2012. By the time I joined gov, organizers were already connected to other historically international [activities such as] the Creative Commons Movement, the Open Source Initiative, the Free Software Movement, and so on.[6]

Within Taiwan, there's a broad community and intellectual tradition that informed the gov organizers. Gov started at a time when mobile social media became prevalent in Taiwan and there were a lot of people who wanted to serve as what we call "civic media people."[7] In Mandarin, we call them 公民媒體人 or 自媒體 [*gong min mei ti ren* or *zi mei ti*], the *self-media*. With my training in social interaction design and crowd lexicography—that means collectively making a dictionary—we hoped to evolve both a new language for, and new strategies of governing, this emerging "self-media." We very quickly encountered doubts. Although previous social movements, including Free Software,[8] had a way to engage people who were already practitioners and people who had already shown their interest and formed interest groups and so on, we did not yet have a methodology to engage people who were there for fun, who were engaging in these movements for what we call "clicktivism," meaning that I have only one second to maybe sixty seconds to engage a social idea. There was no robust methodology in these social movement traditions to engage in these ways. In short, we were asking ourselves how to help transition new social media away from "clicktivism" and consumerism toward something more like intentional, long-term political engagement.

My main contribution was to assist what we now call the "Fast, Fair and Fun" principles, and to design engagements that were both pro-social and democratic in the sense that anyone can participate in this governance. We successfully launched, for example, the MoeDict Dictionary project (萌典) that collected the Taiwanese Hoklo, Taiwanese Hakka, Indigenous Amis, and other now official national languages in Taiwan. The MoeDict—a mega dictionary came out in 2013.[9]

Cheng: So this mega dictionary contributed to the inclusion and sustaining of languages spoken by historically marginalized members in Taiwan. You mentioned that gov was a way to congregate people through and perhaps beyond clicktivism. What are some of the goals that you had when you first became involved in these activities?

Tang: First of all, it is to have fun. I wrote a blog essay, literally called "Optimizing for Fun,"[10] meaning that in order to sustain the broad engagement with citizens, we really need to make it inclusive in a sense that is not just fun for a selected few elites or technologists, but rather, it really needs to be enjoyable to pretty much everybody.

Fun needs to be fair, in the sense that anyone who shows up, regardless of their training, their background, their age, their ethnicity and so on, they could show up at gov hackathon to have fun, to enjoy food together, and to enjoy listening to people's stories and participate in their own storytelling. In that sense, in spirit, gov also drew a lot of lessons from the early community building efforts in Taiwan, which often centered around a sense of building community, sharing our emerging sense of national identity and shared cultural affiliations. So the second goal was to make sure our efforts were inclusive, fun, and rooted in a sense of community.

I'm also a meta-organizer in the sense that I design the mechanism that enables other people's organization. For example, I work closely with the National Development Council on their petition platform at Join.gov.tw.[11] Our contribution is to merge it with the regulatory preannouncements, with the participatory budgeting, with the National Auditing Office's data and things like that, so that people can have a *full lifecycle* understanding of all, not just budget, but also the regulatory changes that the government brings to the table. Instead of just the *what* of policy, people can participate also in the *how* of policy making, the *why* of policy making, and that enables multiple community organizers to expand their outreach and empower their community. For example, in this new petition platform there's a way for users to engage meaningfully with the ministries on the one hand but also with other social sector organizers on the other.

The longer-term goal is to democratize the thinking around democracy. Because in many other established democracies, only very few people actively work on democracy. Here I include for example people who work on gerrymandering, which is also working on democracy. Citizens, by and large, participate in only uploading bits of information every four years. It's called voting. Their day-to-day life is not that involved with democracy. But in Taiwan, having the benefit of being a very new democracy, everything is malleable in the sense that if people think we need to have a referendum, then we design a referendum. The referendum mechanism by itself is currently undergoing another change, but we're maybe at the fourth revision.[12] The Constitution is at maybe the sixth or seventh amendment.[13] So this is a really important part of what we are doing: We are not only acting democratically, in the sense of being inclusive and transparent, but we are consciously trying to help each other to reimagine what democracy can be in Taiwan.

Democracy in Taiwan is a flexible project that everyone can contribute to. People who advocate for a safe participatory budgeting, or deliberative democracy, or Presidential Hackathons, and other ideas such as Open Government,[14] can all see that idea put on the table within their lifetime. There's a real chance for their designs to be integrated into democracy proper. So in addition to fun and inclusion, I would also say one of our broad goals is helping users to imagine innovations in democracy itself, to see democracy as a technology that is open, inclusive, and flexible.

Democracy as a Technology of Resistance

In the beginning of the interview, Minister Tang explained that an active citizenry in Taiwan has historically intertwined with international movements, particularly those of technologically based organizing. The conversation then shifted from Tang's involvement with grassroots communities to their view toward democracy as a living organ to be (re)designed for greater inclusivity.

Chiaoning Su: I would like to discuss a relevant topic, which is more about the role of technology in government. Your role changed over the years from an outsider of the institution as a community organizer to your current position as part of the institution. In your previous interview with *Harvard Business Review*, you stated that democracy is a technology and that radical transparency helps decision-making. Can you explain these two concepts?

Tang: Technology as the broadened definition shows [that] it's any applied science that will have an impact, negative or positive, on our lives. Democracy certainly is a decision-making technology. Previously, in the Greek imagination of democracy, it's mostly people who walked around from the markets, the agoras, to the acropolis having a conversation among themselves. On Wikipedia, there is this large flowchart of how the Athenian democracy works.[15] You can see something very much like a flowchart for a semiconductor or a computer program board. There was a very strong mechanism design view in the early Greek democracy. When we design democracy correctly, then peoples' ideas can add to each other and flow freely for the betterment of the democracy. If we don't design it correctly, then they detract from each other and polarize the polity. I mean it in the original sense. Of course, many politics have standardized some sort of representational democracy, and it has become the dominant reference when people use the term "democracy." For example, people nowadays think about the members of the parliament and the ministers when it comes to the idea of democracy. However, that's not the only configuration. Similar to designing semiconductors, we can try different layouts from two-dimensional to three-dimensional layouts when building a democratic nation. In a polity, we can try, various different ways for people in different positions to come to a general understanding of how well a democracy functions without having to wait for four years. That's what I mean by "democracy as a technology," which means that people can cocreate, experiment, and improve it. It is a collaborative process of multiple inputs designed for maximizing positive impacts on people's lives.

Radical transparency means transparency at the root for a democratic polity. For example, this conversation is on the record. I have a recorder right here, and I will send you the transcript to coedit for accuracy before we publish it in the public domain. People then have a general understanding of the ideas in our conversation. This is what I have in mind when I use the term "radical transparency." It invites better understanding as opposed to if people only read the final redacted form, which is a voice that has already been streamlined. Understanding the zigzag, the *how*, not just the product, and the what, of policy making is essential for people to have a more informed, contextualized understanding of democracy and policymaking. This is in our Freedom of Information Act (政府資訊公開法) which allows for draft stage meetings to be published if it serves a public purpose. I do this for a vast majority of the internal meetings that I chair, and for all interviews with the media, researchers, and lobbyists. Interestingly, this also means that lobbyists always lobby for the common good. No lobbyist who meets with me would lobby for something that's only good for them, but not for other people. So that is an additional benefit to being transparent with the public about how the government functions.

Su: This is the prime example of direct participation in democracy.

Tang: I think it's a precondition for meaningful direct participation, but it's not by itself participation. This is just the transparency part where we try as much as possible to show the process of decision-making. As government officials, we can indeed redact it after all, but retaining as much information as possible provides the context of policymaking for people to see democracy in action. Now, when people are interested in the policy, for example, around the policy of the design for social movements, chances are they will search on search engines and rediscover our transcript, and then this can be attributed to our names. Maybe you get an email some weeks down the road saying they have a different take on a particular part in the interview. I get such emails all the time because I publish transcripts of the meetings that I chair. I get corrections and more input from the citizenry. But if I only publish the decisions, then I have no way to get helpful ideas. This is coupled with a general, inclusive attitude. In Mandarin, it's called 開門造車 (*kai men zao ju*), which can be roughly translated as "Building cars behind open doors," and 你行你來 (*ni xing ni lai*), "If you can do it, come and do it." The idea is that if people think of a better idea after seeing open conversations that led to any particular policy, they are in a much better position to suggest amendments or alternatives to the policy as opposed to if they have no context about the making of that policy. This level of transparency offers a space for continuous improvement of democratic governing.

Su: That's actually a wonderful strategy. Just to expand on the idea of radical transparency and then connect that with pandemic governance. We are still in the middle of this COVID-19 global pandemic, and Taiwan being described as a successful experience using a democratic way to manage the pandemic. Can you tell us a little more about Taiwan's unique ways of managing the early spike of this pandemic, particularly in the midst of China's disinformation campaign against Taiwan? How do you see the role of technology and radical transparency in this process?

Tang: Certainly. The most observable feature of the Taiwan model is that we countered the pandemic with no lockdown at all, and we countered infodemic, which was associated with the COVID-19 pandemic. In some jurisdictions, infodemic caused even more harm than pandemic itself. We countered the infodemic with no administrative takedown. "No lockdown and no takedown" is the distinct feature of the Taiwan model.

Radical transparency played a central role in achieving the Taiwan model because if the government cannot take anything down from the media, or tries their best not to, lockdown any buildings and cities, the government must rely on the general population to understand the epidemiology, to understand the facts around this virus. For example, if there is a significant number of people, maybe one third of the population, who refuse to wear masks, then we can't do anything truly effective to control the spread of the virus. We can do our best to ramp up the production to twenty million masks per day. We can do our best to distribute them evenly and fairly to the pharmacies and convenience stores. However, if people get caught by the conspiracy theories, or by other non-scientific views on wearing

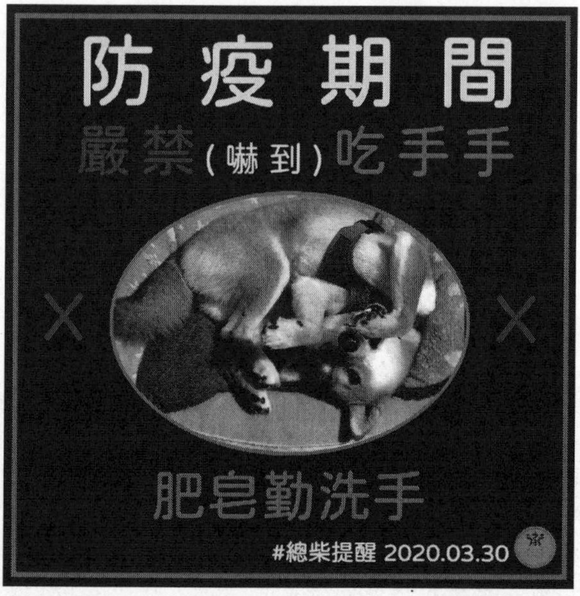

FIGURE 1. "ShibaInu puts hands in the mouth/*chi shou shou*." Image by Ministry of Health and Welfare of Taiwan.

FIGURE 2. "Promoting masks wearing in multiple languages." Image by Ministry of Health and Welfare of Taiwan.

the masks, then none of our efforts would work. We would probably have to lock down at some point.

To mitigate the impact of infodemic, getting the right communications to the people by using a blend of "Fast, Fair and Fun" principles becomes very important. For example, I often jokingly say that while in Minister Chen Shih-chung of our Ministry of Health and Welfare is the most important spokesperson during the pandemic, Shiba Inu Zongchai is the most important spokesdog.[16] There is a team of people in charge of engaging with emerging Zongchai-related hashtags to communicate factual information to the public. They literally live with this dog. After Minister Chen finishes the daily press conference, the team then take new pictures of the dog and use them to explain to the public about the policy. For example, the team popularized mask uses by taking a photo of the dog putting its foot to its mouth and telling people that wearing a mask would prevent yourself from 吃手手 (*chi shou shou*, putting your hands in your mouth). The mask is there to protect your own face against your own unwashed hands (see figure 1). These images convey public-health related message in a fun and immediate way. They are also widely available to those with a smart phone or internet connections.

These communication strategies are very important because they enable people to remix the message. If it's me or Minister Chen talking about wearing a mask, people may understand. They may even comply, but it's unlikely they will share it that much. But because it's such a cute dog, people will share the information much more than they do with the conspiracy theories. We also made sure that there's plenty of room literally in the picture for the people to translate it to their local languages. For example, this one has been translated to more than four or five different languages. (See figure 2.)

These communication strategies made sure that people receive clear and scientific information in a way that is conductive to social sharing. They have a pro-social outcome. Because of this Fast, Fair and Fun communication infrastructure, we made sure that none of the conspiracy theories are valued and stay circulated for long. These "vaccines of the mind" are very funny and reached a lot of people very quickly.

Su: I too pay attention to that kind of social media messaging put forward by Taiwan's public sectors. I personally found it super effective and also very entertaining. In the meantime, I saw a lot of critics stating that the government used the social media language on the one hand to simplify the policy and on the other hand to manipulate the public opinion. Do you share that kind of view?

TANG: The main critique was that when some of the social media messaging came at the expense of specific people, specific business or specific groups, it became what we call 出征 (*chu zheng*, go on an expedition or go into a battle).[17] In other words, the critique was about the risks of anyone turning the messaging into attacks on particular groups instead of sharing the message by laughing about it. It therefore could encourage revenge or vengeful attitudes toward those with whom one disagrees. That is a valid critique.[18] I would say that the public message from our ministries very rarely encourages vengeful behaviors. However, there have been certain cases, and so there are pitfalls in this strategy that we need to be very wary of them. As public ministers, we do command a lot of trust. If we squander that trust because people believe we engage in *chu zheng*, it's not easy to earn it back. At some point when the trustworthiness is reduced, all messages essentially backfire.

SU: This is really to showcase that democracy can be inclusive, participatory, and fun. We can also see how technology can play a significant role in social movements or in a revolution. Ever since the Arab Spring in 2010, people across the world talk about the role of technology in social movements, or in radical political actions. Do you see the differences or similarities in terms of how technology is being used to achieve contentious political actions in different Asian localities?

TANG: Asia is a really big place and it is hard to make generalizations, but I will try anyway. First of all, in Asia, we see technology not just as something that is in the natural sciences or something that is only for the industrial usage. There is a long tradition of what was called "appropriate technology," meaning that people use existing technologies in a way that fits their local needs without asking for permission from the original designers of the technology, or even understanding of its design. During the COVID-19 pandemic, a really good example is how people use the traditional rice cookers to clean the mask, to kill the virus but not the mask. I am sure that the rice cooker makers did not think about this particular use case when they made their technology to cook rice. It turns out that not having a steam vent is actually really good in this situation. Without adding water, the design of a rice cooker makes the temperature very predictable and it can actually be used to clean the masks. Now, that is appropriate technology, because it is something social, something people can contribute to, and that everyone has an easy access to. This usage is wildly outside of the original imagination of the designers.

In Asia, there is a participatory nature of reappropriating technologies in an appropriate way. You can see this, for example, in the Sunflower Movement in 2014 Taiwan and the Umbrella Movement in Hong Kong. In the same year, people repurposed the various communication technologies that were not designed for the streets to fight against the ruling governments. But then we used them on the streets anyway, and modulated those technologies so that they fit a street profile. People who developed those technologies, for example, Hackpad, or Twitch,[19] sometimes have to cater to those people on the street so that the sheer volume of usage doesn't negatively affect their other paying customers. This way of using platforms outside of platformer's original design is a common characteristic around the use of digital technology in Asia for social movements.

Inclusive Technology as a Resisting Vehicle for National Consciousness

At the end of the interview, we asked Minister Tang their view of the growth of Taiwanese national identity during the tumultuous U.S.–China relations since the late 2010s. Tang explained communication technology for inclusivity as a key element to solidify identification with Taiwan and to maintain stability under unpredictable international influences.

CHENG: Thank you for sharing your view about the role technology plays in empowering people and the government for common good. Researchers have been studying ways that technology, especially digital technology, shape identity and vice versa. One example would be how social and national identities were impacted by social movements and how technologies facilitate that. From the recent years' surveys done by National Chengchi University, we're seeing an emerging trend of the Taiwanese national consciousness. What do you think might be technology's roles in this trend?

TANG: With my broadened definition of technology, I would definitely place the national healthcare system into the technology parts that enable such consciousness. Our constitutional amendment very specifically stipulates that the country has an obligation to run universal health care for all its citizens. People have experienced coverage under the National Health Insurance, especially in time of COVID. And, it has shaped self-identification for those who are eligible for our universal health care. Some may not officially be citizens. They may be residents on work permits who have worked, for example, in the long-term care industry in Taiwan. They are considered "Taiwanese people" under the national health care system and in terms of how we should offer protection to them. Because our national health care system enables all individuals to act and be cared for as a collective, it is an important and imperative strategy to counter COVID as a nation.

In other jurisdictions, for example, we have seen immigrant workers being excluded from or getting less attention in the national dialogue among their citizens when it comes to the pandemic. Therefore, it is more likely to have an outbreak in places where the immigrant workers are. In Taiwan, all of us are protected by the universal health care. All of us are entitled to the medical mask rationing system and notification system,[20] and the quarantine system. I would say all these systems are also technologies that, layered on the National Health Insurance system, shaped a stronger national identity.

In the National Chengchi University survey that you just mentioned, we see two peaks of national consciousness. One is during the first year of COVID and another one is around 2014, the year of the Sunflower Movement. I think that movement also pioneered the many uses of social technology, specifically live streaming technology. People who were not necessarily in Taiwan could tune in to a live stream and felt strongly connected to a real deliberation about what to do about the trade agreement between Taiwan and China. Anyone who invested a significant amount of time in that online space felt a stronger link to the Taiwanese identity, almost by definition. Because when viewing a live stream, unlike watching it on TV, anyone who felt that they had something to say, they could type it or shared it on the media that was being shipped by live streams. They then could join in as one of the voices brought to the deliberation spaces around the parliament. I think live streaming technology played a large role in 2014. And it's not just in Taiwan, the Umbrella Movement in Hong Kong also made copious use of that then new live streaming technology.

Cheng: What Minister just shared reminded me about how this collective consciousness extends beyond the national boarder of Taiwan. With all your experiences in open technology, radical transparency, and participation, what is your view toward Taiwan's future, particularly under the U.S.–China relations?

Tang: I often say that Taiwan's future direction is upward and skyward. As anyone who has been to the Taroko Gorge can attest, we're caught between the Eurasian plate on one side and the Philippine Sea Plate on the other. They bumped into each other all the time, causing endless earthquakes. We are very resilient. It's not like we can prevent the earthquakes from happening, but we can prevent negative consequences of earthquakes from happening.

On the upside, literally on the upside, each earthquake pushes the top of Taiwan—the Saviah or the Patungkuonu, or the Jade Mountain, the Yushan—upward by a little bit. Every year on average, Yushan grows by two-and-a-half centimeters (0.98 inch). To me, it symbolizes Taiwan's capability to foster rough consensus and common values out of seemingly zero-sum fights. For example, the social forces of those for and against marriage equality, shaped the social innovation in Taiwan, which was the truly pioneering innovation of "marrying the bylaws but not in-laws (結法不結姻, *jie fa bu jie yin*)." That's a uniquely Taiwanese social innovation.[21] And that's in direct response to the two referenda and the one Constitutional Court ruling.[22]

I can go on with these types of examples, but the point is that because people who remember the time of the Martial Law don't want to go back to the top-down censorship.[23] People who are aware of the information manipulation and disinformation crisis do not want to sit there and do nothing. Again, we have to figure out a Taiwanese model of humor over rumor. That is our information playbook, a unique innovation that is now seen in a broad application across the world. I guess we will keep doing so. We will keep doing innovations that meld the seemingly irreconcilable positions and then deliver innovations that are truly good for everyone.

In Taiwan, we have long considered communication as a human right. In the constitutional amendment, in the same clause that said universal health care is the government's duty, it also said that learning and having access to communication and speech must also be universal in Taiwan. These formed what I refer to as the social core. This is important. If you have a digital democracy, as we have, but if you leave out certain groups of people, denying them access to broadband, then what you are essentially doing is excluding them from policy making. That is profoundly anti-democratic. We are really serious about the universality of not just broadband access but also media competency, digital competency, and all the requirements for each and every citizen to be included in the policy making. For us, digital inclusion is the true goal. Innovation and governance are important instrumental values on our way to inclusion.

After Russia invaded Ukraine in 2022, we once again reached out to Minister Tang for their views on how technology might play an important role in countries like Taiwan and Ukraine to defend their democratic ways of living.

Su: Hi, Minister Tang. Good to speak with you again. It has been almost a year since you shared your views with us. Today's world is a very different place because of the war between Russian and Ukraine. Informational technology has played a major role during this ongoing war. With your expertise, what lessons can Taiwan learn from the ways that communication technology has been used in the Russian-Ukraine war?

Tang: When we last talked in early 2021, top-down authoritarian decision-making processes were still hailed as "efficient" by political commentators; liberal democracies were often written off as less efficient. Nowadays, they don't say that anymore, as everyone can see that although authoritarian regimes could be efficient at times, the lack of check-and-balance and real-time feedback means it could also commit to strategic mistakes very efficiently. Thus the case for democratic resilience is stronger than ever before.

As for lessons for Taiwan: On the counter-disinformation side, the "notice & public notice" and "humor over rumor" tactics of effectively out-memeing the authoritarian propaganda worked really well for Ukraine, reinforcing our belief that civic journalism is preferable to administrative takedowns in terms of infodemic resilience.

Finally, it's notable that before the invasion, Ukraine already set high standards in digital democracy, first through their open-source ProZorro procurement platform, and then through participation platforms such as e-dem.ua, based on the Diia digital citizenship framework that was put to immediate use during the war. Echoing our own experience countering the pandemic and infodemic, this clearly shows digital democracies—motivated by a shared urgency and clarity of purpose—offer unparalleled capacity to deliver outcomes that respond to emerging challenges.

Our conversations with Minister Tang are testaments to their deep convictions—utilizing technology in the most appropriate way to hold an open and inclusive space where information flow and knowledge creation is transparent and accessible for all. This is the Taiwanese way of building consensus and identification unbound by geographic boundaries. Democratic countries and societies that face unwelcomed intrusions are learning and working with each other to survive and thrive. In the time of volatile global and regional geopolitics, transparency and openness to verifiable contributions are the ultimate resistance for self-determination.

NOTES

1. Andrew Leonard, "How Taiwan's Unlikely Digital Minister Hacked the Pandemic," *Wired*, July 23, 2020.
2. This conversation has been redacted for the purpose of the book.
3. G0v Taiwan is an online community created in 2012 with a conviction that a transparent government is imperative for democracy. Bimonthly, g0v hackathons are held to openly exchange ideas to solve the most pressing problems in the society. See "COMMUNITY PROJECT g0v Hackathons | Open Culture Foundation (OCF)," http://ocf.tw/en/p/g0vdathon/.
4. "Taiwan's Revolutionary Hackers are Forking the Government," *Wired UK*, April 5, 2018.
5. Carl Miller, "How Taiwan's 'Civic Hackers' Helped Find a New Way to Run the Country," *Guardian*, September 27, 2020.
6. Creative Commons is a global movement in which non-profit organizations offer free licenses so that creators who wish to make their work available to the public can do so. See Creative Commons, November 16, 2016, https://creativecommons.org/2006/11/16/ccasaglobalmovement/. Open Source Initiative, https://opensource.org/. For more information on these movements, see Christina Dunbar-Hester, *Hacking Diversity :The Politics of Inclusion in Open Technology Cultures* (Princeton: Princeton University Press, 2020).
7. For example, see Center for Civic Media at MIT "Group Overview Center for Civic Media," https://www.media.mit.edu/groups/center-for-civic-media/overview/.
8. For information on the Open Software Movement, see http://understandingtheurban.qwriting.qc.cuny.edu/2017/03/15/free-software-movement/.
9. This website also has a Google application. 萌(MOE) means "to spout." Borrowing from

Japanese, it lately has morphed into the slang meaning of "adorable." This online mega dictionary provides translations in English, French, and German, in addition to major languages in Taiwan. It reflects the vibrant and diverse characteristics of Taiwanese society. See https://play.google.com/store/apps/details?id=org.audreyt.dict.moe&hl=en_US&gl=US.

10. Audrey Tang, "-Ofun: Optimizing for Fun," *Speaker Deck*, October 21, 2012, https://speakerdeck.com/audreyt/ofun-optimizing-for-fun?slide=34.
11. Established in 2015, this council provides an open channel for citizens to participate in discussing, supervising, proposing, and responding to policies. "Public Governance of Taiwan in the Digital Age: E-Participation," National Development Council, https://www.ndc.gov.tw/en/Content_List.aspx?n=C3C5AABC54ECEA0D.
12. In 2019, the Referendum Act was passed, determining that biannual voting would happen in August on the fourth Saturday. Legitimate voters must hold National Identification Cards. Central Election Commission, "Referendum Act," Laws & Regulations Database of The Republic of China (Taiwan), June 21, 2019, https://law.moj.gov.tw/ENG/LawClass/LawAll.aspx?pcode=D0020050.
13. The Constitution of the Republic of China (Taiwan) was established in 1947. "Constitution of the Republic of China (Taiwan)," Laws & Regulations Database of The Republic of China (Taiwan). January 1, 1947, https://law.moj.gov.tw/ENG/LawClass/LawAll.aspx?pcode=A0000001.
14. Taiwan Presidential Hackathon was launched in 2018 with the goal to invite "data owners, data scientists and field experts" to collaborate and solve pressing issues for public good. It included an international track in 2019. "International Track," The Presidential Hackathon, https://presidential-hackathon.taiwan.gov.tw/en/international-track/. For more information on Taiwan's involvement in the Open Government Partnership, see "Social Development: Open Government National Action Plan," National Development Council, https://www.ndc.gov.tw/en/Content_List.aspx?n=0DA7FCD068C7ECF5.
15. "Athenian Democracy," *Wikipedia*, January 23, 2022, https://en.wikipedia.org/wiki/Athenian_democracy.
16. Wang Amber, "Virus Outbreak: Mascots Embraced for Virus Prevention Campaigns," *Taipei Times*, February 20, 2020, https://www.taipeitimes.com/News/taiwan/archives/2020/02/18/2003731193.
17. The concept of *chuzheng* refers to organized online trolling. For more on this concept in the context of Taiwan and China, see Guobin Yang, "Performing Cyber-Nationalism in Twenty-First-Century China," in *From Cyber-Nationalism to Fandom Nationalism*, edited

by Hailong Liu, 1–12 (New York: Routledge, 2018).

18. There have been vigorous debates over the impact of the Taiwanese government's reliance on memes and social media platforms to communicate with the public. On the one hand, memes convey lucid and poignant meanings to a wide range of audience within a short amount of time. On the other hand, light-hearted social media may risk oversimplifying complex issues—or worse, placing harsh judgements on individuals' lifestyle and morality. See Xiwen Chen, "Tsai Zhen Fu Wang Hong Hua? Xue Zhe Dian Wu Da Feng Xian Zhen Yao Bian Wang Hong Dang Dao" [Officials in Tsai's administration became internet celebrities: Scholars pointed to five risks], *United News Network*, January 17, 2019; Qiao Se Fen, "Yan Suan Fa Xia De Tai Wan Gong Quan Li" [Taiwan's public power under algorithm], *Initium Media*, May 5, 2020; Lin Yu Tsang and Chen Fang Yu, "Do Zhe Lai Han: Tai Wan Li Shing Tao Luen Kong Jien De Ya Suo Dao De Han She Mo Yo Kuan?" (Letter to editor: What led to the shrinking space of rational discussions in Taiwan?], *Initium Media*, May 23, 2020.
19. Hong Kong students relied on Twitch to organize and amplify messages during the anti-extradition protests. Blizzard, an American video game company that owned the platform, faced heavy criticism for banning its users from supporting the Hong Kong protests. Twitch's parent company, partially owned by the Chinese tech conglomerate Tencent, denied the criticism and blamed the ban on an algorithm. See Charlie Wood, "Blizzard Denies Reports that It's Banning Twitch Viewers for Pro-Hong Kong Chat," October 21, 2019, https://www.businessinsider.com/blizzard-denies-banning-twitch-users-for-pro-hong-kong-chat-2019-10.
20. During the early stage of the pandemic, to reduce public anxiety over the shortage of masks, the Name-Based National Masks Rational System was implemented whereby masks were expropriated by the government. People could buy nine masks biweekly with their National Health Insurance card. See Po-Sheng Ko and Jen-Yao Lee, "Analysis of Taiwan's Mask Collection and Plan Evasion during the COVID-19 Pandemic," *International Journal of Environmental Research and Public Health* 18, no. 8 (April 14, 2021), https://www.ncbi.nlm.nih.gov/pmc/articles/PMC8070768/.
21. This statement plays with the phrase of "結髮 connecting a married couple" and "結法 connecting the laws" based on their shared pronunciation. Through this playful language, Taiwanese LGBTQ advocate groups employed the legal strategy to separate the traditional cultural view of marriage, which is closely intertwined with family structures, from the legal view toward marriage, which treats individuals as separate entities. This strategy contributed to the legalization of same sex marriages in Taiwan. See Elaine Jeffreys and Pan Wang, "Pathways to Legalizing Same-Sex Marriage in China and Taiwan:

Globalization and "Chinese Values," in *Global Perspectives on Same-Sex Marriage*, 197–219 (Cham, Switzerland: Springer International Publishing, 2017).

22. In 2017, Taiwan's Constitutional Court ruled that same-sex couples should be equally protected by law. In 2019, Taiwan's parliament passed a bill to legalize same-sex marriage and made Taiwan the first country in Asia to do so. See Laurel Wamsley, "Taiwan's Parliament Legalizes Same-Sex Marriage, A First in Asia," NPR, May 17, 2019, https://www.npr.org/2019/05/17/724222598/taiwans-parliament-legalizes-same-sex-marriage-a-first-in-asia.
23. From 1949 to 1987, the Nationalist Kuomingtang (KMT) enforced martial law in Taiwan. It was one of the longest periods of martial law imposed in a nation. "Taiwan Ends 4 Decades of Martial Law," *New York Times*, July 15, 1987.

Acknowledgments

This project carries tremendous weight as individual, societal, national, and global disruptions have occurred since its inception. In the early stage of completing this book, one editor decided to withdraw from the project over concerns of retaliation as their academic freedom was evaporating. One contributor, in fear for the safety of their activist participants in Hong Kong, had to stop their involvement in this project—a decision communicated via an alias email account. Another contributor with strong publication and teaching evaluations lost their tenure-track position at a university in Hong Kong with no explanation. Although there was not a specific accusation, the political nature of their research is suspected to have been the cause. Each of these individual oppressions occurred while people all over the world were fighting against authoritarian regimes.

It is within this context that we came together as a collective to analyze resistant communication in Taiwan and Hong Kong. We are deeply grateful for the Michigan State University Press for the space to voice our concerns. To Catherine Cocks, the editor-in-chief, and Stephen Hartnett, the series editor, we thank you for your invaluable insights and support in this collection. We are fortunate to work with Anastasia Wraight, our project editor, throughout this process. Working on this volume pushed us to think more creatively about the critical roles of Taiwan and Hong Kong in the era of heightened U.S.-China rivalry. We see the promise in highlighting the non–state-focused resistance from both societies. Many contributors broadened the scope of their research concerns and came to realize that what happened to Hong Kong and Taiwan is closely connected with the geopolitical dynamics around the world.

Writing from the margins can be lonely at times. We could not have finished this book without many individuals who shared their expertise. Taiwan's digital minister, Audrey Tang, took time from their busy schedule to share the role that communication technology has played in Taiwan's resistance movements. Omedi Ochieng graciously offered his intellectual insights. And Taiwanese photographer Ken Chin-yuan (柯金源) generously granted us permission to use his art as the book cover. We hope this text adds to future resistant efforts by amplifying voices from the people whose dignity and ways of life are under threat.

Contributors

Chin-Chung Chao is professor of communication at University of Nebraska at Omaha. Her primary research interests span conflict management, leadership, intercultural communication, organizational communication, and media communication. In 2020, she edited the collection *Asian Woman Leadership: A Cross-National and Cross-Sector Comparison*, one of many examples of her distinguished scholarship. It won two Outstanding Book Awards at the 2021 NCA Conference. She has served on the editorial boards of the *Journal of Intercultural Communication Research* and *Negotiation and Conflict Management Research*.

Hsin-I Cheng is associate professor in the Department of Communication at Santa Clara University. Cheng's work appears in the *Journal of International and Intercultural Communication*, *International Journal of Communication*, *Western Journal of Communication*, and *Women & Language*. Her first book, *Culturing Interface: Identity, Communication, and Chinese Transnationalism*, received the 2009 Outstanding Book Award from National Communication Association's (NCA) International and Intercultural Communication Division. The book is a critical ethnography unpacking several Taiwanese and Chinese communities living and working on the U.S.–Mexico border. In 2021, she published her second book,

Cultivating Membership in Taiwan and Beyond: Relational Citizenship. In this work, Cheng develops a theoretical concept derived from Taiwanese experiences, and shows its application to citizenship development in other cultural contexts. This book received the 2022 Book Award from NCA's Asian American Pacific Caucus and Communication Studies Division.

Andrew Gilmore is an assistant professor of communication studies at Central State University. He explores how Hong Kong's pro-democracy advocates have enacted strategies of resistance through mechanisms such as the creative performance of national identity and the use of transportation infrastructure, the urban environment, gender constructions, and mundane items and rituals. Andrew's scholarship has received awards from the National Communication Association, the Western State Communication Association, and the Association for Chinese Communication Studies. His research has been published in the *Journal of International and Intercultural Communication*, *Flow Journal*, and numerous titles published by Michigan State University Press and Waveland Press.

Iam-chong Ip is currently visiting assistant professor at the Graduate Institute for Social Research and Cultural Studies, National Yang Ming Chiao Tung University in Taiwan. He taught cultural studies at Lingnan University in Hong Kong from 2002 to 2021. His research focuses on cultural experience, political identities, and ICTs. His most recent publications include *Hong Kong's New Identity Politics: Longing for the Local in the Shadow of China* (2020) and journal articles about Chinese migrants, urbanism, and state power.

Micky Lee is a professor of media studies at Suffolk University, Boston. She has published in the areas of feminist political economy, and information, technologies, and finance. Her latest books are *Dis/ability in Media, Law, and History: Intersectional, Embodied AND Socially Constructed?* (2022, coedited with Frank Rudy Cooper and Pat Reeve), *Media Technologies for Work and Play in East Asia: Critical Perspectives on Japan and the Two Koreas* (2021; coedited with Peichi Chung), *Information* (2021), *Alphabet: The Becoming of Google* (2019), and *Bubbles and Machines: Gender, Information, and Financial Crises* (2019).

Wei-Ping Li is a PhD candidate at the Philip Merrill College of Journalism at the University of Maryland. Before attending the PhD program, she was a journalist covering financial and legal news in Taiwan. She is also a lawyer licensed to practice in New York State and has worked as a consultant and researcher examining digital rights policy. Her research has focused on disinformation, propaganda, and media laws and policy.

Wen Liu is assistant research fellow at the Institute of Ethnology, Academia Sinica, Taiwan. She received her PhD in critical social psychology at the Graduate Center, City University of New York. Informed by affect theory, critical race studies, and queer theory, she studies diasporic Asian American movements and subjectivities in the context of U.S.–China inter-imperial rivalry. She has coedited a book volume, *Reorienting Hong Kong's Struggle: Leftism, Decoloniality, and Internationalism* (2022).

Chiaochun Su holds an MPS from New York University and is the creative director of 23Design. She specializes in information design and interactive storytelling as applied to various fields. Based on her interest in science and culture, much of her work at 23Design leads to exhibitions advocating for important social issues. She received an honorable mention for the 2020 MUSE Award with her project entitled "ENERGYM." She has previously published in the *Journal of the National Taiwan Museum*. Currently, she is working on her MBA in *entrepreneurship* and innovation at National Taiwan University.

Chiaoning Su is assistant professor in journalism and public relations at Oakland University (OU). She served as the 2018–2020 president of the Association for Chinese Communication Studies. Her previous work on disaster journalism and East Asian geopolitics has been published in *Media, Culture and Society*, *International Journal of Communication*, *Asian Journal of Communication*, *Communication Review*, and *Taiwan Journal of Democracy*. She is the recipient of the 2020 Honors College Inspiration Award and the 2021 Teaching Excellence Award at OU. Prior to her academic career, she worked as a communication specialist at Ogilvy Public Relations and for several political campaigns in Taiwan.

Ming Xie is assistant professor at West Texas A&M University. Ming earned her PhD in public administration from the University of Nebraska at Omaha and another PhD in cultural anthropology from the Graduate School of Chinese Academy of Social Sciences in Beijing. She is particularly interested in non-profit organization management and communication, social media, emergency management, and intercultural communication. She has served as guest editor for *China Media Research* and *Negotiation and Conflict Management Research* and won top paper awards at the annual conferences of International Communication Association and National Communication Association.

Hsin-i Sydney Yueh is associate teaching professor in the Department of Communication at the University of Missouri. Her research examines how culture shapes communication in various groups and communities. Her book, *Identity Politics and Popular Culture in Taiwan: A Sajiao Generation*, received the Outstanding Book Award for the International and Intercultural Communication Division at the 2018 National Communication Association (NCA) convention. The earlier version of this book was awarded the Outstanding Dissertation Award in the Language and Social Interaction Division at the 2013 NCA conference. Yueh's research has been published in NCA journals, such as *Journal of International and Intercultural Communication, Communication and Critical/Cultural Studies*, and *Critical Studies of Media Communication*, in addition to specialty journals focusing on East Asia, China, and Taiwan. Yueh was the recipient of a Taiwan Fellowship in 2021 from the Ministry of Foreign Affairs, Taiwan.

Index

Page numbers in italics refer to figures and tables.

G

H

I

X

Y

Z